Surviving War,
Oceans Apart

Surviving War, Oceans Apart

Two Teenagers in Poland and Japan Destined for Life Together

YANEK MIECZKOWSKI

McFarland & Company, Inc., Publishers
Jefferson, North Carolina

Unless otherwise noted, all photographs are from the author's collection

ISBN (print) 978-1-4766-9210-4
ISBN (ebook) 978-1-4766-5289-4

LIBRARY OF CONGRESS AND BRITISH LIBRARY
CATALOGUING DATA ARE AVAILABLE

Library of Congress Control Number 2024019387

© 2024 Yanek Mieczkowski. All rights reserved

No part of this book may be reproduced or transmitted in any form or by any means, electronic or mechanical, including photocopying or recording, or by any information storage and retrieval system, without permission in writing from the publisher.

Front cover images: the Mieczkowski family on vacation, approximately 1938, *left to right*: Aniela, Janusz, Bogdan, Tadeusz, Zbigniew; the Kawakami family approximately 1938, three years before WWII began: *left to right*: Yasuko, Hagi Onozoki, Shizuko, Hiroshi, Seiko, Echi, Kazutoshi, Suguru.

Printed in the United States of America

*McFarland & Company, Inc., Publishers
Box 611, Jefferson, North Carolina 28640
www.mcfarlandpub.com*

To my Ithaca, New York, classmates—at South Hill, Boynton,
and Ithaca High—and to the people of Otaru, Japan,
and Bydgoszcz and Warsaw, Poland

Table of Contents

Acknowledgments — ix
Introduction — 1

Part I—War Begins
1. Bydgoszcz, Poland—Living and Leaving — 7
2. Otaru, Japan—A Good Life by the Sea — 25

Part II—War Devastates
3. Warsaw at War — 43
4. War in a Japanese City — 66
5. Uprising! — 78
6. "That morning devastated us" — 91
7. Death Hits Home — 98
8. Doing Something Strange with Seaweed — 112

Part III—Determined to Bounce Back
9. From Soldier to Prisoner — 127
10. The Tough Transition — 148
11. New Goals, New Country — 162
12. Clashing Countries to Clashing Cultures — 178

Conclusion: The War Never Left Them — 191
Sources for Further Reading — 205
Index — 207

Acknowledgments

This book is possible because of Bogdan Mieczkowski and Seiko Kawakami Mieczkowski. Their story, survival through World War II, and willingness to share their experiences have provided a unique narrative on the conflict, one that gives a transnational perspective to the war. During a period spanning several years, they sat patiently as I dunned them with questions about their respective lives in Poland and Japan before, during, and after the war. I have kept the wording as close to their original recollections as possible, at times quoting them directly.

Layla Milholen, my editor at McFarland, deserves immense credit for this book. Layla expressed interest in the manuscript from the moment I mentioned it to her, and she showed steadfast faith in it. Because of teaching responsibilities, I had to ask for multiple extensions, and each time Layla was more than patient and understanding.

The staff at the Warsaw Rising Museum have supported this project generously, interviewing me about it and providing photographs from their excellent archives. I would like to express deep gratitude to Aleksandra Duda, Joanna Jastrzebska-Wozniak, Aleksandra Trzeciecka, and Museum Director Jan Oldakowski. The Warsaw Rising Museum is one of the best I have ever visited anywhere; for anyone traveling to Poland's capital, it is a must-see.

At the Stalag XB POW Camp Memorial in Sandbostel, Germany, Ines Dirolf and Günther Justen-Stahl helped me to arrange a visit, and Günther answered many of my questions about the camp and its wartime operation.

My cousin, Mateusz Danielak, met me in Warsaw, along with his family members, and they gave me insight into the extended Mieczkowski family stretching back generations. Mateusz, who is a helicopter pilot in the Polish Army, has been my wingman of sorts in Poland, helping to get one of my earlier articles on my father's World War II experiences translated into Polish and published.

While writing the manuscript, I assigned an early iteration to a graduate U.S. History seminar that I taught, and the students had constructive suggestions and questions. I would like to thank Robert Covert, Seth English, Luke Kasbarian, George Kotlik, and Mel Vasquez.

Malcolm A. Swanston, founder and content director for themaparchive.com, has been my friend for more than two decades. He provided all maps for both editions of my presidential elections atlas, so I naturally turned to him for maps to help readers visualize Otaru, Warsaw, and Poland during the war. I am grateful to Malcolm for hosting me when I have visited him in England, and I was delighted when he signed on to this project. When it came to this work, Malcolm gave plenty of compliments and encouragement, which were sustenance to me.

Friends and colleagues have helped me in innumerable ways, including proofreading the manuscript and offering input so valuable that it was priceless. I would like to acknowledge Hervey Priddy, James Patterson, Boyden Marison, William Shelton, and Dennis Duval. Robert Taylor, Professor and Dean of the College of Psychology and Liberal Arts at the Florida Institute of Technology, read the manuscript and also welcomed me aboard FIT as a faculty member. I have taught full-time at five different schools; Florida Tech has been the best, comprising a marvelous combination of great students, faculty colleagues, location, athletic teams, institutional mission, and a cosmopolitan environment that includes students from across the country and around the world. Readers wishing to contact me may reach me through my FIT email address: ymieczkowski@fit.edu.

Two friends who have monitored the progress of this work at every stage, vetting the manuscript and giving tons of advice, have been Michael Green of the University of Nevada, Las Vegas, and Leo McCue, with whom I graded the Advanced Placement U.S. History Exam for many years. For their keen insights and editorial wisdom, I am deeply indebted.

This book centers on three cities on opposite sides of the globe—"oceans apart." I have visited Bydgoszcz, Warsaw, and Otaru a number of times. During each visit, I was struck by their beauty and the placid lives citizens lead there today—in complete contrast to what World War II residents endured. I think of the people there, on opposites sides of the earth, and I wish them the peace and good fortune that the war generation never got to enjoy.

Introduction

In 1986, forty-one years after World War II ended, my parents, Bogdan and Seiko Mieczkowski, were having dinner at the home of friends John and Doris Ivey in Ithaca, New York. My father and mother were telling the Iveys about the hardships their respective families experienced during World War II. They described extreme scarcities of food and consumer goods, the suspension of schooling, military threats, and worst of all, the deaths of family members. The suffering was seared into my parents' memories, making their experiences seem vivid and real again.

After hearing my parents' wartime accounts, Doris exclaimed, "Someone should write a book about everything that happened to both of you during the war!" This is that book.

Growing up under my parents' guidance and tutelage, I heard stories from them about World War II—how devastating it was, how much their families suffered, how it changed their lives. With the usual insouciance of youth, I listened without comprehending, and I failed to appreciate the enormity of the conflict and their roles in it. I also took for granted the stability that a family can enjoy during peacetime, if they are lucky enough to avoid war and its concomitant disruptions and bloodshed. The World War II generation, unfortunately, never had that luck.

A multi-ethnic family, with parents who crossed different oceans to arrive in America, creates a household rich with cultural diversity, but it presents challenges in understanding one's ancestral history. During my childhood years, Poland was immured behind the Iron Curtain, and for many reasons—which this book will detail—my father was reluctant to return there until the country regained its freedom. On the other side of the world, Japan was distant, and travel there was expensive. I never got to meet my Polish grandparents, and I only met my grandparents in Japan once, when I was four years old. I did not return to Japan or visit Poland for the first time until the twenty-first century.

My trips to Poland and Japan made my parents' past come alive to me, and I wanted to write about their lives during the war and their immigration to the U.S. My interest in history made me more conscious of the need to record their stories so that future generations will know more about the past—especially a seminal event like World War II and how it affected humans around the globe. While my impetus for writing this book was personal, it also stemmed from the responsibilities that historians feel to preserve the past.

In this regard, one blandishment I have for readers is that you, too, may have important histories that should be memorialized. You may have relatives or friends who lived through critical events—or you yourself may have had such experiences—and the story may be sitting right in front of you, hiding in plain sight. I would urge you to record the details and massage it into a history that a larger audience and future generations may read and enjoy.

I spent countless hours interviewing my parents and asking questions, and I tried to capture their precise words as they related their accounts. I have adopted a braided format, alternating chapters between Bogdan's and Seiko's accounts, beginning with my father's, so that the odd-numbered chapters are his, while the even-numbered ones are my mother's. This pattern continues until the Conclusion, which describes how Bogdan and Seiko met, got married, started a family, and continued their careers. (I originally conceived of this book as my parents' joint memoir of World War II, and I wrote early drafts in the first person; ultimately, though, I decided to switch the manuscript to the third person to reflect my own narration, tone, and writing.)

In writing history, I usually focus on U.S. presidents, who by the very act of attaining America's highest office have attained an Olympian status. This kind of history is "top down," from the vantage point of movers and shakers who led a branch of government, formulated policy, commanded armies, and created national and international headlines.

Compared to presidents, my parents might seem like ordinary figures. They offer a "bottom up," worm's-eye view of history. But they did extraordinary work during World War II, requiring great courage, diligence, and perseverance—traits they displayed amply in our household. My father faced enemies, joined battle, and stared down death with no real weapons—as he recalled, without even a knife. My mother lived with her family in a cramped house with no running water, working seven days a week in a war factory when she should have been enjoying normal teenage life. Although my parents loved the classroom and were dedicated students, they had to sacrifice their education for the war effort. They had to accept the occupation of their respective countries, along with whatever treatment their occupiers doled out to them. These were unusual circumstances that demanded extraordinary qualities to survive.

Besides the enormous disruption to their lives, what was also striking was the patriotism that Bogdan and Seiko showed. My father's love for Poland was clear. It tore him apart to see the German Army invade his country, take over his home town of Bydgoszcz, and destroy the beautiful and historic capital of Warsaw. He was willing to risk his life to fight the Nazis, and after the Allies defeated them, he still burned with the desire to free Poland, this time from the Soviets, and he prepared to do so. My mother demonstrated her devotion to Japan, as did her school classmates and residents of her hometown of Otaru. They dedicated their war efforts to the Japanese emperor, and they obediently accepted the harsh restrictions and admonitions to work, sacrifice, and see their country to victory, which they firmly believed would be theirs.

Three salient themes define my father's and mother's wartime and postwar experiences. First was the *devastation* visited upon them and their families threatened to ruin them in every way—emotionally, physically, spiritually, and financially. Second, they both endured what Americans did not when World War II concluded—*defeat*. The Warsaw Uprising of 1944, which began with optimism and brimmed with energy, ended with appalling loss of life for Poles. During the Uprising, Bogdan witnessed fellow fighters die, suffered severe injuries himself, and experienced death within his own family. When Bogdan surrendered and endured seven POW camps, he watched comrades succumb to the harsh conditions and feared for his own life and limb. The defeats cascaded down in a period of only a few years, almost too much for him—or anyone—to absorb in such a short period.

Living on Hokkaido, my mother and her family were more insulated from the hardships visited on the Japanese living on Honshu, the country's main island, but she still felt the harsh hand of war and tasted bitter defeat in a country and culture where the idea of surrendering was unthinkable. People in Seiko's hometown of Otaru withstood onerous restrictions and intrusions into their lives, constituting invasions of privacy that liberty-loving Americans would find intolerable. Defeat shattered faith in the government and in the divinely protected superiority of the Japanese, a trope that the people of the country had believed for centuries. They emerged from the war exhausted and disillusioned.

During one period when I worked on this book, the Covid-19 virus wreaked havoc around the globe, prompting economic shutdowns, restricting family and social activities, disrupting school, preventing travel, and worst of all, killing millions. People will reflect on this period as a horrible time, just as World War II survivors looked back on that conflict as the worst experience of their lives. Luckily, during the Covid crisis, we had comforts that the World War II generation never would have dreamed of, including home delivery of food, smart phones for communication, streaming videos and other Internet services, Zoom calls, and many implements and activities that could keep spirits up and human connections strong. During World War II, especially in countries like Poland and Japan, citizens had far fewer ways to get through each day with a sense of hope and normality. Just surviving took a remarkable reservoir of optimism and perseverance.

Here the third theme comes into play. Despite adversity, setbacks, and worlds broken beyond repair, Bogdan and Seiko showed *determination* to move forward, surmounting their sorrow and plotting new paths. They refused to let the war destroy them; instead, they adapted to the circumstances and survived.

It took diligence, too. When children grow to become adults, they marvel at how hard their parents worked, and with good reason. During the war, my parents kept grueling schedules outside their homes, and they helped with domestic chores as much as they could. After the war, they assumed new roles and supported themselves. Freed from the conflict's horrible constraints, they set ambitious goals, always working hard at sundry jobs to support themselves.

Their most important aspiration involved education. Both Bogdan and Seiko showed a drive for self-betterment, and despite war, they tried to squeeze in schooling. After the war, their determination to learn led them to leave their families and study in the U.S., eventually earning advanced degrees. They met in America, and their adopted country enabled them to transcend their bitter war experiences, enjoy fulfilling careers, and above all, have a family. World War II had threatened to take almost everything from them. In the end, ironically, the war gifted Bogdan and Seiko tremendous opportunities. It gave them the freedom and impetus to travel halfway around the globe, embark on a grand adventure, and start anew.

But the war never left them. It continued to be a defining experience in their lives, shaping their views, creating permanent habits, and filling them with powerful memories. Their wartime experiences and the fallout from them marked an incredible journey, which began on opposite sides of the world, oceans apart.

PART I

War Begins

— 1 —

Bydgoszcz, Poland—Living and Leaving

I. In a Dentist's Chair When War Came

The war began in Bogdan's country. He heard it start.

In the summer of 1939, Bogdan Mieczkowski was a fourteen-and-a-half-year-old boy, living in Bydgoszcz, a city of 130,000 in northwestern Poland. The date was September 1, and it began as a routine Friday. The school year had not yet commenced, and in the morning Bogdan walked to downtown Bydgoszcz, fifteen minutes from his house, to have a regular visit with his family dentist, Dr. Sobocinski. As they finished the appointment, Bogdan heard a heavy rumbling in the far-off distance. It sounded like a typical late summer thunderstorm, and the noise made no great impression on him or his dentist.

"Bogdan, let's make another appointment," Dr. Sobocinski said. That statement was so normal, so casual and routine, and they both assumed that the future was theirs to control. Looking back, Bogdan was later struck by how innocent the words were.

The sounds they heard that day represented the shattering of their world. As they soon learned, they were not thunderstorms, but explosions marking the outbreak of World War II. Neither of them had any way of knowing that these were the booms of doom, starting a conflict that would destroy much of their country and many of its people. Later, Dr. Sobocinski was arrested and tortured as part of the Nazis' systematic effort to wipe out Polish leadership classes, including anyone with an advanced education. While they eventually released him, Dr. Sobocinski died from his wounds. Bogdan could not imagine that fate befalling his dentist, a relatively young man with a robust, athletic build. He was not the only one to suffer. The Nazis arrested the Bydgoszcz mayor, paraded him around town, and then executed him, along with other city officials.

The war was to affect Bogdan and his family in tragic ways as well.

II. Family Life in Bydgoszcz

On that day, history was catching up with Poland. Sadly, Poles were accustomed to it. Over the centuries, nearby nations had pressured and remade Poland's borders, and invasions and annexations pockmarked Poland's past so much that a common expression among Poles was that their country had "no history, just neighbors." Neighbors tended to be strong and truculent, and Poles had resisted them. At school, Bogdan and his classmates listened to teachers' lessons about the so-called "partitions" that marked Polish history. In land area, Poland had been one of Europe's largest nations; nonetheless, by the mid-eighteenth century, Swiss-born philosopher Jean-Jacques Rousseau warned Poles, "You are likely to be swallowed whole," adding that they should try to avoid getting "digested."

Rousseau was right. In the late 1700s, the nearby nations of Russia, Prussia, and Austria began to annex what was then the Polish-Lithuanian Commonwealth and crushed a Polish resistance movement that tried to drive them out. In 1795, these three countries conquered and divided Poland, an arrangement that wiped the nation off the map. The disappearance of an entire country might seem difficult to conceive today, but it was true; Poland vanished. In fact, the Polish national anthem, *Jeszcze Polska nie zginela*, which means "Poland will never die," was composed in 1797 and refers to the Polish people's fervent desire to keep their country alive, despite its past partitions and disappearance.

Throughout the nineteenth century, Poles chafed under the rule of the three subjugating powers, and nationalism stirred hopes to reclaim their country. Indeed, they tried to get their country back. In 1830 and again in 1863, Poles in the Russian sector rebelled, but the Russians overpowered them. Russian rule left a legacy of bitterness toward these neighbors, and the feelings grew worse over the next decades.

World War I benefited Poland by weakening its historic adversaries. Germany and Austria-Hungary lost the war and part of their empire, while Russia had to withdraw from the conflict after the Bolshevik Revolution. The Versailles Treaty of 1919, which ended World War I, restored Poland as a nation. After a hundred and twenty-four years, Poland existed again, and the country rejoiced in its new independence. It could now rebuild its economy and government, consolidating infrastructure, communications, and other elements that constituted nationhood. The country even gained access to the Black Sea again through Pomerania, a region it received from Germany. Poles, it seemed, had won a just reward for their brave resilience. Like the mythological phoenix, the country rose from ashes, and thereafter Poles celebrated November 11—the date of the World War I armistice—as Independence Day.

1. Bydgoszcz, Poland—Living and Leaving 9

Poland, reborn in 1919, as it looked on the eve of World War II. The country's borders—and its political status—were to change dramatically after the war (map by Malcolm A. Swanston).

Bogdan Mieczkowski arrived on the scene shortly after Poland's rebirth. He was born on November 8, 1924, in Bydgoszcz, and he remembered the prewar years there with an almost lyrical fondness. Until the conflict started, his family led a happy, stable, even luxuriant life. Bogdan had an older brother, Zbigniew (whom the family called by the Polish nickname "Zbyszek") and a younger brother, Janusz. They had pets, too, a dachshund, Filut, plus a larger dog, Minerva, which they kept chained outside their house as a watchdog.

Bogdan's mother Aniela was a fervent reader and talented piano player. In a reception room adjoining their living room, she played classical music daily, and above her piano they kept a caged yellow canary, Macias. A devout Catholic, Aniela graduated from a private school administered by nuns, located near Posnan. Every Sunday, the family went to church, and Aniela attended weekdays by herself. She showed her deep faith at home, too; before cutting bread loaves at family meals, she used her knife to make the light sign of a cross on each loaf.

The children called their mother *mamusu* (pronounced "mamushu," with the accent on the second syllable), and she led in celebrating religious holidays, which had a central role and importance in their lives, punctuating points of the year. At Christmas, they engaged in the Polish tradition of breaking wafers and kissing one another. They sang carols, decorated a tree, and burned a small forest of candles. For Easter Sunday, they painted eggshells and had a special meatless meal after honoring the holiday at church.

Bogdan's father, Tadeusz, was the family leader. With dark brown hair and striking blue eyes, he exuded a sense of authority and physical robustness. He stood only five feet seven inches tall, but he towered with determination and ability, and he took life seriously. Having little sense of humor, Tadeusz seldom joked, and he had a stern but gentle formality to his bearing. Although he called his sons by name, he also addressed them individually and collectively as *chlopaku*, which meant "boy." They called him *tatusu*, which is an endearing version of *tata*, the Polish version of "dad."

Growing up just north of Warsaw in the late 1800s and early 1900s, Taduesz did not know Poland as a nation when he was a boy. The Russians controlled the schools, and in 1905, students protested this arrangement by going on strike, marking a social revolution that showed Poles' continuing efforts to end the partitioning of their nation. As with prior rebellions, the students' effort failed. The Russians suppressed the uprising and retaliated by punishing students with so-called "wolves' tickets," which prevented them from getting an education in Poland. Tadeusz was counting on this avenue for advancement—he aspired to earn a college degree—and he felt stuck.

In a daring move, Tadeusz went to America to study engineering at Chicago's Armour Institute. He knew little English, and his college yearbook noted that Tadeusz "pursued his studies here in the face of obstacles that would have daunted most of us, and [he] has the respect of all who know him." Tadeusz had a trait that impressed anyone who met him: he had a fantastic work ethic. After earning his degree in 1915, he stayed in the

U.S. to gain citizenship and acquire more business savvy, working several jobs, including one in Louisiana.

In 1920, Tadeusz returned to the newly liberated Poland and parlayed his American education and work experience into building a thriving business. He co-owned a construction company called Impregnacja—"Impregnable." The enterprise had a brick-making plant in Bydgoszcz and a factory in Naklo, a town northwest of Bydgoszcz, which made tarpaper for covering roofs. Each factory occupied more than an entire city block.

The Bydgoszcz factory was impressive. Encircled by a long fence that stretched far into the distance, its grounds covered several acres. Railroad locomotives delivered materials to the plant, and the facility included a storage depot for building materiel, which Tadeusz bought wholesale and then sold to individual contractors. The factory smokestacks belched smoke, which—although an environmental insult—signaled the company's vibrancy.

The plant was a mile away from Bogdan's home, and he and his brothers often walked there on weekends, when they were off from school. One man and his family lived at the site in a large building adjoining the brick-making facility, and he watched over the entire facility when it was not in operation. When he saw the boys come to the factory grounds to visit, he recognized them and let them enter. Once they were inside, the factory was so vast that they had no fear of getting caught loitering or playing around. One of Bogdan's friends, Zbigniew Tymowski, even brought a pistol belonging to his father, and the boys entered one of the large brick-drying buildings and engaged in target practice. They did it on Sundays, when the factory took a respite, so no workers were around. Each time they fired the gun, the sound reverberated loudly around the building. They tried to hit the top of a broomstick with the gun, but it was such a small target that they never succeeded.

When the factory operated, Bogdan was fascinated to watch the workers make bricks. Tadeusz's employees numbered more than a hundred, and they practiced a skilled trade. Machines dug out clay from a large quarry on the premises, and workers added the right mix of water and sand to make raw bricks, cutting the mix into brick-size blocks. They transported them into buildings that looked like barns, with roofs but otherwise open to the elements. Inside any of these barns, Bogdan could see thousands of bricks drying. He sometimes touched them, and usually they were still moist, but they had to lose water content or else they would give off dangerous amounts of steam while they were baking. After the bricks dried for a few days, workers loaded them onto metal carts and wheeled them into another building housing multiple kilns. On the second and third floors workers shoveled coal into furnaces, generating tremendous heat—up to two thousand degrees Fahrenheit—that baked the clay into bricks, giving them their red color and hard texture. Next, the workers took the bricks to storage areas where they cooled, and after that truck drivers shipped them out to their destinations. Usually, they went to construction companies that had contracted to buy Tadeusz's building materiel.

While the factory was on the outskirts of the city, Tadeusz had a spacious office in downtown Bydgoszcz, where he did most of his work, visiting the plant only occasionally. Bogdan liked to visit his office because it was in the center of town, where he could watch traffic and feel the frisson of urban activity. An added attraction was that the office building had an Italian ice cream store on the first floor, and Bogdan loved to get snacks there. The Brda River (pronounced "Bur-dah," with the accent on the second syllable) cut through Bydgoszcz, and Tadeusz's office was just a block away from it. The walk from the Mieczkowski house to downtown took just a little more than ten minutes, and from Tadeusz's office, Bogdan could cross the river and enter the expansive city square, which bustled with shops and restaurants. A textile mill in the downtown area gave Bydgoszcz the feel of a small industrial city—tight-knit enough to be community, yet large enough to hum with dynamism and progress.

Most of all, Tadeusz's company made Bogdan proud. Whenever he saw the large sign outside the factory, with the word "Impregnacja" emblazoned on it, a sense of achievement surged inside him. He could see buildings in Bydgoszcz that contained Impregnacja bricks, and he felt himself beaming to see his father's products throughout the city. Close to their house, for example, stood a five-story apartment complex, built with Impregnacja bricks. In essence, the company helped Poland to rebuild after its rebirth as a nation.

Tadeusz was a disciplined man of business, devoted to his work. In the early afternoon he often repaired home for a quick lunch, took a nap to regain energy, and then returned to his office. He was absent from home a lot, and at the end of the workday, he came back tired. To unwind, he sometimes drank a small amount of bourbon or smoked a cigar—simple indulgences that he later gave up during the war. Through his hard work and business success, Tadeusz maintained a family tradition. "Mieczkowski" translated to "Sword man" in English, and the family had a crest, which Tadeusz displayed in the house. The crest was rich with martial imagery: at its center was a scimitar that penetrated a horseshoe, and a series of spears adorned a garland, topped by an arrow above a knight's helmet. While it wasn't unique—other families shared the identical crest—it symbolized that the Mieczkowski family belonged to the Polish nobility, and with that status came the talisman of socioeconomic achievement. Aniela came from an impressive pedigree, too. Her father, Jozef Kapelski, was a medical doctor, and he had looked after many families in the countryside where he worked. Partly because of their

1. Bydgoszcz, Poland—Living and Leaving 13

devotion to their careers and family, Bogdan's parents were austere in personality. His mother was dedicated to the church, and his father to his work.

As a business leader, Tadeusz felt a sense of civic responsibility, and he took a prominent role in the community. He belonged to the city council, which consisted of Bydgoszcz's business tycoons, making decisions on managing the city. His company kept him busy enough, and the city council added to his burdens. When the city council held meetings, Tadeusz came home in the evening even later than usual.

Even though his work was demanding, Tadeusz was a dedicated father who provided extremely well for his family. If he had any hobbies, it was family, and he expended all of his energies in looking after his wife and three sons. His business empire afforded them a comfortable life. They lived in a large, sturdy, five-bedroom home, which Tadeusz built using his factory's bricks and cement. When the house was completed, the workers displayed a garland and received special tips to celebrate the occasion. Overlooking a park, the house at 2 Wsypanskiego Street had balconies on the second floor and was situated in an affluent neighborhood. (Built more than a century ago, the house still stands today, as durable as ever.)

Tadeusz and Bogdan Mieczkowski outside their home in Bydgoszcz, 1929. Ten years after this photograph was taken, the family fled this house for Warsaw.

Bogdan and Seiko Mieczkowski outside the former Mieczkowski home in Bydgoszcz, 2010. Tadeusz's construction company built the home to last—and it has, for more than a century.

At home, the Mieczkowski family employed a cook, Truda, a single mother with two children, and she prepared delicious meals. Poles were celebrated for their love of meats, especially pork and ham dishes, and the house always had an adequate supply of protein for the three Mieczkowski boys, who were active and growing. They also had a domestic servant, Frania, a young girl who shopped, cleaned, and served Truda's meals.

The Mieczkowski family had two cars, including an American-built Willys Overland and a Tatra, which was a Czechoslovakian make (named after the Tatra Mountains located in southern Poland). The Willys Overland Company had been producing quality cars for two decades and was a prominent automaker in the U.S. But the Tatra was unreliable and broke down frequently. The nice aspect of the Tatra, though, was that it was a company vehicle, and Impregnacja gave the family a chauffeur who drove them on longer trips (an arrangement that reflected an era when the automobile was still a relatively new household appurtenance, and families who could afford one often employed a driver to shuttle them around). The chauffeur was a German naval veteran of World War I who had served aboard a U-boat, and the warm friendship the Mieczkowski family developed with him illustrated, on a small scale, the stable relations between Poland and Germany at the time. In fact, the Mieczkowskis' next-door neighbor in Bydgoszcz was a retired German couple, and all told, Germans comprised about ten percent of the city's population.

During summers, Bogdan and his family vacationed along the Baltic Sea. Tadeusz also owned a small hotel in the city of Rabka, nestled in the Carpathian Mountains, which sprawled more than nine hundred miles through central and eastern Europe. The hotel, called Margrabianka, had two floors and fourteen rooms, along with a common dining area that had a grand piano. Although the hotel was another part of Tadeusz's business holdings, it was also his labor of love, allowing him to gain a restorative respite from the pressures of running Impregnacja. There the family took winter vacations, where they loved to ski, which was a popular pastime among Poles. Occasionally, they went there for summer vacations, instead of going to the Baltic. Many people can remember the pool where they first learned to swim, and for Bogdan and his brothers, it was at Margrabianka, which had an open-air pool, uncommon in Poland at that time. During summers, they also visited Aunt Hala, Aniela's younger sister, who had married Tadeusz's brother Ludwig, creating additional ligaments joining the two families (such arrangements were not uncommon in Poland). Hala managed a farm, called Lutomek, in western Poland. Her farm was an impressive operation, where she grew wheat and rye,

The Mieczkowski family on a ski vacation before the war (left to right): Zbigniew, Janusz, Bogdan, Aniela, Tadeusz (unknown girl sits in front).

owned twenty muscular draft horses, and maintained a pond stocked with fish.

Outside of family, school stood at the center of the Mieczkowski brothers' lives. They were good students; their father made sure of it. Because of the excellent education he received in the U.S., Tadeusz emphasized the importance of their studies, and he encouraged and prodded their learning. At home, they had a library on the first floor, and Bogdan and his brothers had book collections in their respective rooms. The first-rate public schools in Poland helped, too. The boys took pride in their local high school, which was a short walk from their house, and they wore two-piece navy blue school uniforms with their school number (814) emblazoned on one sleeve. Among the subjects they studied was German language, and Bogdan grew adept at speaking it. Tadeusz hired a German woman to look after Bogdan and his brothers, and she spoke in German, which increased his knowledge of the language. Bogdan got so proficient at it that people asked him, especially seeing his fair complexion and light brown hair, if he were German. That result pleased Tadeusz, since he wanted to use every opportunity to enhance his boys' education, including with foreign languages. Their education would help them in life, he believed, and whatever bad fortune might befall them, no one could take away their schooling.

In prewar Poland, Bogdan and his family enjoyed a good life. It was like a period of bright sunshine before a deadly storm.

III. War Clouds on the Horizon

The political and military threats to Poland stretched back years; in fact, storm clouds darkened over Poland immediately after its rebirth, threatening its newly won independence. In 1920, Soviet leader Vladimir Lenin threw the Red Army against Poland, sparking the Russo-Polish War. This conflict featured the spectacular 1920 "Miracle on the Vistula," during which Marshal Jozef Pilsudski beat back advancing Soviet troops at Warsaw's Vistula River, marking a turning point in the war. The next year, the Treaty of Riga concluded the conflict and granted Poland more territory at Russia's expense. Although it had emerged victorious, Poland still considered the Russians to be oppressors, and the conflict left an even greater residue of bad blood between the two countries. The Soviet territorial concession rankled Russians, and one veteran who was especially aggrieved was Joseph Stalin, who thereafter plotted revenge against Poland.

Other dictators, present and future, coveted Polish territory. Adolf Hitler, who had become Germany's chancellor in 1933, annexed Austria five years later, achieving *Anschluss* (union) between Germany and his birth country. His aggression led to the infamous Munich Agreement of 1938, in which British Prime Minister Neville Chamberlain tried to "appease" Hitler by permitting him to take the Sudetenland in Czechoslovakia, a new country that the Treaty of Versailles created, as he promised no further territorial acquisitions. In March 1939, Hitler's troops took the rest of Czechoslovakia. It was "the greatest day of my life," Hitler pompously declared. At this point, he was capturing territory that had no historical connection to Germany; it was land belonging to Slavic people.

Following this German attack, Great Britain pledged to defend Poland's independence. Bogdan was just fourteen years old, so these events were somewhat abstract to him. He sensed that the world was snaking through convulsive twists and turns but would emerge onto a straight path eventually. Back in the days without television, he saw no footage of German troops entering Czechoslovakia, which kept him from visualizing and discerning how ominous these happenings were. At one point, officials at his Bydgoszcz school were concerned enough to hold a special assembly to prepare students for the uncomfortable idea that war could engulf them. They sang patriotic songs, and the teachers affirmed that Hitler would not conquer their country. Later, when the Germans invaded Poland, many of these teachers died.

Despite what the teachers said, events accelerated toward war. On August 23, 1939, German Foreign Minister Joachim von Ribbentrop met with Soviet Foreign Minister Vyacheslav Molotov in Moscow. There they signed the Ribbentrop-Molotov Pact, a nonaggression treaty in which Germany and the Soviet Union agreed not to attack each other for ten years. No longer worrying about Soviet interference, Hitler could now engage in more territorial aggrandizement.

Soviet President Joseph Stalin, the cobbler's son who had spurned the priesthood to pursue radical politics, was the other great beneficiary. The cunning Stalin (which was his adopted name, meaning "man of steel") had won control of the country after a decade-long power struggle following Lenin's 1924 death (even though Lenin had warned that Stalin was too brutal to be leader), and he was bent on acquiring territory and transforming his backward nation. The Ribbentrop-Molotov Pact allowed Stalin to build up Soviet forces to pursue both aims.

The treaty also contained a secret agreement that the signatories withheld from the media: Germany and the Soviet Union agreed to divide Poland. This conspiracy became public knowledge only after the Soviet Union invaded Poland. As events bore out two years later, Hitler had another devious plot, aiming to use Poland as a corridor of attack into the Soviet Union. The Ribbentrop-Molotov Pact gave him breathing space, keeping Stalin at bay while Hitler developed and then unleashed his plans. It also bought Stalin time and distance. For Stalin, who mistrusted Hitler, ganging up on Poland provided a way to neutralize him.

The whole scheme was stunning. Throughout the world, people assumed that these two countries were ideological enemies and bitter rivals. Yet the pact allowed their leaders to engage in a political sleight-of-hand to pursue deeper motives. For Hitler and Stalin, it removed their worries about conflict with the other. Here, Poland was key. One of the only ways the two antagonistic countries could reconcile their differences was in a treaty using Poland as bounty, to be divided up between the two conspirators. Bogdan's country, barely two decades old as a reconstituted nation-state, was to be cleaved in two and again might disappear.

Poles felt safer and relieved when Great Britain responded with the Anglo-Polish Alliance. On August 25, 1939, England signed a treaty pledging to defend Poland against attack by any European country. The alliance seemed a way to dissuade Germany from more territorial grabs and defuse the brewing crisis in Europe.

On September 1—the day Bogdan sat in his dentist's chair—Germany smashed through Poland. Hitler's control of Czechoslovakia allowed him to attack Poland from the south as well as west and north, catching Poland in a pincer movement. As if they were a gigantic lobster claw, German army divisions began to squeeze shut and crush Poland. The German invasion force comprised one and a half million troops. They used 1,500 tanks and more than a thousand airplanes; it was no wonder that, as Bogdan concluded his dental appointment, the invasion sounded like thunder.

Two days later, Britain and France declared war on Germany. World War II had begun. Defending his aggression, Hitler claimed that the German people needed *lebensraum*—"living space"—in central and eastern Europe. In truth, he wanted nothing less than to rule Europe. Over the next few weeks, Hitler's army executed *blitzkrieg*—lightning war—speeding over Poland using fast tanks and bombers, overwhelming the country. Although the Polish Army fought courageously, it lacked the sophisticated tanks and aircraft that the Germans possessed.

As it had been throughout history, Polish independence was in grave danger. On September 17, the danger mushroomed. At 4:00 a.m. on that day, the Soviet Union poured in 600,000 troops over the border and occupied Poland's eastern half. The Soviets confiscated homes and businesses and declared themselves owners and rulers of eastern Poland. Like all Poles, Bogdan felt his country was stabbed in both the front and back—attacked by Germany to the West and the U.S.S.R. to the East—caught off-guard and paralyzed. The two most brutal dictatorships in history had dismembered his nation. Of Poland's two million troops, only 700,000 soldiers were afield at the time, and they proved no match for the combined forces of Germany and the Soviet Union.

Later, Americans, Brits, and other westerners would have different feelings toward the Soviet effort in World War II, because the blood that the Russians spilled in fighting Hitler illustrated their sacrifice and contribution to the Allied war effort. Poles had another view of the U.S.S.R. The Soviets were the enemy, conspiring with the Germans and invading their country. The Soviets might have been allies to the U.S. and the U.K., but they were no allies to Poles. They connived with Germany to disfigure Poland and kill its people.

Poles fought to preserve everything they had, but for too many, this effort was hopeless. By early October 1939, one hundred thousand Poles had fled the country, initially escaping to neighboring countries such as Hungary and Romania. Many of them continued to trek westward, reaching France and Britain. (The following year, Poles made great contributions during the Battle of Britain, denting Hitler's armor by repulsing his attempt to take to the British Isles, handing the German dictator his first major defeat.) For millions of Polish families, World War II meant the destruction of the lives they once knew. Bogdan's family was one of them.

IV. Flight from Bydgoszcz

Hitler's troops reached Bydgoszcz quickly, since it was little more than one hundred miles from the western border with Germany. The Nazis overran the city, killing upper-class citizens, eventually executing 15,000 Bydgoszcz residents. Tadeusz Mieczkowski was a prominent target. He had "industrialist" on his Polish identification card. That word and profession, coupled with his status as a part-time citizen-administrator in Bydgoszcz and his American college degree, meant that the Germans would murder him. Eventually, they executed most members of the city council, giving a clear indication of what fate had awaited Tadeusz.

Bogdan and his family needed to flee. Leaving meant abandoning their house and everything they owned. When Bogdan returned home from Dr. Sobocinski's office, there was no time to pack clothes or childhood memorabilia. His family took only what they were wearing, rushing to evacuate the house. They even had to say good-bye to their dogs. Bogdan was particularly saddened to leave Filut behind. He was a cheerful, obedient dachshund who had learned various commands, such as sitting and waiting for food, and the boys had enjoyed teaching him. After September 1, Bogdan never saw Filut again.

Events now controlled them. From this moment onward, Bogdan and his family had to move swiftly with the current of action, wherever it took them. They had no time to feel sentimental about abandoning their home. They had no chance to communicate with childhood friends and their parents to learn their plans. They had no moment even to process any thoughts or feelings. Were they to stop and let their emotions get in the way, they would make themselves vulnerable to the Germans and jeopardize their lives.

Bogdan did not realize it at the time, but he was leaving Bydgoszcz for good, which meant his life was changing permanently. Bogdan rarely saw the city again, returning only a handful of times. (During one visit, Bogdan passed by the Impregnacja factory. The large hole where workers used to dig clay for bricks was filled in, and the factory sat idle. Today, it is long gone, replaced by housing.)

Although Bogdan's parents had not even a moment to grab food, they did take every zloty of cash they had because they knew they would need it. Aniela loaded the boys up in the Tatra and drove out of the city, under the agreement that Tadeusz would find them later at a prearranged location. As his mother drove them out of Bydgoszcz, Bogdan saw a man's body lying in the street. As a teenage boy, he could barely comprehend the notion of a dead body, yet there it was. They had no idea what had happened to him—it might have been a Bydgoszcz resident, or perhaps a German parachutist—but they took it as an ominous sign.

After a day, Tadeusz joined the family in the Willys. Abandoning the Tatra, he decided to take his family to Kobryn, a city 270 miles east of Bydgoszcz, near the Soviet border, where his sister Marysia Czapska lived (today, Kobryn lies in the western part of Belarus, just outside Poland). As they traveled east, Bogdan saw fleets of German planes flying overhead, slicing through the sky and casting dark shadows on the ground. These were invaders, penetrating deep into Poland, menacing and intimidating. They were killers, Bogdan thought, and he struggled to absorb that fact. As they sped toward Kobryn, nervous and edgy, they saw the effects of German strafing: burnt-out shells of houses, dead livestock, and even human bodies. Bogdan sensed that these invaders controlled everything, including the power of life and death, but events were moving too quickly for him to feel fear. He felt numb, overwhelmed by the cascade of events. Inside the car, they just drove along swiftly, almost mechanically, with too much happening at once to process the implications.

Tadeusz thought his family could find shelter with Marysia and her husband. When they reached the city, it seemed oddly peaceful, and they felt they had found refuge from danger. Marysia's house was simple, lacking even an inside bathroom, which forced everyone to use an outhouse;

1. Bydgoszcz, Poland—Living and Leaving

fortunately, the weather was still mild in September, so no one suffered freezing temperatures during the necessary trips there. Overall, at Marysia's home, Bogdan and his family were able to enjoy good meals and catch their breath.

The tranquility soon ended. Two days after the Mieczkowskis arrived, county officials ordered that families be evacuated on buses. With gasoline now scarce, Tadeusz decided to abandon the Willys and join the exodus. They climbed aboard a bus and traveled east to escape the Germans, almost reaching the new Soviet border marking their occupation of Poland, but then they backtracked to flee the Soviets, the eastern invaders.

Bogdan and his family were zigzagging, and as they now traveled west, at one point the bus slowed and shuddered to a stop. "What on earth is going on now?" Bogdan wondered. He craned his neck to look out the windshield and saw a roadblock. The bus doors flung open. A civilian dressed in black, wearing a red armband, stepped aboard and spoke in Yiddish, telling the driver to proceed to Brest, a city thirty miles west of Kobryn that had gained fame as site of the Brest-Litovsk Treaty of 1918, which allowed the Soviet Union to withdraw from World War I. Now the Soviets controlled the city (today, like Kobryn, Brest lies in western Belarus).

When the family got to Brest, darkness had settled in, and the bus stopped at a jailhouse. In front of that building stood two Soviet tanks, one with its loud motor running, a physical reminder that they were now in the Soviet-occupied zone of Poland. They got off the bus and, once inside the jail, they saw more black-clad civilians, all wearing red armbands.

The invasion of Poland involved a hierarchy of victims, and Bogdan began to witness the first stratum of Poles to suffer: police officers. The black-garmented authorities were processing a long line of Polish policemen, who were probably headed to forced labor in the Gulag, the horrid work camps in Siberia. Police represented Polish authority, and the Soviets were abolishing the police force so that their new regime could supplant it and control Poles. Policemen also had guns, and the Soviets needed to strip Poles of countervailing weapons. So the officers, who had represented order and authority in Bogdan's old world, were reduced to nothing. Inside one room, Bogdan heard a policeman scream, "They are torturing me! They are beating me!" The door to the room slammed shut, and only muffled cries seeped out, which soon grew silent.

A wise rule was to obey anyone who had guns and power, and it was clear who was in control now. The Soviet authorities ordered Bogdan and his family to the second floor. There they found a large common room with about two hundred Polish citizens, and everyone spent the night there, sleeping on the bare floor. In the morning, Bogdan could hear more cries of men being tortured. Sitting on the floor, a police officer's wife hastily shredded his uniform to protect his identity and prevent him from being beaten. Under a blanket, her husband was shaking, which made the blanket vibrate as if it were alive. Their fear of what might happen to him was chiseled into their faces.

For a long time afterward Bogdan wondered about this couple's fate, but whatever it was, he knew his family got lucky. Tadeusz and Aniela were middle-aged parents from the German-occupied part of the country, and they were responsible for three teenage boys. Because of these factors, their captors released them. But they knew this reprieve was only temporary; they had to keep moving. If they stayed in Brest, the Soviets would catch them again and deport them to Siberia. Conditions in the city compelled them to leave, too. Store shelves were stripped bare, uprooted people roamed the city, drifting like ghosts—many of them sleeping in the railroad station—and the Soviet authorities conducted sweeping arrests in which they jailed civilians en masse.

Tadeusz decided to risk returning to Kobryn alone so that he could retrieve the Willys car, which would give his family mobility. That move almost cost him his life. The Soviets arrested him and marched him under armed guards to a jailhouse interrogation room. He had no idea of what would happen to him; they could have discovered his identity and killed him. Instead, after a tense period of uncertainty, they let him go. The psychological and emotional strain on him reached a breaking point. When he rejoined his family, he sat down next to Aniela, recounted what had happened, and began to sob. It was the first and only time Bogdan ever saw his father cry.

Tadeusz, though, was a brave man, not one to be paralyzed by emotion. With responsibility for his family's lives resting in his hands, he made a decision: they had to go to Warsaw. The journey there was risky, since they first would have to evade Soviet authorities in Poland's eastern zone, and then slip past German troops to the west, because the capital lay west of the Molotov-Ribbentrop line that Soviets and Germans used to divide and conquer Poland. Moreover, German forces tightly controlled Warsaw, clamping down a curfew and imposing martial law. But if they could make it to Warsaw, they could seek refuge with one of Aniela's relatives who lived there. The city's large population would allow them to blend in better, affording them safety in numbers. Security through anonymity seemed the best bet to survive.

After two unsuccessful attempts, the Mieczkowski family finally left Brest by train, getting to the town of Siemiatycze, and from there they reached the Bug (pronounced "Boog") River, which runs just west of Brest and a hundred miles east of Warsaw. (After the war, Stalin annexed the area that they traveled through, east of the Bug River. Poland would never

1. Bydgoszcz, Poland—Living and Leaving 23

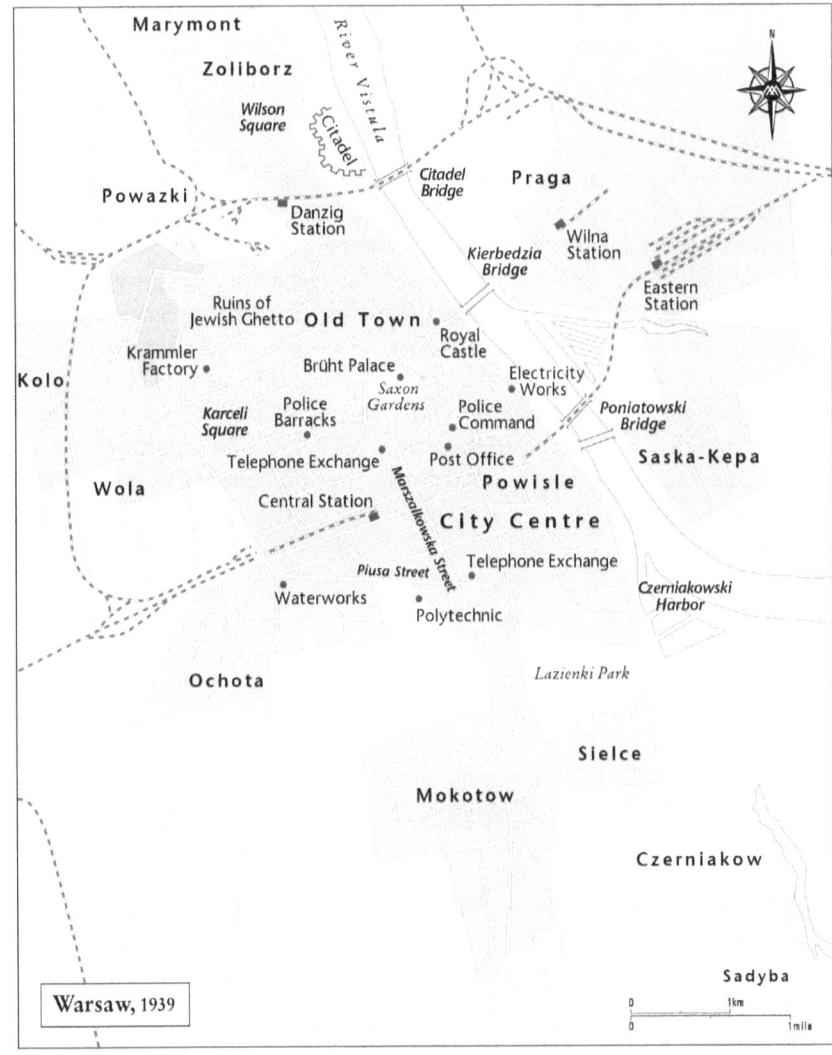

Warsaw during World War II. The Mieczkowski family had an apartment on Piusa Street, just west of Marszalkowska Street (map by Malcolm A. Swanston).

regain that territory.) They boarded a boat and crossed the Bug at night from the Soviet zone into the German one. Nine people were aboard. The others might have been secure and prosperous people just days earlier, like Tadeusz, but now they were all refugees from terror, their futures uncertain, fleeing in the darkness. Everyone stayed silent as the water lapped up against the boat, and they made slow progress toward the other shore. Luckily, the night was calm, because the boat sat perilously low in the water, and Bogdan touched the water with his hands, feeling cold splashes during the whole crossing. After they landed and debarked, they walked two miles to a train station and took a train to Warsaw. Bogdan was amazed that trains were running at all amidst the chaos, but in a few hours, they got to the city.

It was late November 1939, and Warsaw looked ruined. Bogdan and his family had to take a horse-drawn cart to a relative's apartment. A college professor, he sheltered them for a few days until they found an apartment. (They learned that later in the war, the Germans shot the professor's wife.) After looking for a rental unit, Tadeusz obtained a place on the top floor of a three-story building at 46 Piusa Street (named after the pope), a short block from Marszalkowska Street, a main downtown thoroughfare running north-south through the city.

Thus began Bogdan's life in Warsaw, where he would stay for most of the German occupation, until more perilous events propelled him elsewhere.

— 2 —

Otaru, Japan—A Good Life by the Sea

I. A "Fighting Condition" at Pearl Harbor

The announcement stunned Seiko Kawakami. In Japan, it was already December 8, 1941. The country's time zone put it thirteen hours ahead of the U.S., and on that day the Kawakami family's home radio crackled with a news bulletin. Japan's bombers had fought American warplanes at Hawaii's Pearl Harbor naval base.

"Early this morning, in *Shin ju wan* (the Japanese word for Pearl Harbor), Japanese military forces went into a fighting condition with American forces," the broadcast said. The Japanese government controlled radio broadcasts and carefully crafted the wording, so the announcement skirted around a fact that Seiko learned later: Japan had attacked the U.S.

Hearing the news, Seiko's older brother Suguru jumped up in shock. "Wow!" he exclaimed. "War has started!" Once he settled back down, the two siblings sat in their family's small living room and listened intently as Prime Minister Hideki Tojo announced, "Now the emperor has proclaimed that war has begun."

This war would devastate the Kawakami family and change their lives—and their country—forever.

II. Japanese Militarism

At the time of Pearl Harbor, Seiko was a twelve-year-old girl living in Otaru, a city in Hokkaido, Japan's northernmost island. Seiko was in sixth grade, the final year of elementary school in the Japanese system, and though they were only children, she and her classmates sensed that tensions had been building between the U.S. and Japan for decades. In school, history was one of Seiko's favorite subjects, and she learned about the litany of actions from other nations that slighted the Japanese, stretching back generations. After the Sino-Japanese War ended in 1895, China ceded to Japan the Liaodong Peninsula in northeastern China, jutting into the Yellow Sea, yet Russia, Germany, and France forced Japan to relinquish this gain. Many Japanese felt that the episode showed their country was weak, a less muscular power that had to accept the dictates of stronger nations. The country simmered with discontent at such insults and sought more international respect. So when the Russo-Japanese War broke out in 1904, it was especially important for Japan to win as a way to overcome a lingering sense of shame. Japan emerged victorious the next year, gaining international respect that it felt was long overdue.

The end of World War I seemed to set preconditions for future conflict. Following the war, the Allies refused to include a racial equality clause in the Versailles Treaty, even though Japan had pressed for it, creating a void that left Japan disgruntled. Only two major countries emerged from World War I physically unscathed and stronger than they were before the conflict—the U.S. and Japan—and they seemed on a collision course.

The decade of the 1920s paved the way for further confrontation. At the 1921 Washington Naval Conference, which tried to slow the naval arms race, participants forged an agreement, the Four Power Treaty, in which the U.S. and Great Britain consigned Japan to lesser strength by forcing it to accept a lower naval tonnage, along a 5:5:3 ratio—assuring American and British superiority. The Japanese begrudgingly called it a "Rolls Royce, Rolls Royce, Ford" formula. In 1924, another slight came when the U.S. Congress passed the National Origins Act, which set quotas and effectively banned Japanese immigration into the U.S.

Despite fraying relations with the U.S., Japan felt that its global standing was gaining ground. At the 1928 Summer Olympics in Amsterdam, track and field star Mikio Oda garnered Japan's first ever gold medal when he won the triple jump. But the reaction seemed to show Europeans accepting it more graciously than Americans did. News reports said that the Dutch hosts presented Oda with a bouquet of flowers when he was about to have dinner one evening, and he was surprised and flattered. Among Japanese, such stories created the impression that the Europeans saw Japan more as an equal, whereas the Americans refused to acknowledge its growing strength.

For generations, territorial acquisition provided a path to gain world prestige and acquire natural resources, and Japanese militarists clearly subscribed to these ideas. This thinking was common for the time and helped to explain Germany's push for "Lebensraum." In 1931, Japan took a first step of its own in that direction by taking Mukden in Manchuria, a territory that was part of China. At the League of Nations, China protested the Japanese aggression, but in 1933, Japan withdrew from the League. Four years later, the so-called "Marco Polo Bridge Incident" occurred, during which Japanese and Chinese troops skirmished at a bridge near Beijing, marking the outbreak of a full-scale war. Japan then invaded China, capturing Beijing, Shanghai, and Nanking and signaling the start of world war in Asia. What Seiko learned about in school, though, was much different. China touched off the war, her teachers said, acting as the aggressor, and Japan was rightfully winning, its power expanding.

Japan aspired to empire. For centuries, a key measure of a country's greatness was how much territory it held and how many resources and people it controlled. For subjects, colonialism was a wound that sliced deep into a country's soul, oppressing people and hamstringing economies and national aspirations. But for the mother country, the practice was a point of pride and a tangible sign of national greatness. Like other ambitious nations, Japan wished to enhance its global standing, and it looked to expand its territorial reach. But to the Japanese, the West tried to elbow them aside in their own backyard, the Pacific Ocean. European powers like the Netherlands had controlled the "Dutch East Indies" for centuries, while the U.S. was the newcomer, acquiring the Philippines and Guam as spoils of victory after the Spanish-American War of 1898. Later, in October 1941, when Hideki Tojo became prime minister, he inveighed against the "ABCD" powers that restricted Japan in the Pacific—America, Britain, China, and the Dutch.

Japan was trying to enlarge its "Greater East Asia Co-Prosperity Sphere," which it had originally conceived as a self-sufficient bloc of nations comprising itself, China, and Manchukuo, acting in concert to oppose Western domination and imperialism. Now it was trying to enlarge this concept by gaining control of Southeast Asia, eyeing the Philippines, British Malaya, the Dutch East Indies, and more. Japan prided itself on being the workshop of Asia, using raw materials to churn out manufactured goods for the entire Pacific region. But the country's problem was that, as an island nation, it depended heavily on imports. For example, it obtained two thirds of its oil from the U.S., and critical metals and minerals like scrap iron, salt, and copper all came from abroad. These additional areas would provide resources that Japan needed to achieve greater industrial might, and they would also slake Japan's thirst for empire. In essence, the Japanese planned to supplant the U.S. and European powers as colonial rulers of Asia.

In school, Seiko felt the effects of this policy in lessons that limned Japan as the proper king of the Pacific. In late 1937, she and her classmates felt their country's growing pains when one incident affected them. They had to pay a small donation to help Japan compensate for the sinking of the U.S. gunboat *Panay*, which Japanese aviators had bombed while it was anchored on the Yangtze River near Nanking. Two American sailors died, and scores were wounded; the Japanese government apologized and offered to pay an indemnity. At school, teachers told Seiko's class that the government had "a guilty feeling," as they put it, about the damage the military had caused, and Seiko had to ask her parents for five sen, which was the approximate equivalent of an American dime. One sen could get two pieces of candy at a store, so for a child, five sen was a small fortune.

The teachers' words and the tiny treasure the children relinquished allowed them to glimpse the larger significance of what happened. The quick amends after the *Panay* incident showed that both sides—Japan and the U.S.—were eager to avoid war, and as schoolchildren, they accepted the government's explanation and patriotically helped to pay the indemnity.

But over the next four years, U.S.-Japanese relations deteriorated. When Japan occupied France's Indochina colonies in 1940, the U.S. responded by embargoing scrap metal exports to Japan. The next year, Japan drove further into Indochina, and the U.S. froze Japanese assets, a move that deprived Japan of the ability to buy oil, which was a serious economic blow. Although Seiko had no way of knowing it as she listened to the radio on December 8, the attack on Pearl Harbor was part of a scheme to acquire more territory and oppose U.S. imperialism.

But the Japanese strategy balanced upon many contingencies. A resource-starved country like Japan could not survive a long war with the U.S. The architect of the Pearl Harbor attack, Fleet Admiral Isoroku Yamamoto admired America's industrial engine, expressing pessimism that Japan could defeat the U.S. over the long term, accurately predicting that Japan could prevail for only half a year. In truth, he opposed the Pearl Harbor offensive as inane, but demonstrating his loyalty, he helped to plan it. (His pessimism about Japan's chances of defeating the U.S. increased as the war dragged on, yet he continued to fight, reflecting the obedience that characterized the Japanese.) Once war began, Japanese leaders hoped for a negotiated peace with the U.S., whereby the latter would concede Japanese dominance in the Pacific and thus allow the country to enjoy unchallenged access to the resources that would make it a great nation.

Like so many aspects of the government's war planning, that idea was folly. But citizens in Hokkaido and throughout Japan had little idea of the catastrophe their government was plunging them into so recklessly.

III. Life in Hokkaido

Hokkaido, which means "north sea territory," sits between the Sea of Japan to the west and the Pacific Ocean to the east. In land area, it is

Japan's second largest island, but it is only about the size of the state of Maine. Moreover, when Seiko grew up there during the 1930s, it comprised less than five percent of Japan's population. One reason for this paucity of people was that Hokkaido was comparatively new to Japan. Only in the 1860s did the Meiji government, Japan's new leadership at the time, decide to gain control of Hokkaido, mainly to prevent Russia from seizing it. (In annexing Hokkaido, though, the government displaced many native Ainu people, who had lived there for centuries, and encouraged the Ainu to assimilate with the Japanese, a controversial policy that marginalized them as a people and culture.)

Because relatively few people lived on Hokkaido, it remained bucolic and beautiful after Japan acquired it. It had *onsen* (hot springs), forests, mountains, stunning sea shores, and wildlife that was uncommon in other areas of Japan, including bears, owls, deer, and foxes. Later, when Seiko mentioned to Tokyo residents that she was from Hokkaido, she often got a shocked response, almost like she was from another planet, which was usually followed by a question such as, "So, that means you live next to bears?"

The only Hokkaido city that seemed to be developing was Sapporo, the capital, but when Seiko was growing up its population numbered just a few hundred thousand. Today, Sapporo stands as Japan's fifth-largest metropolis, and during the 1930s Seiko could see inklings of its future growth. When she was in fifth grade, her class went on a school trip to Sapporo. The city's hustle-and-bustle and well-organized street grids, which reflected advanced urban planning, captivated her. The mighty Toyohira River snaked through the city and provided water, while Mount Moiwa, one of Japan's most beautiful mountains, loomed in the distance. The huge brick building of the Hokkaido Prefectural Office impressed Seiko, and Imperial Hokkaido University's campus was a commanding presence. The school seemed to radiate power and authority, and it was renowned for many departments, including medicine, engineering, and agriculture. Although it was just an hour away, Sapporo seemed a world away from the simple life in Otaru.

But even Otaru was a huge step up from Seiko's roots. She was born in 1929 in Yoichi, a speck on the map ten miles west of Otaru, which officially became a "town" after its population reached three thousand during the 1920s. Seiko was the third of five children. Her father, Hiroshi, was a hard-bitten, no-nonsense patriarch who taught science at a vocational school. Hiroshi grew up in Eramizawa, a tiny town north of Sapporo, and he earned a teaching certificate there. Although a bespectacled chain smoker, he was still athletic, swimming and playing tennis regularly. Throughout the day—from the moment he left for work until just before bedtime—he drank copious amounts of green tea, a volume that could have filled a small bathtub daily.

Hiroshi brewed his tea in a *kyusu*, a small teapot, but he frequently misplaced it. One morning, Seiko walked into the family's tiny kitchen and sensed tension between her parents. She asked her mother Echi what had happened, and she said that Hiroshi had once again lost his *kyusu*. Exasperated, she had told him to tie it around his belt so that he would not lose it so often. This irreverent suggestion made him angry, and he felt it upset the natural deference that a Japanese wife should show her husband.

That incident spoke volumes about Seiko's mother, Echi. She was strong-willed in an era where women were supposed to be subservient to men, and society enforced these mores of a docile, deferential female. In public, women sometimes were discouraged from initiating a greeting with a man, such as "good morning" or "good day," and they were not supposed to venture out at night to movies or bars lest their reputations be besmirched. Females seldom had their own careers, deferring instead to their husbands as the family breadwinner. Sometimes, they barely knew their husbands until they were married. Families often arranged marriages by matchmaking, so women relied on a network of relatives and friends to find their husband. The resulting unions sometimes experienced true love, but they also could be distant.

Echi broke the normal cultural restrictions in many ways. Whereas women usually refrained from carving out their own careers, Echi taught at an Otaru elementary school, and she enjoyed a prolific teaching career. She grew up in Esashi, Hokkaido, along the Sea of Japan, and she went to Tokyo to teach at an elementary school but returned to Hokkaido after her mother fell ill. Her journey from Esashi to Tokyo showed her ambition, because it meant leaping from a pin dot town to Japan's capital. Echi was diminutive, standing less than five feet tall, but she was a mountain of motivation and determination. Yet, conforming to tradition, she went to work every day wearing a black-colored *hakama*, a long skirt that covered her legs completely, looking like the bottom half of a *kimono* gown. Most working women wore *hakama*, while men wore Western clothes consisting of jackets and ties.

Hiroshi and Echi never needed matchmaking services. They met when they were both teaching at a school in Yoichi, and they got married and started a family. Besides Suguru, who was born in 1924, Seiko's family included her sister Yasuko, who was two years older than Seiko, her sister Shizuko, three years younger, and the baby of the family, her brother Kazutoshi, who was born in 1935. Seiko's maternal grandmother Hagi, a widow who had taught sewing to the native Ainu people in Hokkaido, also lived with the family, an arrangement common in Japan at that time.

In 1934, Hiroshi and Echi's teaching jobs transferred them from Yoichi

2. Otaru, Japan—A Good Life by the Sea

The city of Otaru sits on Hokkaido's west coast, facing the Sea of Japan (map by Malcolm A. Swanston).

to neighboring Toyohama, which had a population of only five hundred. Toyohama had just one small dirt road running through it, speckled with homes that looked like rickety dollhouses. It was a small, stifling village that seemed a throwback to the nineteenth century, frozen in an older era. Even bears, the unofficial Hokkaido mascot, seemed bored in Toyohama. During the summer, buses traveled along a narrow dirt road burrowed into the hillside and often encountered bears sleeping in the middle of the street.

Toyohama was too parochial for anyone to have educational and vocational opportunities, and Hiroshi and Echi knew that. The town was so isolated that life there could be perilous. No doctor practiced medicine in Toyohama, and if anybody fell gravely ill, residents would gather to help, often creating an unusual sight. They took a house door, turned it into a makeshift stretcher by putting a futon or some bedding on it, and then carried the patient away, walking ten miles to Yoichi with the patient in triage, even during winter.

Seiko's parents itched to leave Toyohama. Because of the primitive medical care there, they got scared whenever any family member became ill, which happened often. Shizuko once suffered agonizing stomach pains, and Hiroshi hired a fisherman to take her by boat to a neighboring town, where he found three skilled doctors who diagnosed an appendicitis attack. Luckily, they caught it in the early stages, but Seiko's parents realized that with five children, they needed to be close to better medical treatment. They waited for an opportunity to get the family to a more modern environment.

That came in 1939, when Hiroshi and Echi landed teaching jobs in Otaru. Packing up all their possessions, Seiko and her family used a combination of ship and train to get to their new hometown. Located on Hokkaido's west coast, Otaru faced the Sea of Japan and had a wide, sweeping port that stretched across the shoreline, as if welcoming incoming ships with open arms. Across the distant horizon, the water blended with the sky. A series of canals and waterways latticed the city, and the streets sloped steeply downward as they moved eastward toward the water. Looming over the city was Mount Teguyama, which commanded a stunning view of the surrounding hills and port below. During the summer, an aerial tram took people to the mountaintop for a breathtaking view, and during winter, skiers tackled the mountain's slopes. Seiko's family was proud that her brother Suguru became an accomplished ski jumper by training on Mount Tenguyama, and people commented on how muscular his legs were.

Winter was the hub of the entire calendar year in Otaru, dragging on interminably. Hokkaido sits at the same latitude as Canada, and during winter, cold winds swept down from Siberia and picked up moisture over the Sea of Japan, buffeting Otaru with cold air and dumping snow on the city. Temperatures routinely plunged below zero degrees Fahrenheit, and snowfall averaged more than seventeen feet yearly. As late as May, mounds of snow still sat atop Mount Teguyama.

Besides snow, Otaru was famous for its seafaring and fishing products. Craftsmen made bright glass buoys that helped to guide offshore fishing boats. Herring was a staple in the city's thriving export trade. Norwegians called herring "gold of the sea" because it brought huge profits,

2. Otaru, Japan—A Good Life by the Sea

A view of Otaru from Mount Teguyama, showing the city's sweeping port.

Seiko Mieczkowski, pictured in 2016 in downtown Otaru. The city's canal system is one of its most beautiful features.

and fishing communities worldwide revered this small silver fish from Otaru. Some merchants and fishermen in Otaru got wealthy from the herring trade. One merchant built an opulent castle outside the city, and Otaru residents dubbed it *nishin gotten* [herring castle].

Herring and other fish gave many people in Otaru decent lifestyles—and a great diet. The freshest sushi Seiko ever tasted was in Otaru, and her family ate raw fish regularly. In addition to herring, fishermen harvested scallops in the cold waters off Hokkaido, which Seiko and her family always ate raw, and they also enjoyed flounder. Just as Americans eat beef jerky, the Japanese salted and hung fish to dry and then ate dried fish year-round. With fish, Otaru's long winters worked to residents' advantage. The cold temperatures induced fish to build up layers of fat, adding a succulence to their taste.

In addition to fish, Otaru's export trade included agricultural goods like soy beans and potatoes, which streamed into the city from farms located in Hokkaido's interior. A merchant fleet took these products around the world, sailing especially to Sakhalin Island, the Soviet Union, Korea, and European ports. In tying their fortunes to farming the land or fishing the sea, most Otaru residents earned income but not wealth, living decently but never extravagantly.

Japan's three other islands—Kyushu, Shikoku, and the main island, Honshu—were more industrialized than Hokkaido, and by the 1930s Japan had become a true global power, ranking seventh in the world in economic strength. It also had military might, and the Sino-Japanese War, raging since 1937, gave Japan a chance to flex its martial muscle. By the late 1930s, Japan had withdrawn from all international naval agreements, freeing it to amass more armaments. Japan built the world's third-largest navy, and it boasted battleships of the fearsome *Yamato* class, which had a 64,000-ton displacement, thick armor, and heavy guns. In a dramatic, visible way, the Japanese navy demonstrated that the country had come a long way from earlier in the century, when it had to rely on Great Britain to build its first battleships. Japan seemed ready to make a statement to the world.

IV. Spartan Beyond Belief

Otaru was far enough from Tokyo that residents felt little impact from the Sino-Japanese War and continued life as normal. But the war against America would be different. This was total war, and soon after Pearl Harbor, Otaru residents noticed subtle changes. As government-imposed rationing hit the city, bakeries and clothing stores closed, and staple foods like rice and soy sauce became scarce or even disappeared. Shortages wrought by war affected everyone, and Seiko witnessed a sad sight when storeowners shuttered their shops for good.

Hiroshi and Echi rented a small, one-story house in Otaru, shoe-horning eight family members into five rooms—a kitchen, living room, bathroom, and two bedrooms. All told, the house was no more than seven hundred square feet. The small bathroom had no tub or shower stall, and Seiko and her family washed in a public bathhouse, as most people in Hokkaido did. For the two bedrooms, it was four persons to a room: Hiroshi, Echi, and the two youngest children—Shizuko and Kazu—took one, while Hagi, Suguru, Seiko, and Yasuko occupied the other.

The house had no running water, so like most families, the Kawakamis took metal buckets to a nearby well, located about forty yards away. It had a large metal handle that they pumped vigorously, which was tough work in itself. During each trip to the well, they collected about three gallons of water in three buckets and then hauled them back to the house to use for every purpose—including drinking, cooking, and washing clothes. This task was particularly arduous during winter; the Kawakami children trudged through snow that came up to their thighs, all the while carrying the heavy buckets. Because he was the eldest son and thus shouldered the most onerous chores, Suguru did most of the water carrying, but Seiko often went to the well with rice, which she washed on site and then took back to the house. Six different families used this particular well, so it sometimes ran dry, and when that happened everyone waited hours for it to replenish itself.

A house with no running water is like a car without gasoline and oil, and a reader might have trouble imagining the hardship that missing essential imposes. Getting water from that well was vital, and for the eldest Kawakami children—Suguru, Yasuko, and Seiko—a huge part of their childhood consisted of lugging buckets from the well to their house. Once they had the water buckets at home, they conserved every drop, knowing that any water they consumed would necessitate more arduous trips to that well. No matter how much everyone tried to save water, though, the reality was that eight family members needed and used it, so they had to make those trips willy-nilly—and frequently.

No running water meant no flush toilets, and the Kawakami house had a simple in-house john as the bathroom. Many homes had actual outhouses separate from the residence, so for Seiko's family, having a bathroom within their house was a privilege. But the toilet was crude; it just dumped into a large wooden chamber pot that sat below the floor. Every week, a man came to the house to haul away the waste; it was a tough task, and the children sometimes watched him do it, with a mix of fascination and revulsion. He made the task more unsavory by working with his bare hands, never using gloves. (Once, Shizuko saw him taking a break and eating a sandwich—which he did without washing his hands, she reported with horror.)

The family's house was made of wood and paper, the same flimsy construction that proved disastrous when American aircraft firebombed Tokyo in 1945. In one bedroom, the roof leaked during rainstorms, and the Kawakamis used a bucket to catch the rainwater. The family lay down straw tatami mats in every room except the kitchen, and while they provided a small amount of warmth for their feet, the mats could get cold, too. During winter, they sometimes glistened with a thin coat of ice. In the room where Seiko, her grandmother, Suguru, and Yasuko slept, the fittings and moldings were so poor that a gap between the window frame and the wall around it exposed the room to the elements. Simple caulk could have fixed this problem, but the family had no such resources. During winter, especially when Seiko woke up in the morning, she could see her breath vapor, and when strong winds howled outside, snow actually blew into the room.

An enormous daily operation that fell on Seiko's shoulders was laundry. Outside, the family collected rainwater in a special china bucket. At the bottom, they layered down ashes from their wood stove. Once they got rainwater, they filtered out the ashes and used that water to clean clothes, turning the small amount of ash residue into a simple detergent. After washing the clothes, Seiko hung them on a clothesline behind the house. During winter, they froze, so they looked like stiff, two-dimensional cardboard cutouts. Still, they dried off partially in the winter air, and the exposure to the sun helped to kill germs. The clothes smelled of Otaru snow, a fresh aroma that was always distinctive. Seiko draped the frozen clothes on her arms and shoulders, brought them inside, and hung them in the living room, where the stove dried them further.

By twentieth-century Western standards, the Kawakami house was spartan beyond belief. At night, only two electric lights illuminated it, in a bedroom and the living room. Most homes in Otaru had the same arrangement—two lights for the whole house. Residents had no control over the lights; instead, the city government turned them on and off at regulated times. Citizens' willingness to abide by this schedule bore testimony to how faithfully the Japanese adapted themselves to rules and circumstances they could not control.

Seiko and her family ate meals in the living room, savoring whatever food they had but also the electric light there at the dinner hour. During the school year, the children settled into a customary routine. After finishing supper, they cleaned the table, cracked open their books, and then all five of them studied together at the same table under that one light.

Other than the two lights and a radio, the Kawakamis had no appliances—no refrigerator, oven, telephone, or vacuum cleaner. Not even a toaster. They cooked meals on a hibachi-like grill in the kitchen and also on the living room's wood and coal-burning stove, slightly smaller than a two-drawer filing cabinet, which heated the home during the colder months. During winter, it consumed wood and coal voraciously. Because Hiroshi and Echi were teachers, the local government gave them an allotment of money specifically to buy coal, which made the family grateful that they were in an esteemed profession. The stove protected the family from the Otaru winter—but its heat had limits, as did the supply of fuel. Often, the family ran out of coal and wood, and the house went cold. Then, they had to bundle up even at home, wearing big gowns and gloves to stay warm.

For Seiko, perhaps no single item epitomized the rudimentary conditions in Japan as much as her toothbrush. Made of bamboo, it was the length of a pencil and the head had about twenty holes, where small bristles protruded. It might have looked like a serviceable implement, but whenever she brushed her teeth, bristles fell out. Soon, the toothbrush became useless, and Seiko lost track of how many of these primitive toothbrushes she had to throw away.

Despite the cramped quarters and crude conditions, the house had a radio, which testified to the ability of Seiko's parents to afford a modest income. Many families lacked the means to buy that device, but since they both worked as teachers, Hiroshi and Echi kept up with the latest technology and provided for their large family. They also provided stability and compassion.

The war would test everything the family had.

V. Reading and Schooling

After the Pearl Harbor attack, school became a source of stability for Otaru children, including Seiko. She graduated from sixth grade and by early 1942, she was in 7th grade and thus in high school, because at that time the Japanese educational system comprised six grades of elementary school (with no kindergarten) followed by four years of high school. In seventh grade, she was pursuing studies at Otaru Prefectural Girls High School, which admitted the top 250 female students from the half-dozen elementary schools throughout the city. To gain entry into this school, aspirants had to pass a competitive exam, and Hiroshi and Echi were proud that Seiko had made the cut. Although it was a public school, it charged tuition, but the cost was relatively modest and her parents felt the high school's quality and prestige made the expense worthwhile.

Seiko's parents instilled in their children a passion for learning, emphasizing school and homework. While there was no public library nearby, they kept books in the house, and on one wall of their home they posted a large map of the world. Seiko and her siblings often gazed at the map, with their attention always riveted first on Japan and then expanding outward to other countries, giving them a sense of their nation's place in the world.

Hiroshi and Echi also had a monthly subscription to a variety magazine that was invaluable to Seiko. It brimmed with lively articles, and she dug into the magazine as soon as it arrived. She particularly enjoyed *The Wonderful Adventures of Nils*, a serial by the Swedish author Selma Lagerlof, who won the 1909 Nobel Prize in Literature, the first woman to earn the accolade. Nils was a boy who shrank to miniature size and traveled around the world, so the stories allowed Seiko to learn about regions far from Otaru. She read each of Lagerlof's tales over and over, practically memorizing them.

As most students know, teachers can make a huge difference in their enjoyment of school, and Seiko experienced two instructors from different ends of the spectrum. Her first teacher in Otaru was thoughtless, even cruel. Since Seiko came from a poor hamlet, her pronunciation differed from that of other Otaru residents. Once, when she was reading aloud to the class, she mispronounced the name of a general as "Tai-hyo" instead of the proper "Taisho." Her classmates laughed—and so did the teacher! She repeated it, trying to say it correctly, and they laughed again. The sting of that embarrassment seared like a hot flame. The teacher could have pulled me aside and corrected me privately, Seiko thought, but instead, she participated in humiliating me.

Fortunately, when Seiko finished fifth grade she got a new teacher, Kunimatsu Takakura, and he was a true gentleman. He singled Seiko out for praise when she jumped up and grabbed a parallel bar, even though—or perhaps because—she was one of the shortest girls in the class. "How nimble you are, Kawakami-san," Mr. Takakura said, adding the suffix *-san* as a show of respect. Surprised and grateful, Seiko felt that she could finally enjoy school and learning. In inculcating a respect for education, Takakura-san was second only to Seiko's parents, and she knew that she wanted to keep at it, learn more, and pursue a path for self-betterment. (Takakura was talented himself, and he painted landscapes, one of which he gave Seiko as a gift when she visited Otaru, years later.)

Seiko found that she especially liked the humanities and social sciences—history, literature, and geography. The stories in history fascinated her, and she enjoyed the writing of Japanese novelists like Doppo Kunikida and Natsume Soseki. She wanted to read more of their works and learn more about literature and history. In one of her assigned history books, she remembered vividly a story about explorer Christopher Columbus at a banquet with Spanish noblemen who cast aspersions on his voyages and feats. Miffed, he challenged them to balance a hard-boiled egg on the table, and when none of them could, he gently smashed the egg onto the table, making it stand still and ending the discussion. Seiko assumed that she would learn more such intriguing stories from her history classes, continuing her schooling without interruption.

The war had other plans.

Part II
War Devastates

— 3 —

Warsaw at War

I. Destroying the "Paris of the East"

In 1939, Warsaw was a metropolis of 1.3 million citizens, but it bulged with more people like Bogdan's family, who arrived as refugees. Located in the geographic center of Poland, Warsaw was bisected by the mighty Vistula, Poland's longest river. The Vistula stretched four hundred yards wide and ran 650 miles, emptying north into the Baltic Sea, and it accommodated all kinds of boat traffic. It served as a major trade and transportation artery and gave the city a picturesque feel. Local legend reported that a mermaid named Syrena lived in the river, and portraits and statues of her populated the city. Athletic and bare-breasted, she propped herself upright with her tail and bore a look of serene determination, raising a sword above her head with her right hand and sporting a shield in her left. She appeared ready to join battle, and she would supposedly defend the city in time of danger. If Warsaw ever needed Syrena, this was the time.

Warsaw was worth defending, too, because it was beautiful. Its northern, historic section was called "Old Town," with tall, narrow buildings and cobblestone streets that dated back centuries. Historical luminaries had called Warsaw home, including the city's three C's—Copernicus, Chopin, and Curie. During the late fifteenth century, the famed astronomer Nicolaus Copernicus, who had championed the heliocentric model of the universe, had lived in Warsaw. The composer Frédéric Chopin was born in 1810 just outside the city, and he spent his childhood and teenage years there before leaving for Paris. Marie Curie, the Nobel laureate in physics and chemistry, counted Warsaw as her birthplace and in 1932 had opened a Radium Institute there. Poles were fiercely proud of her, the only scientist to win Nobel Prizes in two fields, and she displayed her own love of country by naming an element on the periodic table that she discovered—*polonium*—after her native land.

Although he had wanted to do so, Bogdan never visited Warsaw before the war, and while he had now made it to the city, he wished he were there under better circumstances. Europeans called the city "the Paris of the East." It was a center of Polish culture, with a national library, museums, theaters, and opera houses. It was a commercial entrepot, with many different stores, and the prestigious University of Warsaw added even more vibrancy to the metropolis. Ruefully, Bogdan thought it would have been an exciting city to inhabit and enjoy during peacetime.

But when the Nazis invaded Poland, they made Warsaw a German district. They blanketed the city with the "Reich eagle," which now appeared everywhere. They plundered artwork and other valuables. Nazi soldiers built bunkers and air raid shelters for themselves at various spots. Marszalkowska Street, the normally busy artery near the Mieczkowskis' apartment, had a reputation as Warsaw's equivalent of Oxford Street in London, lined with restaurants, stores, and boutiques. But the war stifled its glamour. Bogdan seldom saw people eating at restaurants or shopping, and stores withered away.

Everywhere stood reminders of how much of the city the Germans destroyed. One especially regrettable victim was a royal castle one block from the Old Town square. It was a huge concrete edifice with myriad rooms, well-appointed with paintings and ornate furniture like antique clocks. But in September 1939, as the Germans bombed the city into subjugation, the castle was reduced to rubble.

The German invaders aimed to subdue Warsaw, and they attacked it with special savagery. The city refused a German offer to surrender, and its resistance became a whetstone for Hitler's rage. The Wehrmacht punished Warsaw, pounding it with artillery, and then a bombing campaign killed nearly 26,000 people. September 25 was an especially harsh day, when the Nazis unleashed three hundred bombers in a titanic air attack against the city. Two days later, Warsaw surrendered to the Germans. Its resistance had lasted less than one month.

On October 5, city residents saw a satanic figure. Adolf Hitler appeared in person, visiting to confirm that Warsaw was under his control. (The Polish underground resistance, which had already formed, plotted to assassinate him during this visit by detonating explosives near him, but they were unable to carry out the plan.) Hitler wanted not only to destroy the city but replace it with a new town, a project known as the "Pabst Plan" after one of its designers, Friedrich Pabst, which aimed to transform Warsaw into a German city. The first step was to raze it, so that by the time Bogdan and his family arrived, the once beautiful capital was a ruined shell. Symbolic of Warsaw's fate, all the statues of Syrena were destroyed. Citizens would have to look elsewhere for inspiration to defend themselves against the Germans.

II. A Secret Way to Fight the Nazis

For the first months of World War II in Europe, Poland was the only nation that knew the horrors of invasion and conquest. After September 1939, Hitler's aggression abated for the next half-year, a period known as *sitzkrieg*, or "phony war," because of its quiescence. It did not last. In April 1940, Germany swept through Denmark and Norway with ease. The next month, Belgium, Holland, and Luxembourg surrendered to the Führer. Then the Wehrmacht brought the *blitzkrieg* into France. The French army began to collapse so quickly that Winston Churchill, who became the British prime minister in May 1940 when Neville Chamberlain resigned, even proposed a union between England and France, Europe's historic adversaries.

In June 1940, the war suddenly changed. That month, France fell to Germany; it was a moment when the course of world events seemed to shift, with a historically great power falling to the German juggernaut so quickly. France had a proud military tradition that included Napoleon Bonaparte, yet the Wehrmacht needed just six weeks to vanquish the country. Hitler boasted to his wartime ally, Italian dictator Benito Mussolini, "The war is won." In France's Compiègne Forest, just a half-hour northeast of Paris, he imposed the ultimate humiliation by forcing the French to sign the surrender documents aboard the same railroad car in which Germany accepted peace terms after World War I. In Warsaw, Bogdan saw German soldiers parading around and celebrating France's surrender, chanting martial songs that included the lyrics, "Now we will march against England."

At that point, the United Kingdom stood alone against Hitler. In the summer of 1940, during the Battle of Britain, the German Luftwaffe launched devastating air raids over England, including a bombing campaign against London that lasted for twenty-three straight days. But the British hunkered down, and by September, they handed Hitler his first major setback of the war when Germany lost the Battle of Britain, forcing Hitler to shelve plans for Operation Sealion, the invasion of England. That month, though, Germany stiffened its resolve by signing the Tripartite Pact, making Japan an Axis power along with Italy.

The fall of France was a dramatic moment in history, but for Bogdan and other Poles, it was also a turning point in their own war. They had hoped that France would defeat Germany, but now that idea lay shattered. Poles were determined that Britain would not fight Germany alone. Resistance movements such as Poland's became a more integral part of the fight. Especially after France fell, Bogdan recognized the reality that Poles could depend on little help from allies. They had to help Britain, not the other way around, and they also had to fight Hitler on their own terms.

But Poles had to wait until the time was ripe. While Warsaw teetered on the brink of destruction, Bogdan knew that as an individual and family member, he above all had to survive. A key to perseverance, Bogdan believed, was the ability to adapt and then persist, and the new situation put those skills to the test.

Until war struck, Bogdan had the typical concerns of a teenager—friends, sports, hobbies, church, and especially school. The German invasion turned his world upside down. Bogdan was in ninth grade, which in the Polish education system marked the last stage of a first high school, and he was to enter a second high school the next year. Now his learning was dashed; the 1939–40 academic year was done before it even began.

The war claimed life, limb, and property, but it also took valuables that were less tangible, like education. All students, including Bogdan, were losing a full school year, and he had friends who lost more. In Bydgoszcz, he learned that some of his former classmates stopped their formal education for good, which blocked their intellectual growth and career advancement. Usually, they ended up working in manual trades. The premature end to everyone's schooling smothered talent and potential, foreclosing opportunities for a better life even after the war ended.

For some teenagers, the outcome was tragic. Bogdan had abruptly left all his friends behind in Bydgoszcz, never getting a chance to say good-bye, so he was surprised and delighted to encounter Zbigniew Tymowski in Warsaw. Zbigniew was a bright, cheerful friend, and they had always enjoyed visiting the Impregnacja factory together. Besides his good company, one reason Bogdan was pleased to see his old friend again was that he provided a link to a happier life that they knew before the German invasion.

But Zbigniew soon hanged himself. Although Bogdan had no chance to spend time with him before his death, he later met his brother and asked him what had happened. He offered no precise explanation, but he said that Zbigniew had grown anxious and depressed, buckling under the strain of the German takeover. In the end, he saw no way past Nazi rule other than leaving this world. Zbigniew's death was senseless, Bogdan reflected; his friend could have gone on to do much good for himself and society, yet the catastrophe of war snuffed out his life.

That kind of tragedy was only the beginning. The German occupation of Poland was much more malign than their later administration of France, the Netherlands, and other countries. It was not just an invasion. It was ethnic cleansing, aiming to destroy Poland and eventually replace Poles with Germans. To effect this plan, the Germans first wanted to eliminate all leaders—current and potential—in Polish society. They first went after the Polish military, police officers, civil authorities, and business leaders.

Then they targeted education. The Nazis executed schoolteachers, and they sought to stop all education beyond the elementary level. They shut down high schools and colleges; they closed libraries; they banned theater, sports, and cultural activities. The Germans wanted to wipe out the Polish intelligentsia—professors, doctors, businessmen, priests, dentists (like Dr. Sobocinski) and more. Anyone with an education beyond high school was vulnerable.

The German invasion embodied the savage confluence of race and space. The Germans wanted more "living space," and they believed they were entitled to it because of their race. In the scheme of Aryan superiority, Germans thought Polish education and culture were worthless, that Poles were incapable of higher thought, fit only for manual labor. Poles were to become slaves to the Germans.

But Polish authorities did something clever, and Bogdan was grateful for the ruse. They convinced German leaders that an educated work force would be more productive for the German state. So the Germans allowed trade education to continue in areas such as carpentry, masonry, and electricity. They remained leery of so-called higher thought, but the trained manual laborers, working in thrall to the Germans, would help to ensure that the Third Reich would fulfill Hitler's prediction of lasting a thousand years.

Because the Germans allowed Warsaw trade schools to remain open, Bogdan enrolled there. Beginning in the fall of 1940, after a full year's disruption of his schooling, Bogdan was back in the classroom to start the two grades that the Germans countenanced, and he completed the equivalent of a junior high school education. It was vocational training, and the idea was that Bogdan would learn trades like electricity and carpentry.

In truth, he never did. What happened was a secret of World War II that has almost never been discussed or revealed in the decades since. Instead of instructing students in manual trades, teachers furtively sneaked in lessons that were not officially sanctioned, delving into the liberal arts, including history, Polish language arts, Latin, German language, and sciences like biology. Bogdan admired and appreciated his teachers, because they were flouting German orders and risking their lives to teach regular lessons. If the Germans caught them, the teachers would have faced hard labor, concentration camps, or execution.

The teachers took their defiance a step further. According to German rules, students' education was supposed to end after these two years of trade lessons. Instead, Bogdan and other youths received a secondary school education—but under secret conditions. They convened classes at various apartments, where small groups of teachers and students met, sitting around a table, absorbing the lessons and reading and discussing whatever books were available. Since almost no Polish books were published during the war, they relied on books from their teachers' own collections. They met year-round, usually just for an hour or two at a time. The courses were called *komplety*, which meant secret units of learning, and they reflected an effort to "complete" the high school education of Warsaw teenagers. To avoid arousing German suspicions, the classes never exceeded six in number, although through the rumor mill in Warsaw, Bogdan heard that tens of thousands of students took courses in the system. Like everything Poles did under German rule, they followed a decentralized model so as to keep the system amorphous and difficult to detect, and also to avoid creating a conspicuous leadership class that would be vulnerable to execution.

The *komplety* were marvelous, a form of intellectual nourishment. Bogdan felt his mind relishing the exposure to liberal arts, languages, and science. As they studied, Bogdan and his classmates also felt a sense of responsibility, because they were helping to preserve knowledge of Polish culture and history at a time when the Germans were trying to destroy it.

Bogdan felt both grateful and astounded. His teachers risked their lives to instruct so many students, and as far as he knew, they received no pay; certainly, they collected no tuition fees from the students. They worked for the sheer love of teaching, to inculcate lessons in young Polish students so that a new generation of Poles would have the knowledge needed to be responsible citizens and leaders. Ultimately, that is what the *komplety* also represented to Bogdan: a promise for a better future and a form of intellectual and psychological resistance against the Germans. The knowledge the students gained was like a treasure because everyone knew the cost of being discovered was high—their lives.

A real high school diploma, though, remained beyond reach; Bogdan never received one, and he regretted it. But this secret school system allowed him to further his education. Teachers and students tried to keep to a normal schedule of semesters, although everything had to be compressed into a shorter learning span, with brief and sometimes erratic classes, and they relied on cramming and self-study. Although improvisational, the *komplety* courses permitted learning even amidst the carnage of war, but they did even more. They added a sense of routine to teenagers' tumultuous lives. They constituted an act of defiance, and they boosted morale. Importantly, Bogdan's wartime education built a foundation, whetting his thirst for more knowledge. In the back of his mind, Bogdan hoped that it would allow him to gain acceptance into a college, whenever the war ended.

III. Odd Jobs

As important as the ersatz education system was, one necessity took greater urgency: income. The Germans had wrested Tadeusz Mieczkowski's construction empire from him, but he still felt a deep sense of responsibility to provide for his family, only now with limited tools with which to generate a revenue stream and buy necessities. Worse, wartime scarcities drove up prices, and inflation ran rampant in Warsaw. The entire Polish economy limped along, wounded by the German invasion, and the normal activities of producing goods and services suffered severe disruption, which left families struggling to put food on the table.

Tadeusz pawned family watches and jewelry and, ever resourceful, he became a partner in a secondhand store that accepted merchandise such as clothes on commission; in turn, the store sold the items. When Bogdan visited his father at the store during winter, the inside was frigid, and he had the task of firing up the stove and feeding it wood that he had split with an axe. Because Tadeusz remained vulnerable to German capture, he used an alias and changed his appearance, growing a moustache and beard, using a different pair of glasses, and wearing them more often. To throw the Germans further off their trail, the family tried to spread the word that they had fled to Romania.

Bogdan, too, learned to blend into the environment. He was careful to wear nothing that would attract attention, which meant no rings, no military-style boots or shoes, no school uniform. He wanted to convey the impression that he was just a poor, undernourished teenager who posed no threat to German authority. Avoid trouble, Bogdan told himself, and just try to make money. He steered clear of German patrols, navigating a different path whenever he spotted them in the distance, and his life settled into a routine of working, returning to the apartment, sneaking in *komplety* classes, and then sleeping.

Like his father did, Bogdan held down jobs to provide income for the family. His first job, in fact, was a family effort, which began in 1940, their first full year in Warsaw. They obtained tobacco leaves, which Bogdan had never seen before; Poland's climate was too cool to grow tobacco, but as soon as he saw the dried yellow leaves, he understood why people called tobacco the "golden weed," a double entendre because it also provided a path to profits. In the family apartment, Bogdan and his family began a small enterprise in making cigarettes, cutting the leaves into thin slices and then rolling them into small cylinders to fashion homemade cigarettes, which they sold. They often had some that were imperfect, getting torn in the rolling process, and rather than throw them away, Bogdan tried them. In a time of extreme scarcity, the notion of wasting anything—including cigarettes—was illogical. But Bogdan had observed people who were addicted to tobacco, begging smokers to cadge cigarettes off them, and after a brief foray into smoking, he decided he wanted nothing to do with it. He kicked the habit before it began to control him.

Bogdan's next job was outside his home, in roofing. He spent hours atop homes and buildings, nailing down shingles and tiles. The most substantive part of this work involved a railroad freight car repair facility. This job involved heating up molten tar and then pouring it over crevasses to get a watertight seal. The work was tough; standing on the rooftop, Bogdan had no protection from the hot sun or rain, and breathing in the tar fumes was unpleasant. The molten tar was blazing hot, and once, an object fell into it, and a large drop splashed onto the back of Bogdan's hand, creating a large and painful blister.

While Bogdan held the roofing job, he also worked at a railroad station. He knew that everything he did would assist the Germans, who owned the railroads now, and the thought of expending effort to help them disturbed him. But survival came first, and looking like a compliant teenager hungry for odd jobs was the best front that he could assume. Bogdan held the roofing and railroad positions for a few months, and then his employment became eclectic. He dabbled in a delivery business, a shoe-making plant, and a toy manufacturing facility, where he worked a night shift. In 1942, he began the job that provided his steadiest work, at a Warsaw agricultural seed factory and research institute called Udycz, where workers processed grain that they described as "poisonous" so that the Germans would not use them for their food. In reality, the seeds had no poison, and they could be used in bread making. The company also experimented with the seeds to improve their productivity, which was an early form of genetic modification. At Udycz, Bogdan was an office boy, running errands that included going to the post office, usually twice a day.

During the summer of 1943, German military operations gave Bogdan employment on top of his Udycz job. In 1941, the Germans had launched Operation Barbarossa, an invasion of the Soviet Union, and they had an airbase outside Warsaw that they had used in their early maneuvers to launch aerial attacks into the Soviet Union. By 1943, their assault had moved far enough within the USSR that they no longer needed the airbase, so they hired young Polish men to deconstruct it. Like all such work, this one involved arduous physical labor, and Bogdan did it solely to help provide for his family, rather than out of any desire to assist the Germans. One benefit of the job was that the workers received food, mostly potatoes and vegetables, which kept Bogdan from feeling hungry all the time. In truth, he was not just pretending to be an undernourished teenager. He really was, and he sorely appreciated the rare chance to eat a decent meal.

The earnings from these jobs were meager; the reality was that the German and Soviet invasions ravaged the Polish economy. Poles had only a subsistence living, and their lives were circumscribed in every way imaginable. Bogdan and his family confined themselves to their downtown Warsaw neighborhood, and when they needed to get anywhere, they walked or used the streetcar. They wore the same clothes day in and day out, because they could not afford new vestments and could do laundry only rarely. The ascetic existence helped to keep expenses down. The greatest concern was to get enough food to sustain life.

IV. Austerity Everywhere

When it came to food, Bogdan's diet was as spartan as his clothes. Everyone suffered a plunge in food intake in wartime Warsaw, but for Bogdan's family, the contrast was jarring. Before the war, their cook, Truda, made scrumptious, protein-rich meals, featuring Polish classics like bigos (the so-called "hunter's stew," which consisted of pork, sausage, cabbage, sauerkraut, and tomatoes) and pork cutlets with vegetables.

But in wartime Warsaw, Aniela had to assume the roles of food procurer and cook, and those activities took up much of her time. She bought food at a local store that had limited offerings, and Tadeusz sometimes ventured out and slipped beyond Warsaw city limits to buy food. Where Bogdan's family used to eat meat daily, now they ate it just once or twice a year. Once, some residents shot a horse in a courtyard near the apartment and distributed the meat to neighborhood families, providing a rare luxury. Otherwise, Bogdan's family got accustomed to eating potatoes and bread for breakfast, lunch, and dinner—or just breakfast and dinner, since three daily meals became impossible. Often, when Bogdan returned to the apartment from work, Aniela was frying potatoes, preparing to serve them with bread, which was usually as hard as bricks.

Portions were always small. The family had little fruit, and while the apartment had running water, they never had coffee or tea. People who needed something approximating a caffeine buzz used a burnt rye grain and tried to add hot water to make their "coffee." At the agricultural seed firm where Bogdan worked, he obtained sugar. That was like white gold, a medium of exchange that Tadeusz could barter for other goods, taking advantage of people's desire to add sugar to their homemade coffee and other beverages.

Some people dream of food—scrumptious buffets and mouthwatering desserts—when deprived of it. Bogdan's experience was the opposite. During the war, he developed an aversion to talking or even thinking about food, because he hated to torture himself with the thought of something he could scarcely obtain. Summoning all the willpower he could, Bogdan shut it out of his mind and tried to focus on other pursuits. His poor diet had one dividend: even if someone from Bydgoszcz were tempted to betray his family to the Germans for a reward, he or she might have had trouble recognizing Bogdan because he had lost so much weight. His hollow cheeks and gaunt visage bore little resemblance to the robust teenager he was in Bydgoszcz.

While he could not feed his body well, Bogdan tried to nourish his mind and senses. In addition to having the *komplety* courses, he located a library four blocks from his apartment, which miraculously remained open, and he borrowed and read books. Although the German forbade radios, the family had a poor quality one in their apartment, and Bogdan sometimes listened to the British Broadcasting Corporation [BBC]. They started one of their news programs with the opening score from Beethoven's Fifth Symphony, and the news brought the outside world into their cramped, isolated environment.

War suppressed humor and laughter, and few things could make anyone smile amidst the grim circumstances. Still, on a psychic level, Bogdan and his family and friends tried to get even with their enemies by making fun of them. After the June 1941 German invasion of the Soviet Union, as Nazi troops got stuck in the mire of a long Russian winter, they joked that bulletins from the Eastern front reported some German casualties, more Soviet ones, and none among Poles. They cracked jokes about Hitler's being a pig. Mussolini was even easier to roast. In another era, this vain, barrel-chested narcissist would have been almost comical. He ordered odd measures, like outlawing dancing. He led a country that had faded behind other European nations; Italy was a middleweight power with little appetite for war, and the country's military strength sometimes prompted mirth. Yet Mussolini was pompous enough to declare, "My animal instincts are always right." Poles mocked the bizarre alliance between Hitler and Mussolini, the latter six years older than the Führer yet the junior partner. One joke that Bogdan and his friends told was that when Hitler rode his train to meet Mussolini at the Brenner Pass in the Italian Alps, near the border with Austria, he defecated out a train window. As the train reached the station, the obtuse, obsequious Mussolini ran up to the train window and began kissing Hitler's rear end.

Church allowed Poles to sustain some faith. In Warsaw, the Mieczkowski family still tried to attend mass on Sundays, although Bogdan frequently skipped services because he was working and later, soldiering. Showing her great devotion, Aniela still went a few times a week. But the frenetic pace of war cut into church routines, and one priest always conducted services in smashingly fast time. Bogdan and his brothers called him "the record breaker," but his quickness was sensible. War forced cutbacks in everything, even spiritual communications, and to stay congregated in one place was dangerous. No matter how devout they were, everyone knew that one German bomb, well timed and placed, could wipe out an entire congregation.

Electricity rationing limited activities, too. During the day, Warsaw residents had electricity, but at night the Germans cut the current to preserve it for their own undertakings. To fend off total darkness, people used carbide lights. These were the same kind of lamps that miners used, and they burned acetylene gas, which risked explosions. These lights were dangerous, but citizens figured that it was a risk worth taking to continue normal activities past dusk.

In addition to the darkness, Bogdan's apartment had other irritations. Bedbugs ran rampant throughout Warsaw, including at home. During the day, when the bugs were visible, the family members killed them, but they got even at night. In the morning, every family member awoke to see marks on their bodies and small bloodspots on the sheets.

Overcrowding created another inconvenience. Almost miraculously, Aniela maintained contact with her sister after the family's tortuous journey from Bydgoszcz to Warsaw. As events unfolded, the Germans sent Hala and her two daughters to Warsaw, where she found Tadeusz's apartment and moved in with her girls. The five-bedroom apartment now teemed with people. Hala and her daughters took one room, and another of Aniela's relatives came to stay at the apartment after the Soviets killed her

On the balcony of the Mieczkowski family apartment in Warsaw, 1943 (left to right): Janusz, unidentified friend, Bogdan. The following year the Warsaw Uprising began, and Bogdan lost his right thumb.

husband. Because all the bedrooms became occupied, Bogdan slept in various locations. When the weather was warm, he spent nights on an outside balcony; at other times, he slept in the kitchen or in a common area. The situation was a far cry from the family's spacious home in Bydgoszcz.

Bogdan's family had no way of knowing what was happening to that house—or anything that took place in their hometown—because attempting any contact could have exposed Tadeusz. The Germans were undoubtedly looking for the head of Impregnacja so that they could execute him. In Warsaw, the family kept to themselves. Even though they saw and passed by neighbors in the apartment building, they made little attempt to know them.

In addition to risking Tadeusz's life, communicating with people was dangerous because no one could tell if another person were connected with the Germans. Bogdan recalled one man in the neighborhood who wore sunglasses and played violin in front of various buildings, panhandling for cash. He was Polish, and he seemed ordinary and innocuous.

Later, though, Bogdan later learned that the fiddler was spying for the Germans. For a spy, he picked the perfect job, because he had an ostensible reason to stand and observe a wide range of people going into and out of apartments. But really, he was monitoring behavior and consorting with the enemy, reporting to the Nazis what he observed. Eventually, he was discovered, and Poles executed him for his treachery. But his case drove home the point that unless you were absolutely certain, you could not trust anyone, so being neighborly was unwise. Warsaw Poles trained themselves to mind their own business.

So Bogdan and his family were sparing in their social interactions, and Warsaw's battered condition added to the sense of austerity. Residents were living in a sad husk of a city—physically, spiritually, and socially.

V. *One of Mankind's Lowest Groups*

The greatest peril came from the German captors. During World War II, Poland suffered the highest casualty rate of any European country—twenty percent of Poles died—and one reason was that the Germans treated Poles as expendable. In other countries they occupied, the Germans refrained from wantonly killing civilians, just for violating curfew, for example. In Poland, they showed no such restraint.

The Germans viewed Poles as one of mankind's lowest groups, a subhuman race like Jews, Sinti, and Roma (the latter two belonging to a large minority in southern and eastern Europe that the Germans labeled "Gypsies"), and they held Polish life in dim regard. The Nazis brandished a slogan of "Jews, Gypsies, and Poles," lumping together the three groups they targeted for extermination. The Nazi propaganda machine pounded out the incessant refrain that Germans were racially superior, and that mindset helped to explain some of the viciousness that ensued. In Warsaw, Nazi snipers picked off men, women, and children, as if for sport, and they also carried out mass executions. One afternoon when Bogdan returned home, his mother told him that the Germans executed a group just up the road from their building, mowing down more than twenty people. "Roundups" were frequent: Germans snatched Poles from the streets and gathered them together, later torturing and killing them or sending them to concentration camps. Those three groups—Jews, Gypsies, and Poles—suffered incalculable losses. Aniela hosted a Jewish couple from Bydgoszcz who sought shelter in Warsaw, and one evening the husband, restless from being cooped up indoors all day, decided to stroll outside just before the curfew clamped down. That night, his wife waited hour after hour for him to return. He never did.

The Germans employed other ethnic groups to subdue Poles. They imbibed Hitler's swill about racial superiority, or perhaps they had taken a kind of moral sedative, Bogdan conjectured, relaxing normal constraints against evil behavior so that they themselves could survive. Some Ukrainians, for example, acted as mercenaries for the Germans, and Bogdan's older brother Zbigniew, fell victim to this behavior. Zbigniew was a diminutive teenager, standing just five feet, five inches tall, and he once came home with his face bloody and swollen after a Ukrainian man had beaten him up.

This was no isolated incident. No one was safe from anyone or anything. Warsaw was a garrison state, and the Nazis patrolled the streets, forcing residents to live in constant fear. They required that citizens register with them, and Bogdan complied, receiving a card with his photograph, Warsaw address, an identification number, and his work office (or so-called *arbeits* in German). Whenever anyone left their homes, they were taking a risk. The Germans could stop and frisk them, or conscript them to work for them. They forced residents to clear streets so that German military vehicles could pass. Worse, the Nazis abducted citizens, sent them to forced labor camps, or killed them.

Bogdan heard word about Hitler's "Final Solution," the extermination of undesirable groups. One of Bogdan's officemates at Udycz, the agricultural seed company, was a Polish Catholic woman whose husband was arrested for his resistance work and sent to the Auschwitz concentration camp. Showing great devotion, she sent him small parcels of food regularly, but she had no way of knowing whether he received them. A few prisoners were indeed lucky enough to escape. A friend of Aunt Hala's son George—who himself was murdered by Germans—managed to escape, and he told Bogdan about the hunger and primitive conditions in the concentration camp. With pride, he said he still washed himself regularly, even with icy water when the weather was freezing. But his luck ran out. A short time after Bogdan spoke to him, the Germans recaptured him, and he was sucked down into the maw of the Nazi prison system. As to his eventual whereabouts, one clue surfaced when a friend found a piece of paper in which he had scrawled the message that "they are taking us north." That was an ominous sign, because "north" likely meant a cemetery containing Poles whom the Germans had executed en masse. Bogdan never learned anything about his fate.

To survive, Warsaw residents complied with their German occupiers, however repugnant they found it. If they showed intransigence, the Germans would punish the civilian populace and kill more of them. But the instinctive feeling among patriotic Poles was to fight the Germans, and they tried to resist—as long as they could get away with it. Residents wanted to fly the Polish flag, but the Germans would have killed anyone who did so. Because the Germans now controlled all public transportation, they tried to avoid paying streetcar fare so as to deprive them of revenue. Bogdan just got on and off the bus casually.

One day, though, he got caught. The Nazis imposed a segregated seating system, in which only Germans sat in the first car, where the driver was located, while Poles were restricted to the second car. Bogdan was taking the streetcar to work, and the Polish car was packed. He was standing at the front of the car, and because the crowd of passengers was so thick, he did not notice an inspector making his way up the car, asking people for their identification; had Bogdan spotted him, he would have exited at a stop.

When Bogdan saw the inspector, it was too late. Muscling his way through the thicket of passengers, he got next to Bogdan and asked for his ticket. Bogdan told him that he had none; the inspector grimaced, clearly upset, and demanded his identification card. Bogdan handed it over, and he copied down his name, address, and identification number.

For the next several days, Bogdan agonized that there might be a loud knock on the apartment door, with German troops there to escort him away. Thankfully, that never happened. He suspected that the inspector, who was Polish, sympathized with him and decided not to file a report. Bogdan was lucky, and with greater vigilance, he could continue his strategy of avoiding the streetcar fare. But in the scheme of German occupation, it was only a small gesture of defiance.

Bogdan wanted a more potent way to resist.

VI. *Joining the* Armia Krajowa

In the late summer of 1940, with France defeated and the future of Europe looking grim, Bogdan got serious about taking the fight to the

Germans. Within him stirred strong feelings of Polish patriotism, which made his decision to join the Polish resistance movement a natural one. Poles had nothing to lose and faced possible execution anyway, so young people accepted the idea that they would confront their occupiers. Many of Bogdan's friends urged him to take part in the resistance. Zbigniew signed on but proved passive, skipping meetings and contenting himself with watching from a ringside seat rather than joining the fight. He considered himself a scientist in training, and he preferred not to get too deeply involved in skirmishing. Janusz, though, decided to join the battle.

In reflecting on his family history, Bogdan noted an intriguing parallel. Centuries earlier, his ancestors belonged to the feudal peasantry, which was essentially congruent to slavery. (In fact, the term *slavery* likely derived from Eastern European "Slavs," whom Spanish Muslims had enslaved.) But in a 1410 battle, Poles triumphed over German invaders, a victory that enabled Bogdan's forbears to rise to aristocratic ranks and change the family name from the original "Poziomak" to "Mieczkowski," to celebrate the sword that was used as a weapon against the enemy. Centuries later, a new generation of the Mieczkowski family would now again fight to repel Germans from their land.

One evening, at a solemn ceremony in an apartment of some rebel fighters, Bogdan took an oath to join the resistance, swearing to defend Poland and honor its independence. It was also an anti–German pledge, in which soldiers vowed to defeat *Niemcy*, "the Germans." The new recruits stood before the Polish flag, bowing their heads in reverence. The ceremony was short but replete with meaning; Bogdan found it moving, and he took his new responsibilities seriously.

One of Bogdan's first jobs as a resistance fighter was to distribute an underground newspaper, *Biuletyn Informacyjny*, wholesaled in his neighborhood by a married couple who owned a small Warsaw grocery store. Because the Germans controlled all media, Poles obtained almost no news about the war and hungered for information, so they had a vibrant underground publishing industry that churned out newspapers, pamphlets, and books—all at a time when the Germans forbade Polish publications. The newspaper was more like a pamphlet, with regular sheets of paper folded over, totaling ten to twenty pages, which gave word on the war's progress, including battles in Western Europe and the Polish effort to fight the Germans. Bogdan's procedure was to enter the store, as if to shop for merchandise. Upon seeing him, the wife went to the back of the store and brought out the newspapers, which Bogdan hid amongst his layers of clothes.

It was dangerous work. If caught, publishers and distributors faced a painful ending. Were the Germans to apprehend Bogdan carrying the newspaper, they would have tortured and killed him. The couple were also putting their lives in jeopardy, and Bogdan worried about them. He knew they were a "couple," comprising a husband and wife, but he never saw the husband. In keeping with the principle that the less resistance participants knew about one another, the safer and more secure they would all be, Bogdan worked only with the wife, and they never even learned each other's names. She quietly handed Bogdan the papers, and he shoved them deep into his clothes, pressing them against his body.

Two months after beginning his courier work, Bogdan was walking to the store to pick up a load of contraband papers. As he approached the storefront, from a distance he saw that it was shuttered, marked with a piece of paper carrying the Reich eagle and swastika along with some typed text. Pretending to be indifferent to the scene, Bogdan briskly walked past the door, as if he noticed nothing. His pulse quickened, though, and he had a sickly churn in his stomach, because he knew the couple had likely been caught and executed. For the first time in his life, people whom he knew and had daily contact with were now gone, and it was because of the work they were doing in the resistance.

But the Nazis could have caught Bogdan with the couple, and he had other close calls. He was once standing outside his apartment building, and a group of Nazi soldiers arrived to conduct a raid. Bogdan realized that he had hidden contraband newspapers inside a ceramic stove in the family's living quarters. Luckily, though, the Germans came there to inspect another apartment, so they never entered the Mieczkowskis' unit.

Another incident was more frightening. Bogdan was walking along a street, which was mostly deserted, and a short distance away, he spotted a German patrol. His mind raced through alternatives. If he backtracked or crossed to the other side of the street, that would attract their attention, and they probably would give chase. If he continued, he risked being arrested, and anything could have happened to him after that, including torture, deportation—or death.

In a split second, Bogdan decided that he should just continue ambling along, which would help to avoid arousing their suspicions. "Maybe they will just let me pass," he thought. As he got closer, the officer in charge signaled him to stop and then gestured for him to get ready to be searched. Bogdan raised his arms to the sides, and the officer frisked him and felt something in his jacket. Probing for it, he removed a wad of papers and unfolded it, straightening out the layers. Luckily, they were letters from Udycz, written in German, which Bogdan was delivering to a German agricultural office, indicating that Udycz operated in compliance with the German authorities. The officer glanced at the papers, handed them back, and then released Bogdan.

Neither of them said a word. Bogdan could have spoken to him in

German, but the officer asked no questions, brandishing his power through gestures. The whole exchange, which took only a couple of minutes, transpired in a menacing silence.

Bogdan left the area, tremulous but relieved, and as he walked past the patrol, he saw a reminder of how lucky he was. A young man whom the patrol had detained stood there and made eye contact with Bogdan; that day and that moment marked the end of his freedom. Without question, the Germans planned to send him to prison and whatever fate awaited him thereafter.

Warsaw Poles could not continue to live like this, amidst nonstop fear, intimidation, and death. They had to strike back. The resistance movement against the Germans grew in size and intensity, and Bogdan was proud to participate. Beginning with a small nucleus, the Polish AK (*Armia Krajowa*, or Home Army) eventually totaled 40,000 soldiers, which included four thousand women. Most AK fighters were amateurs with no military training or warfare experience, and they came from all walks of life. They were volunteers and received no pay, even though they risked everything. Many fighters were like Bogdan: young students who had little to offer but courage, love of country, and a will to fight. The resistance had a symbol, a "P" superimposed on a "W" (which looked like a "P" with two hooks at the bottom), and it stood for their motto, *Polska Walczy*, or "Poland Fights." During the night, intrepid Poles sneaked out and used chalk to write the symbol on walls and buildings, showing their solidarity and spirit.

Girding to fight the Germans, the resistance took orders from the Polish

Bogdan, Aniela, and Janusz (left to right) at a park near their Warsaw apartment, 1943. Even during the German occupation, Bogdan and his family members could have tranquil moments like this one. The Uprising began the next year.

government-in-exile in London. After the German invasion, the Polish government first fled to Romania, then to Paris, operating there until the Wehrmacht overran France, when it relocated to London. General Wladyslaw Sikorski, who was Polish prime minister during the 1920s, headed this government, operating out of London's Rubens Hotel. Backed by cabinet officers, Sikorski communicated with the Polish citizenry and provided instructions and inspiration for them to keep resisting the Germans. As with all Polish resistance activities, the Warsaw efforts were decentralized to avoid German detection, relying on small groups and individual initiative. They hoped the loosely organized network would be enough to beat the Nazis.

For Bogdan, this was an intense period. He was juggling three major activities simultaneously: studying in the *komplety* courses, working at Udycz, and training with the resistance movement. He was constantly busy. His life was about to get even more intense.

VII. Twin Evils

The resistance began to plan an uprising against the German occupiers. Their patriotic impulses were strong; they wanted to free themselves from the yoke of Nazi oppression and prove that their nation belonged to them, that Poles controlled their own destiny and would tolerate no invaders.

They had another powerful motive for resistance. In June 1941, Hitler commenced Operation Barbarossa. The Non-Aggression Pact of 1939 had always been like an embrace between two vipers, just enough for them to stop hissing but doomed to end quickly. Hitler reneged on the agreement, ordering a German invasion of the Soviet Union, thus opening up a titanic second front in the war. Hitler coveted territory and resources too much to honor the Non-Aggression Pact for long. What was especially stunning was how the Germans caught the Soviets off-guard. They had been massing troops for the invasion, widening roads and constructing new railroads in Poland, and they took over the Soviet-controlled eastern half of Poland, using it to penetrate the U.S.S.R. In Warsaw, Bogdan witnessed hordes of German soldiers snaking eastward, obviously preparing for an attack. The Soviets acted as if they never wanted to confront the reality that Germany would betray them. Poles had little sympathy for them; the Soviets had been foolish to trust them. They deserved each other, Poles felt.

But the offensive into the Soviet Union would eventually drain the Wehrmacht of men, machines, and morale. Moreover, the strange alchemy of war made the Soviets—the invaders of Poland from the East—the Poles' uneasy allies because they now shared the common enemy of Hitler's Germany, which ruled all of Poland. The situation reminded Bogdan of hoary adages like "the lesser of two evils" and "the enemy of your enemy is your friend." That was the nature of an emerging partnership with the Soviets: Poles distrusted them, but they had to work with them.

For years, though, the Soviets had sown the seeds of Polish misgivings. In April 1940, as part of their effort to wipe out the Polish leadership class, Russians executed almost twenty-two thousand Polish Army officers who had been captured in 1939, killing each with a bullet to the back of the head. They dumped their bodies into a mass grave in the Katyn Forest, located just west of Smolensk, a city in western Russia. In April 1943, German soldiers invading the Soviet Union unearthed the burial site. Many of the corpses were still dressed in Polish Army uniforms, with their hands wired behind their backs. There were enough of them to populate a small city. Later, Bogdan later learned that his school gymnastics teacher from Bydgoszcz was one of those officers who perished in the Katyn massacre.

The Germans reported the massacre to Geneva's International Red Cross and blamed the Soviets. Joseph Goebbels, the Nazi minister of propaganda, hoped that exposing the Soviets' murderous actions would create fissures among the Allies. He knew the alliance had discord, and the Soviets lacked true friends in this war; the Stalinist mentality regarded everyone outside the Kremlin as an enemy or potential enemy. Goebbels thought that what the Soviets did was so dastardly that it would alienate the Americans and Brits from the Soviets and break their brittle alliance.

But it failed to work that way. The Soviets dissembled and deflected blame away from their crime, accusing the Nazis instead, saying that the Germans had killed the Polish officers while taking Smolensk. The Soviets thus propagated a long-standing myth that the Germans had committed the killings. This story fit the narrative that the Nazis were evil, and President Franklin Roosevelt accepted the Soviet denials and spread the fiction that the Germans had done it. In Poland, people knew better, and the Russians worried that the truth would soon catch up with them. (It took half a century. The Soviets denied their role in the Katyn massacre until 1992, when the U.S.S.R.'s collapse opened documents and provided irrefutable evidence that Joseph Stalin approved the executions, which the Soviets carried out.)

In London, Poland's government-in-exile demanded investigations of the Katyn Forest massacre. Stalin refused and went a step further. In April 1943, the Kremlin cut off relations with the Polish leaders, feigning outrage that they dared to blame the Soviets for the crime. The next year, the Soviets set up a government in Lublin, a city about a hundred miles southeast of Warsaw, rivaling the Polish government-in-exile in London.

Amidst their own treachery, the Soviets still had to fight an offensive war against the Germans, and they threw them back and drove west, entering Poland and creeping closer to Warsaw. During the summer of 1944, the Soviet Army got within ten miles of the city, and Bogdan could hear their artillery as they fought with Germans. Yet in Poland, the worry was that Russia would try to free the country from the Germans and then claim it won Polish freedom. Poles wanted to liberate themselves. The Polish goal was ambitious: they hoped to rise up and repulse the German occupiers. In so doing, they wished to deny the Soviet Union an opportunity to control them after the war. The Russians needed to recognize the government-in-exile in London as the legitimate rulers of Poland, and the success of a rebellion would force them to do so.

Thus, Poles resolved to greet the Soviets—if they got to Warsaw—as simply co-combatants rather than be liberated by them. During the summer of 1944, pressure built for the Polish resistance to act. In June, Poles heard about the D-Day invasion on the radio, and the news heartened them. D-Day opened up the long awaited second front of the war in Western Europe. It marked the largest military invasion in history, with Allied troops numbering 150,000 on the first day alone. Having dealt with the Germans himself during the occupation, Bogdan knew that they were smart but could be outwitted. The Allies pulled off the ultimate deception by fooling the Nazis into thinking that they would land at Pas de Calais, the French city at the point where the English Channel was narrowest, spanning a little more than twenty miles. Instead, the Allies struck at the beaches of Normandy, almost two hundred miles to the West.

The world owed a tremendous debt to the soldiers and paratroopers of D-Day, who faced daunting German defenses in the form of mines, artillery, and concrete blockhouses with rapid-fire machine guns. D-Day also had surprises. The Allies encountered soldiers who surrendered without a fight—and found that some were Polish, not German. The Nazis, who were starved for manpower, had conscripted them by giving them the choice of either fighting for Germany or languishing and likely dying in POW camps. To save their skin, these Polish POWs chose the former, but they gave up peacefully before the Allied onslaught. In one case, the surrendering Poles even warned the invading Allies about landmines; in another, two American soldiers captured fifty Polish POWs, who docilely surrendered and thus stopped their dreaded labor for the Germans.

In Warsaw, Bogdan and other residents sensed that D-Day was a turning point in the war. One week after the invasion, the Allied forces in France had mushroomed to half a million. On August 25, the Allies liberated Paris. With Allies advancing from the West and the Soviet Union battling Germany to the East, the two armies could crush the Wehrmacht.

Poles felt that the end of the war would be coming soon, likely by the end of 1944, yet at the same time, they knew the Allied troops were still far from Poland.

Poles had to act on their own.

VIII. Readying for Rebellion

Earlier in the year, Bogdan had experienced his own personal turning point, which allowed him to devote more attention to military training and Poland's independence. In January 1944, he finished the *komplety* school and, in effect, graduated. His teachers and classmates held a small, quiet ceremony in an apartment, and everyone stayed there overnight. The graduation was subdued and sub rosa, with only a half-dozen attending. They could put nothing in writing because if the Germans had captured it, anyone named on the document would face execution or concentration camps. But Bogdan felt satisfaction that, in the eyes of their teachers, they had received enough schooling to achieve the equivalent of a high school diploma. That achievement gave Bogdan confidence that he could now shift his focus and concentrate on Poland's future, which meant armed rebellion.

Warsaw had witnessed one uprising already. The invading Germans grouped Jews into a ghetto district, where they could control and begin transporting them to concentration camps. In April 1943, Jews in the city's ghetto rebelled against the Nazis rather than be sent to their deaths. But the Nazis had the advantages in numbers and weapons, and they quickly stamped out the uprising, which lasted just twenty-seven days. As a coup de grace, Nazi troops ended the fighting by savagely blowing up the Great Synagogue, a magnificent building designed by architect Leandro Marconi that had opened in 1878. At one point during this uprising, Bogdan saw smoke wafting up from the burning ghetto. All told, more than 20,000 resistance fighters died, and the Germans sent survivors to concentration camps at Treblinka and Majdanek. The precedent of an uprising was inauspicious—especially with the rebels lacking weapons to fight the well-armed Germans—but the new Polish resistance resolved to try.

This was serious stuff, because resistance fighters would be putting their lives on the line to defend Poland. They took crash courses in warfare. Bogdan quit his job at Udycz and studied full-time to be an officer, even though the military operations offered no pay. "But this involves Poland's future, and this endeavor," Bogdan thought to himself, "is more important than any job I can hold." He was proud when he received a promotion to the rank of sergeant cadet officer. He attended small resistance meetings, usually with only a half-dozen attendees, so that the planning could remain inconspicuous.

Bogdan's unit was Gustaw Harnas, named after the officer who was leading them (although Bogdan never got to meet him personally). Even though he and unit members all began spending hours together, they knew one another only by first names, pseudonyms, or even numbers. Bogdan's number was 1668, but in general, his new colleagues and friends called him "Bogdan," and that was it. They did not know his last name, and he did not know theirs. In case the Germans captured any of them, the less personal information they knew, the less they could betray and endanger their comrades, even if they were tortured.

The rebels worked on an ad hoc, decentralized basis, meeting in limited groups inside various apartments, coordinating efforts through word-of-mouth and a network of couriers. It was imperative that the Germans suspected nothing so that when the day came, they could catch them by surprise. Once again, Bogdan was glad to be in Warsaw rather than in Bydgoszcz, because his hometown lacked the population that would provide a critical mass for resistance. People there could not organize and resist the way they could in a metropolis, and a result, Germany simply overpowered and absorbed Bydgoszcz, and no resistance effort grew there.

At their meetings, the rebels studied military tactics and learned how to operate pistols, grenades, and flamethrowers. Since they lacked real weapons, they reviewed diagrams, so their training was more theoretical than practical. Bogdan also saw working parts—just parts, because they were easier to bring to meetings covertly—of certain weapons, including a rifle, pistol, hand grenades, and a British-made Sten submachine gun. Bogdan studied them and tried to memorize how they worked.

Bogdan had fired guns before, but never in combat. He had shot the handgun belonging to Zybigniew Tymowski's father. At Aunt Hala's farm, Tadeusz took Bogdan and his brothers duck hunting, and they used shotguns. Bogdan hoped that he could gain a gun to fight the Germans, and almost miraculously, a few days before the Uprising was to begin, he was visiting an apartment of a fellow insurgent and he obtained a submachine gun, which he put under a raincoat he was wearing. But he soon relinquished that gun to other resistance fighters.

In a way, that was good. During the training and planning phase, if the Germans had caught Bogdan with a weapon, the punishment would have been lethal. He knew of one incident where they apprehended two rebel Poles who had guns; one of them was Bogdan's friend, Przemek Madja. They both landed in prison, and Przemek was executed. Stories like these acted as cautionary tales, so the insurgents temporarily accepted the dearth of weapons, hoping that when the time came for actual combat, they would have them.

They would fight the Germans militarily, but just as importantly, they would battle them on spiritual and patriotic terms, which might give them the edge. In shutting down schools, the Nazi invaders had miscalculated. Had they kept schools open, talented and educated Poles would have stayed in the classroom. As it was, intelligent and motivated citizens joined the resistance, giving the movement its most capable leaders and fighters. Inside their hearts they all had a burning goal. They would approach the Germans with feline stealth and attack. They would kick them out of their city and country—and do it quickly. They would send a message to them and future invaders that they should never trespass on Poland.

Poland would be free again, and they would make it so.

— 4 —

War in a Japanese City

I. Propagandizing the War

As the people of Otaru quickly learned, a vital aspect of war was the government's effort to win hearts and minds. The Japanese government used two tools in its official armature. One was religion. In daily life, Japanese people practiced Shinto, which was supposed to be a unique and superior religion, reinforcing the notion of Japanese supremacy. From the war's beginning, citizens went to Shinto shrines to pray for success in the war and wish for good luck for soldiers. They did so with fervor on the eighth day of each month—because for them, the war started on December 8—praying in special ceremonies and agreeing with the government's blandishments that they had to win the war.

The other official organ was the school system. After parents, teachers were the most immediate authorities in students' lives, and they drenched their pupils with warnings about the Allies, their evil character, and their ill intent. Students accepted these claims at face value, and in this respect, they got quite an education. Teachers inculcated an understanding of history, science, math, and literature—but also bedrock values, and these instructors grew overt about how their flock should view the world.

One way that Seiko could see this process was in English language instruction. Her desire to learn English provided a theme to her education, and school allowed her to pursue this ambition. During the 1942–43 school year, Seiko's teachers taught English as a class subject, recognizing it as an important language, but perhaps also to prepare students to understand their wartime adversaries, the Americans and the British. Ironically, in the early 1930s, authorities had done the opposite, telling Japanese people not to use English or sing American songs. Americans, after all, were a malign race, teachers told students already then, not to be trusted. They even wanted to avoid American terms like "baseball," and so the sport was known by the Japanese name *ryakyu*. If any students used an English word or phrase, teachers delivered a stern reprimand. "No!" they fumed, "You are being anti-Japanese." Of course, these directives came down from the government, so Tokyo showed that it exercised tight control over the population, with the intent to wipe the slate clean of any U.S. influence.

The erasing process happened with music, too. Before Japan went to war against the U.S., Seiko learned a small canon of American songs, often using the English words for the chorus while inserting Japanese lyrics into the verses. She learned and sang tunes like "Go Tell Aunt Rosie," "London Bridge Is Falling Down," "O, Susanna," "Swanee River," and "Twinkle, Twinkle, Little Star." Once the war started, that music stopped. Instead, radio stations played classical music, especially Ludwig van Beethoven's symphonies; he was German, and Japan was a wartime ally of his country.

Throughout history, war's greatest casualties have always been life and limb, but in Japan, another casualty was the truth. In various ways, the government dissembled, as Seiko later learned. This showdown, it stressed to the Japanese citizenry, was a *seisen*—a holy war, or literally a "saint war"—and it was caused by the American and British belief that they were superior to the Japanese race, which they saw as yellow and inferior. So the students' duty, their teachers instructed them, would be to lead the Asian people and get rid of the Westerners, who were self-indulgent and animal-like, even devils. If they attacked the Japanese homeland, they would take away women and girls, raping and killing them, and they would turn Japanese men into slave laborers. As Japanese citizens later learned, these characterizations distorted the Americans and Brits beyond recognition.

Textbooks reinforced the government's official line. One of Seiko's texts featured a letter from a Japanese mother to her son, who served as a sailor, in which she beamed with pride that her son served in the navy. Yet the mother added that she had yet to hear of any noble or great exploits of her son, which disappointed her. She admonished him to show bravery for Japan and devote his life to fighting the war to achieve victory for his country. Seiko and her classmates accepted these sentiments as proper for parents, and a number of schools—including Seiko's—performed a play in which children acted out the roles of the mother and her son.

Various idioms, which Seiko heard in school and on the radio and saw on posters, drilled discipline and patriotism into people's minds. One was *zeitaku wa teki da*. *Zeitaku* means luxurious life, and *teki* denotes enemy, so the expression meant that people should chase away all thoughts of extravagance or frills. During the war, the Japanese looked upon such items with disdain, because if they were to enjoy any indulgences, that meant they were denying those very items—and worse, necessities—to the military. A similar expression was *hoshigarimasen katsu made wa*, which mean "until we win, we do not want candy, rice, or anything else." Any behavior that deviated from these aphorisms appeared to oppose the military and weaken the national will to fight.

Propaganda clotted the public mind, and the process began with the young. As schoolchildren absorbed these official lessons, they grew determined to fight to the end. After all, it was their teachers who doled out these instructions—so naturally, they believed everything. On the radio, the government gave further encouragement by always stating that Japan was winning the war. This effort to propagandize the struggle continued until Japan finally surrendered. The Americans, too, propagandized the war, using simian and vermin imagery to depict the Japanese, portraying them more harshly than German and Italian adversaries, which reflected a desire to avenge Pearl Harbor but also the rancor and racism that infected views on both sides of the Pacific Ocean. The war was cruel and unforgiving.

II. Setbacks

Wartime strategy often boils down to gigantic gambles, and Japan's calculus against the U.S. reflected that. Originally, the thinking was a devastating blow at Pearl Harbor would nullify the U.S. Navy's strength, and then the European war would attenuate American power, which many Japanese viewed as decadent and "soft." The U.S. would then quickly sue for peace in the Pacific.

The Japanese military followed up on Pearl Harbor by achieving planned conquests. The year 1942 started with Japan in command of the Pacific theater, controlling vast portions of Southeast Asia. The Philippines was a U.S. colony, and on December 10, Japanese troops landed on Luzon, the largest island in the Philippines and home to Manila, the capital. The Japanese advance forced General Douglas MacArthur to seek shelter in Manila Harbor, where he set up base. U.S. troops disdainfully called him "Dugout Doug" for burrowing into safety, but in March 1942, President Franklin Roosevelt ordered him to evacuate the Philippines for Australia. In leaving the islands, the general uttered his famous vow, "I shall return." By early 1942, Japan seemed even to be threatening Australia.

Yet during the next months, the tide of war in the Pacific turned. In May, during the Battle of Coral Sea, U.S. forces repulsed the Japanese navy. Following this setback, Admiral Yamamoto planned another attack at Pearl Harbor, but by mid-1942 Hawaii was too well protected. So, looking for some kind of reprise of the Pearl Harbor raid, Yamamoto fixed his gaze on Midway, an atoll more than a thousand miles west of Hawaii, hoping to lure the Americans far out into the Pacific to cripple their navy.

4. War in a Japanese City

In June 1942, the Battle of Midway lasted three days, and a key indicator of success or failure was the aircraft carrier. Seiko recalled that the Japanese government reported to its people that the country lost two carriers in this fight. In reality, four were destroyed, and Midway became the decisive battle of the Pacific theater, putting Japan on the defensive and handing it losses from which it never recovered. Thus began a three-year U.S. offensive that meant setback after setback for Japan—and mounting hardships for civilians all the time.

Just like Germany had done before World War I, Japan invested considerable resources and expense in building up its navy, hoping that military branch would enable it to make and keep territorial gains and ensure its status as a great nation. Much as Germany had experienced, the results were miserable. By late 1942, the U.S. had naval superiority in the Pacific.

The Americans triumphed at the Battle of Guadalcanal, in the Solomon Islands, which lasted through the last months of 1942 and into early 1943. U.S. forces, even while giving first priority to the European theater, battered the Japanese military and stretched its navy thin. It was a muscular display of American strength, showing an ability to fight in two large theaters of war simultaneously and make strides in both.

One aspect of the Japanese government's propaganda machine was to put the best sheen on bad news, leading people to think that Japan was winning the war at every stage. In truth, Japan was experiencing more setbacks in the war. In May 1943, U.S. forces dealt a devastating blow in the Aleutians when they retook the island of Attu, which Japan had seized a year earlier. Two thousand Japanese troops perished trying to hold Attu, while the American death toll was only half that amount. In August 1943, the U.S. regained Kiska, the other Aleutian island that Japan had taken earlier in the war. By 1944, news dispatches could scarcely avoid a candid truth. The media reported that the fight against the Allied powers was not proceeding the way the Japanese government thought it would.

The Japanese media tried to cover for the country's allies, but they, too, experienced setbacks. Once Germany invaded the Soviet Union, Japanese newspapers constantly reported that Hitler's army would take Leningrad, Russia's second-largest city, located on the Baltic Sea. The anticipated capture of Leningrad dominated the news, and the siege of the city, which began in September 1941, lasted 900 days. But in January 1944, Seiko was surprised to learn that the siege ended with the Soviets victorious. Leningrad had repulsed its German invaders, who retreated. The unexpected turn of events elevated the Soviet Union's prestige, burnishing its image in a way that lasted for the rest of the war and beyond. Leningrad awakened the Japanese to the notion that the Axis powers might be losing the war, and that would deliver a crushing blow to Japan and its global standing.

Seiko detected that the Japanese government's emphasis on winning the war grew more desperate. To add military manpower, the government proclaimed that all students in state-run institutions of higher learning would be allowed to graduate in the fall of 1944 rather than the following spring. One student who received his diploma early was Seiko's older brother Suguru, who majored in economics. In November 1944 in Tokyo, the Ministry of Education held a ceremony for these early college graduates. At that point, Suguru had already made a momentous decision. He had enrolled in the Japanese navy to begin training as a kamikaze pilot, reversing the normal sequence for young men who joined the military. Instead of graduating from school and then enlisting, he first signed up and reported for naval training earlier in 1944, so that when the commencement exercises came in September, he was already a member of the navy.

Ostensibly, Hiroshi and Echi were proud of Suguru and thought his military service was honorable, especially because he joined the navy, which was a point of pride for the Japanese, who regarded that branch of service as a national treasure. Like all loyal and patriotic Japanese, Seiko's parents appeared determined to sacrifice at great length to see their nation's struggle succeed. But outwardly, that was what Japanese parents were supposed to say. It was the only allowable utterance. Inside, Hiroshi and Echi felt pained and fearful for their son and the unknown future he now faced, but they revealed those sentiments only to each other. Before friends, they expressed their pride in Suguru and hoped for his safe return.

III. Coercions and Restrictions

The war sacrifices were indeed draining, and while the spiritual strength of Otaru residents remained intact, they grew weary. Three years into the war against the Allies, the conflict was taking a toll on all of its citizens, including students. The war created demographic distortions, which had ripple effects across society. Military service siphoned off young men, and on Otaru streets, the sight of them became rare. Farms, factories, and fisheries experienced labor shortages because male workers had joined the military.

People did whatever they could to earn income, and a shadow economy became more pronounced than in usual times. Street vendors walked in Seiko's neighborhood, chanting out their wares and services. One man draped small packets of boiled tiger eye and kidney beans along a stick that he balanced on his shoulder. Women came around singing "o-hana [flower]," and families bought bouquets because they used them in ceremonies to honor ancestors. The most memorable vendor was a gentleman who walked around during the summer months. In a slow monotone, he chanted out *barikan, kamisori, hocho,* meaning "hair clippers, razors, knives." He would follow with the verb *tonginasu,* or "sharpen," with a slight upward inflection, in effect asking if anyone needed these blades sharpened.

Relatively low at the outset, living standards in Otaru plunged further. During the 1930s, the worldwide Great Depression had suppressed food production, as had the war with China. Now, the fight against the Allies scythed down food supplies, and government at all levels imposed strict rationing. The national government ordered cities, including Otaru, to supervise citizens, and each household received a notebook in which it recorded its family members and their consumption of goods. The government had no qualms about embarrassment: if the father of the house had a mistress, he was even supposed to record that. Each home had to be forthright and deferential, with no room for privacy. Simply put, the Japanese were a people who did what they were told to do. They felt strongly that they should never breach proper codes of conduct, and anyone who did would feel an unbearable sense of shame.

The government's intrusion into personal lives meant that local officials came to every house and collected these notebooks, and families then received instructions on the designated stores where they had to shop to receive staples like food and clothing. No household got enough of anything, but everyone had to make do with what they received. Anyone who transgressed from the rationing regimen faced punishment, so Seiko and her family adhered to the restrictions faithfully. This was an authoritarian government, after all, exercising tight control over its citizenry.

Townspeople faced other constraints. Authorities feared that any shaft of light shooting from a home at night could turn a whole neighborhood into a bombing target, so in their dimly lit homes families had to pull down window shades and practice blackout conditions. Officials strictly enforced this edict. When darkness fell, they walked around inspecting homes, and they bellowed warnings such as "Kawakami-san, we can see your lights! This is a government order. Shut off your lights or pull down your window shades more tightly!" If Seiko and her family members failed to comply, they threatened to send their father to jail. This behavior, which went beyond strictness and resembled arrogance, exerted raw power, compelling families to obey. Since they lacked candles or lanterns, the Kawakamis had to get used to darkness during the evening, and often they just went to bed early.

Villages and cities created groups called *tonarigumi,* comprising household wives, and on certain days they practiced emergency drills.

Seiko's mother, who belonged to Otaru's *tonarigumi*, took part in them. During these exercises, the women wore long pants instead of kimonos, and they simulated what measures they would take in case enemy bombs created huge conflagrations in the city. The women dipped brooms into water and ran around, furiously swatting the wet broom heads onto the ground, trying to stamp out imaginary fires raging in the streets. Each household also had to make preparations for bombing attacks. At the Kawakami home, they followed instructions by digging a large hole outside their house. The idea was that they would rush into the crater during a bombing attack.

The Kawakamis took all these preparations seriously, but in retrospect, they were absurd. Seiko and her family later laughed at how ridiculous the *tonarigumi's* wet broom exercises were. They never used the crude bomb shelter outside their home, and it collected rainwater during warmer months and became a breeding pool for mosquitoes.

But the orders and coercion continued. One directive said that any family with gold or silver jewelry should relinquish them so that the government could gain more revenue. Hiroshi had a gold watch, but because it was valuable to him, he hid it rather than giving it up. Families were supposed to donate their cats and dogs so that the military could use the fur to make coats for soldiers. Pets became scarce.

That was a problem. Many Japanese families, including Seiko's, owned cats, partly because Japanese culture regarded felines as having a talismanic charm—especially calico or "tortoiseshell" cats, which had a mixture of orange, black, and white fur. The *manniki nekko* was a staple of businesses, a calico cat figurine or picture displayed at store and restaurant entrances, standing with its right paw upraised to beckon customers; the Japanese believed it would bring prosperity to an establishment. Ship crews kept calico cats aboard because they thought they would help to ensure a safe voyage, warding away the spirits of drowned sailors (the Japanese viewed whitecaps as the ghosts of drowning victims). Cats also served a functional purpose. Rats and mice infested flimsy houses, and cats controlled this problem at low cost to homeowners, who barely had to worry about providing food for the cats because they feasted on vermin.

As long as Seiko could remember, her family always had a cat, and during the war, they had one they adored. They named her *San Ke* ("Three-Color Fur") because she was a calico, and they could not bear the thought of her being slaughtered for the military. Under austere wartime conditions, cats had short lives, only about seven years, and the family treasured however much time *San Ke* had with them. They refused to give her up, never daring to take her outside, not even to a veterinarian, fearing that to do so would betray her existence. For friends and neighbors who had already met *San Ke*, if they asked about her, Seiko and her family just said that she had run away.

War nibbled away at some liberties and pleasures, and it devoured others. The military gulped down Japan's resources, especially food. The country's best supplies had to go to soldiers fighting on the front lines, so civilians assumed a lower priority. During the war, Seiko and her family never saw red meat, milk, or bread, which was true for virtually all Otaru residents. For protein, they ate lots of herring and flounder. Potatoes were another staple, although in winter their quality deteriorated so much that store potatoes were sometimes frozen and black. Some of Hiroshi's friends shared their fishing catch or homegrown potatoes with the family, and they were always grateful for this generosity.

Two mainstays of the Japanese diet suffered restrictions. Hokkaido's climate was too cool to grow rice, and most of the country's crop went to soldiers. Otaru residents received rice imported from China, but it was often spoiled. When Seiko's family opened a rice bag, a foul odor often sprung forth, and before cooking, they had to scour the rice for bugs and then wash it repeatedly. Miso paste was a second staple that was limited, so they seldom consumed the miso soup that they normally ate daily.

The government restricted what citizens could eat, and conversely, it also told them what they should eat. This coercion included a directive to harvest and eat pumpkins. As a crop, pumpkins required little maintenance, and they provided beta carotene and other nutrients, so authorities figured they would be a sensible way to ease food shortages. But other than soup or bread—a luxury like pie was out of the question—the range of palatable pumpkin products was limited. Still, Seiko and her family dutifully grew pumpkins in their small garden, as did other families, and Seiko noticed an odd result. In looking at her friends, she detected a faint, orange hue to their skin, which must have come from the high consumption of beta carotene. Caricatures of Asians typically showed them as "yellow," but this was a new twist on the stereotype—orange skin.

Although the Allies never bombed Otaru, residents died indirectly from the war. Because feral dogs, cats, and other animals roamed city streets and scavenged for food, authorities put out cakes of poison. Thinking they were edible, one of Seiko's neighbors—who, like everyone else, was chronically famished—ate one and died. A more protracted case involved her school math teacher, a reserved, scholarly man who became a recluse, staying at home even though he had no idea how to cook or take care of himself. Once, Seiko and a few of her classmates took food to him, and he hobbled weakly to the door to receive them. He looked like a man in a death spiral, and no act of kindness could save him.

Throughout 1942 and 1943, everyone could feel the tight squeeze of shortages, but by 1944 it grew more severe. The government rationed coal, so at night Seiko and her family stopped feeding the stove, and the whole house was freezing when they woke up in the morning. With clothing in short supply, no one in Otaru had new clothes, and everyone experienced more trouble in Otaru's brutal winters. As in all homes, in the Kawakami household, if anyone accidentally broke a china plate or drinking glass, they knew they would have to do without a replacement, and the same held true for pots and pans that wore out, especially because the military grabbed any scrap of metal for wartime use.

The war took supplies and provisions, but the greatest theft was stealing childhoods. Shortages robbed children of simple joys. Japan imported more than eighty percent of its sugar, so when war against the Allies started, it became virtually nonexistent, making candy a rarity. Once, Echi heard two young boys outside the Kawakami home, one of them savoring a piece of hard candy. "May I suck on that candy, just for a minute?" the other boy asked. Sharing a candy might seem crass, but the war pushed everyone—including children—to extremes.

Another alien item was chocolate. Seiko never saw it during the war, and one classmate said that her younger sister, encountering a chocolate bar for the first time, feared it might be toxic and begged her parents not to eat it. Before the war, Seiko loved drinking hot cocoa, but she had to give that up as well.

Childhood seemed much more barren without favorite indulgences. In the eyes of children, war was like a bandit, invading their lives and stealing smiles and laughter, and sources of happiness, taking what they liked and enjoyed, and never caring at all.

IV. Everything for a God

For all the sacrifices and restrictions the Japanese endured, they took comfort that they were doing everything for an overriding purpose. They dedicated their efforts to Emperor Hirohito, whom they referred to reverentially as the "Emperor," rather than by his surname. Supreme dynastic ruler of Japan since 1926, when a new constitution took effect, he was the sun god—an omnipotent living deity whom the Japanese believed descended directly from the Sun Goddess Amaterasu. Such was his power that they were not even supposed to look at him because it allegedly would hurt their eyes. They never heard his voice, and most Japanese had not seen his picture, so they had little concept of his physical appearance or attributes.

But there was no need for that. The popular belief was that the emperor's entire family resided above the clouds, and they were beyond being human. The imperial family used the chrysanthemum flower as its symbol, and they were known as the "Chrysanthemum Throne."

As children, Seiko and her friends believed so completely that the emperor was a god that they wondered if he had to stoop to normal bodily functions like using the bathroom. They had many conversations devoted to this quandary of human—or divine—nature. Ultimately, they assumed the answer was no. They could not imagine it. After all, why would a god need to urinate or defecate? The mere thought was a *lèse majesté*.

When Seiko attended elementary school in Otaru, the campus had a small structure, called a *hoanden*, which was the size of a tool shed. Sturdily fashioned with stone and concrete, it was built to last. An iron fence encircled the *hoanden*, and only the schoolmaster could open the locked gate and enter inside. Schools throughout Japan had similar *hoanden*, and this tiny building was a monument to the emperor. Whenever pupils and teachers walked by it, they had to pause and bow. Even a student running late for class would still have to stop and display the required reverence.

On ceremonial days, like the emperor's birthday, the headmaster of Seiko's school opened the building, took out the emperor's portrait, and placed it on the stage in the gymnasium, where they held an assembly to celebrate and sing the national anthem, *Kimi ga yo*, which meant "His Imperial Majesty's Reign," whose lyrics used the metaphor of a small stone gathering moss that would last for a thousand years, like the emperor's reign would. (This song remains Japan's national anthem today.) During class, teachers commonly set aside time and said, "Now, stand up, let's pray for the emperor and our country." Students always felt the emperor's presence, as if he were watching over them, and the tangible tributes to him furnished reminders of his reality, even if they never heard his voice and could never hope to see him.

In addition to being the sun god, Hirohito was commander-in-chief of the Japanese military, and he proclaimed that young people needed to support the government. In school, Seiko's teachers reinforced this message; one teacher was especially truculent about the emperor. "I am the emperor's subject," he warned, "and if you students defy the emperor's principles, then I have the right to kill you, just like samurai could kill peasants in earlier times during Japan's history." For young children, these were chilling words, putting the fear of the emperor in them and forcing them to comply with whatever their teachers demanded.

The country had to prevail in the war, teachers exhorted, saying that everything they did was vital to that effort, even acts as simple as digging up potatoes in their gardens. In the spring of 1942, just before summer vacation began, Seiko's teachers told the students to walk five miles to a beach south of the city along Otaru Bay, a spot where residents sunbathed and swam during the summer. The students wore backpacks, in which they packed water canteens plus rice balls with pickled plums, the latter symbolizing the Japanese flag because they had white rice surrounding a circular core, just like the rising sun on the nation's flag. They walked with umbrellas, too, because the school principal urged, "Just as military soldiers must carry guns, you will carry umbrellas." The point of the exercise was to test the pupils' physical stamina, and even more importantly, their dedication to the war and the emperor.

Every few months, Seiko and other students went as a class to a Shinto shrine to pray. Most cities in Japan had such shrines located on hilltops, and Otaru's was at an especially high elevation, so students had to climb a long distance on stone steps to get there. Most Japanese families also had a *jinja* at home, a small shrine that honored deceased relatives, usually containing photos of the loved ones. Family members put offerings of food, such as small cakes, within the *jinja* to console the souls of the departed. Once the war broke out, the custom was to place food in the *jinja* to serve soldiers who were away at war, with the idea that the practice would bring good luck to the servicemen and help real food materialize before them. The ritual was a spiritual way for families to contribute to the war effort.

Sennin bari ("one thousand people's needlepoint") was another patriotic project. Seiko and her classmates made cotton belts, emblazoned with the image of a tiger in the center, for soldiers to wear around their waists. They put red stiches into the belt, aiming to embed a thousand such marks. (The number one thousand—*sen*—has symbolic and spiritual importance in Japan. For example, one belief is that a person who folds one thousand origami cranes will win the good graces of the gods and be rewarded with good luck.) They sometimes stood on street corners and asked passers-by to help them insert a stitch to complete the needlepoint. In Japanese folklore, the tiger had special significance, symbolizing an animal that would venture a thousand miles and travel that same distance back home. The belts implied that once the war was over, the soldiers would return to Japan unharmed. When Seiko completed her *sennin bari*, she gave it to her older brother Suguru, and he appreciated the gift and its meaning as he prepared to leave home.

In wartime mythology, the lore of the Japanese soldier's thousand-stitch belt loomed large, and it crossed the ocean. Later, when Seiko was living in the U.S., she was amused to see it surface in the popular 1970s American television series, *The Six Million Dollar Man*. In an episode entitled "The Last Kamikaze," bionic man Steve Austin encountered a Japanese soldier who lived on a Pacific island, believing thirty years later that World War II raged on, refusing to surrender. He almost killed Austin, who later saved his life. The show concluded with the old warrior offering

Austin the ultimate gift of gratitude—his thousand-stitch belt. (While a quaint Hollywood drama, the episode was inspired by the real-life story of Hiroo Onoda, a Japanese lieutenant who hid for twenty-nine years in a Philippines jungle, finally surrendering in 1974.)

But like Japan's war effort itself, the thousand-stitch belts were more spiritual than substantive. While they sometimes constituted a point of pride for soldiers, they were inconvenient. Their quality was so poor that they unraveled. Because soldiers could seldom bathe, the *sennin bari* stunk of sweat and dirt. Worse, they became hotels for fleas and lice, and soldiers often threw them away. When Japanese soldiers returned from the warfront, far from expressing gratitude, they often complained about these shoddy belts.

None of that mattered. The people of Otaru were armed with an arsenal of accouterments to fight this patriotic war, and they were prepared to take more action.

— 5 —

Uprising!

I. Sizzling with Success

In late July 1944, word spread that the Warsaw Uprising would soon start. The planning seemed more muddled than meticulous, but the *Armia Krajowa* was an improvisational army, and members had to act in strict secrecy, which hindered communication and coordination. For several weeks, Bogdan had been with a new unit, and he received tentative word that the Uprising would begin operations on Friday, July 28. That day, he patrolled Warsaw with a submachine gun hidden under his raincoat, and then the rebels gathered in their resistance groups and waited. But nothing happened, so they dispersed and waited for more definitive orders.

The next target date was Tuesday, August 1. This time, Bogdan rejoined his original unit at an apartment on Marszalkowska Street, leaving the machine gun with the other group, and he prepared to commence military operations. General Tadeusz Komorowski, a renowned cavalry officer, led the operation in Warsaw, acting in coordination with the Polish government-in-exile in London. The tactical decisions on the Uprising took place at the local level, but the London leaders provided help in organizing the overall effort. In Warsaw, fighters received instructions to begin congregating in small groups in apartments to ready themselves. Waiting in an apartment that was home to one of his unit members, Bogdan and the others felt anxious, and they chatted to brace up their spirits. Messengers brought word that the effort would begin at 5:00 p.m., which became known as "W" hour (from the Polish verb *walczyc*, which means "fight"). By beginning the operation during the late afternoon rush hour, Polish military leaders felt that they could catch the Germans off-guard.

So contingent was the nature of the resistance that right up to "W" hour, the Polish soldiers were still uncertain whether the rebellion would take place at all. In a vague, hazy way, they knew that the call could come to begin, but nothing was firm or official. Bogdan received instructions that when—or if—the Uprising commenced, he would report to a specific

5. Uprising! 79

apartment, one of many meeting places scattered throughout Warsaw that would act as nerve centers for operations. For now, it was just a tense, white-knuckle waiting game, and if the operation truly started, everyone would know through word of mouth and through noise and disruption in the city.

On August 1, 1944, at 1700 hours, it started.

Bogdan received word that the Uprising was taking place, and he and his unit hit the streets. The early evening air seemed to crackle with energy, and they worked feverishly. First, they had to build barricades. This project was peremptory, and civilians helped as much as they could. They needed to prevent German tanks and infantry from penetrating any sections of Warsaw where the rebels gained control and provide protection for the rebel army. Poles used anything available to build the barricades—metal rails, sandbags, pavement stones, furniture, and rocks—and they overturned streetcars and automobiles. Using these materials, they hurriedly constructed a barricade network throughout the city, and building and rebuilding them became a constant activity. As soon as the Germans knocked them down, soldiers and citizens speedily rebuilt them. Bogdan helped a group of people overturn a streetcar for one barricade, and as the massive car crashed down on its side, Bogdan thought about how they were using a perfectly good vehicle as a shield that German tanks might damage or destroy. But that destruction was part of war, and they used whatever implements they could to achieve an advantage over the enemy.

For the Uprising to succeed, the effort needed the sheer manpower displayed in building barricades, and luckily, the Poles had the advantage here. Initially, the insurgents outnumbered the Germans. By August 1, the Polish Home Army comprised about 45,000 soldiers versus 25,000 German troops. The rebels needed to tilt the balance even more in their favor. They rooted out German spies to disable the Nazi information network, and during this time the true identity of the violin-playing panhandler near Bogdan's apartment was unmasked. They had to capture or kill German soldiers and get their equipment and weapons, and they could show no mercy.

The insurgents' strategy was to gain as much of the city as they could and beat down the Germans any way possible. Two key pressure points that the *Armia Krajowa* targeted were the Poniatowski and Kierbedz bridges, which spanned the Vistula River, although they never managed to secure either. They wanted to capture railroad stations, too, but they met only limited success with that objective.

Initially, Bogdan found himself in the center of Warsaw, near the main train station, as he and his unit tried to claw their way onto as much territory as possible. Early in the fighting, Bogdan got a gory look at war

When the Warsaw Uprising began, insurgents and citizens built street barricades, using any available material—concrete slabs, earth, and felled trees. The rebels had few weapons, but visible on the ground are *filipinki*, or Molotov cocktails, which were vital in their fight against Nazi tanks (from the collections of the Warsaw Rising Museum).

when shrapnel cut off the tongue of a member of his unit. One of Bogdan's first assignments was to stop attacks from tanks, the vital cog in the Nazis' military machine, which they used to demolish buildings and ram through AK barricades. Their counter-weapon was *filipinki*, or as they also called it, the "Molotov cocktail," a name that the Finns had given to the gasoline-filled bottles after the Soviets invaded their country in 1939, derisively referring to the Soviet foreign minister ("Molotov," his acquired name, meant "hammer" in Russian).

Because most gas stations shut down, Bogdan and his fellow fighters inserted long tubes into car gas tanks and siphoned fuel with their mouths. They then used any kind of glass container they could scrounge up, usually wine or vodka bottles. Sometimes they inserted a wick in them, but more commonly, they filled the bottles three-quarters with gasoline and aimed to throw them at tank motors. The gasoline would splatter, and the next step—dangerous, involving fast hands and split-second timing—was to throw a lit, gasoline-soaked rag against the tank. The idea was to cause an engine fire, disable the vehicle, force the crew to evacuate, and then overwhelm them, with the rebels relying on their bare hands to disarm and fight the crew.

5. Uprising!

Because Bogdan no longer had a submachine gun, he was left with nothing to fight with—not even a knife. Years later, he learned that only fourteen percent of Polish fighters had weapons, a statistic that matched his recollection and suggested their dire chances. They relied on captured German arms, Allied supplies, and homemade guns. In underground factories, the resistance movement made crude grenades. Usually, these were just a cloth rag enclosing an incendiary substance, although some were sophisticated enough to have a timing mechanism.

Polish snipers managed to kill Germans, but ammunition was scarce, and they had to conserve bullets. The *Armia Krajowa* embraced the expression *Kazdy Pocisk Jeden Niemiec*—"Each Shot, One German." Those soldiers who had guns had strict training to fire only at visible targets rather than shoot randomly. The Germans suffered no such shortages. At their disposal were planes, bombs, tanks, machine guns, and ammunition galore.

But the *Armia Krajowa* improvised. Soldiers threw stones at the Germans and used *filipinki*. Once, Bogdan crouched in a deep, bombed-out crater at a street intersection; he waited for German tanks, and he even saw one a half-block away, but none came close enough that he could hurl a *filipinki* at it. At night, he heard German tanks, with the drivers gunning the loud diesel engines to intimidate the Poles. As if knowing the peril that awaited them, the tanks never came within throwing distance. It was frustrating. Bogdan and other soldiers had better luck in crashing lit Molotov cocktails against advancing German foot soldiers, using them as crude flame throwers.

As these tactics showed, the *Armia Krajowa* was a true rag-tag army, and the guerrilla nature of their fight was visible in other ways. In war, uniforms imbue soldiers with an esprit de corps and a sense of pride. *Armia Krajowa* uniforms consisted of only regular clothes supplemented by red-and-white armbands, signifying the Polish national colors and also providing a visible way to recognize comrades. The armbands bore the Polish eagle and the "PW" symbol, and the fighters wore them with pride. Some resistance fighters wore the uniforms of Warsaw firefighters, while others raided German storage units and obtained vests and helmets. Once the fighting began, they took helmets from dead or captured German soldiers. To prevent misidentification, they emblazoned the German helmets with Poland's red-and-white colors. Bogdan had only his street clothes supplemented by a blue beret, which many resistance fighters wore, plus the armband.

The Polish Army extemporized with other necessities. Communicating was difficult because their whole effort was so decentralized, and Warsaw's physical characteristics compounded the problem. The city comprised various districts, and the German occupation isolated them from one another. To frustrate their efforts further, the Germans cut off telephone service in the city. The Poles relied on a courier system that ran through streets and descended into canals, sewers, and tunnels. These all became vital arteries, and even small boys and girls ran messages and ammunition through these channels. It was dangerous, dirty work. Bogdan witnessed men emerging from canals and sewers like creatures in a horror story—smelly, caked with grime, and unrecognizable.

On the second day of the Uprising, the AK retook the city's power station and main post office. The power station generated electricity to run stores, hospitals, and factories, and Warsaw Poles hoped that the post office would help their communications. The flush of initial success exhilarated them, and their energy and enthusiasm ran high. During these first days of the Uprising, Bogdan saw a group of German POWs held captive in a park near his apartment. They looked miserable and defeated, like rats that had been drenched in water, and the sight boosted Bogdan's spirits. Additionally, he was proud that Poles could treat their prisoners humanely, despite the cruelty and atrocities that the Germans had inflicted upon Poles for years.

In its first days, the Uprising appeared to sizzle with some success. The rebels had regained their freedom, it seemed, and were quashing the evil surrounding them. In liberated areas, Poles celebrated, displaying the national flag for the first time in five years. Warsaw was functioning again as a city run by Poles, and it could act as a beacon for the rest of the country to win back control. On the first evening of the Uprising, two battalions of Bogdan's companies gathered in an apartment. Solemnly, they knelt down and prayed for more success, and they sang patriotic songs, including the Polish national anthem.

After years of defeat and oppression, Warsaw Poles had caught the Germans off-guard, clawing back control of sixty percent of the city. They began thinking optimistically, and a general estimate Bogdan heard was that they could defeat the enemy in ten days. Meanwhile, the Nazis' war against the Soviet Union was going badly, and their losses on the eastern front gave Bogdan and his fellow fighters further confidence that the Germans were a beaten group. They thought that they could quickly overwhelm them and finish the task.

II. Combat and Close Calls

In the first week of fighting, Bogdan commanded four fighters in a detachment charged with defending an entrance gate to a building.

5. Uprising!

Nearby stood a dark-colored pick-up truck. Bogdan ran up to it and, looking inside, he noticed that the door was unlocked, and the keys were in the ignition. He climbed into the cab, grabbed the steering wheel, shifted the gear into neutral and depressed the clutch. He turned the key, but the engine would not turn over. Luckily, the truck faced the building, so Bogdan climbed out of the cab and asked for help. He and his men gathered around the truck, secured their footing, and prepared to push the truck inside the gate. Their plan was that once they got it within the building courtyard, they could siphon its gasoline to make Molotov cocktails.

As they began to nudge the truck forward, straining to gain more momentum with every inch, they heard the roar of a diesel engine, and they looked down the street. A German tank appeared, churning toward them and swiveling its turret in their direction. At once, they darted away from the truck and sprinted toward the building.

The truck exploded. The tank's round hit it square-on, sending metal fragments flying everywhere. Just as they heard the impact, Bogdan and his men made it inside the building. Panting furiously, they leaned against walls and tried to catch their breath, thinking about what to do next and preparing to run again if the tank drew closer and threatened them. Across the hallway from Bogdan, one comrade gestured toward his torso. Bogdan looked down, and he could not believe it. Blood splatters covered one side of his jacket, even though he was feeling no pain.

Bogdan could not see where the wound was—or how badly he had been hit—but blood was dripping from the side of his head onto his jacket. Shrapnel must have sprayed everywhere and caught him somewhere on his temple or cheek. Adrenalin seemed to be blocking out the pain, but he might have been seriously hurt.

Bogdan relinquished command of the unit and ran to get help at his company's first aid post. There, medics and nurses cleaned and bandaged his wounds, the worst of which was a cut above his left ear, which was dripping blood. One nurse made a white dressing that she wrapped around his head. It looked good, even picturesque, but Bogdan got rid of it that very afternoon, after wearing it for only a few hours. His bleeding had stopped by then, and the bandages were white and conspicuous, which would have given the Germans a target. (More than a decade later, in 1955, Bogdan visited a chiropractor who found shrapnel still embedded in his left cheek.)

One the third day of the Uprising, Bogdan's unit had to guard a post office, which the AK had gained control of but worried would be the target of a German counter-attack. As Bodgan walked into the building, he noticed the body of a German soldier. He and his unit went to the second floor and prepared to defend the structure, but no German offensive came. While they waited, they explored the building and chatted with young girls who worked as couriers, carrying messages among different units. With obvious pride, one girl said that German bullets blew two holes in her skirt, just between her legs, as she ran. "This young lady has tons of courage," Bogdan thought.

The fighting raged on. Warsaw became a cockpit of conflict, with deadly combat taking place from building-to-building and even room-to-room at close range. Often, Polish insurgents battled the Germans on the same floor of a building, just yards from them. Bogdan heard bullets whizzing past him, and he felt like David fighting Goliath, armed only with Molotov cocktails. The venues where they fought also showed how raw and rudimentary their efforts were. They faced the Nazis through basements, sewers, and the carcasses of buildings, ducking from one hiding spot to another while avoiding the open streets, where they were vulnerable. The battles had no orderly tactics; they were the archetype of elemental street fighting and guerrilla warfare. If the enemy tried to flush them out into the open, the insurgents instead dispersed deeper into hiding places.

Although the Poles notched early successes, the Germans always reminded them of their unassailable advantage—they possessed modern weapons. At one point, Bogdan led a detachment that defended the second floor of a building, while Germans occupied the ground level. The Polish rebels lobbed homemade grenades downstairs, and then Bogdan peeked down the stairwell. He saw nothing, but he could hear clatter, which meant Germans were there. He raced back toward an apartment.

Whoosh! A roar emanated from behind him. Bogdan turned around to see a bright phantom leap up the stairwell. "Flamethrowers!" he thought, trying to figure out where to run next. At times, Bogdan carried one himself, and he watched in amazement as they shot out flames for up to fifty yards. From the ground floor, this German one could probably have reached the top level of the building. Once again, Bogdan cursed their lack of guns. A soldier operating a flamethrower was vulnerable—a visible and easy target to hit with a gun—and he wished one of his guerrilla fighters could have done it right there.

But as it was, Bogdan could have been burned alive. The German flamethrower sparked fires in the building, and some of his men frantically tried to stamp them out. The conflagration spread too fast to extinguish; they had to evacuate. Bogdan ordered his squad to withdraw to an adjacent building, using a large opening in the wall connecting the two structures. Moments after his unit fled from the first building, a violent explosion shattered the structure, and it collapsed in a gigantic cataract of rubble and dust, letting out a loud wail of death as it came down. By mere seconds, Bogdan and his unit had avoided annihilation.

5. Uprising!

The Germans had brought the building down by using another weapon—the Goliath, a small robotic tank. About the size of an office desk, it emitted a loud growl, like a deep-throated lawn mower, and Nazi soldiers steered it by using wires from a remote control box. Polish soldiers feared the Goliath; it carried devastating explosives. Rebels tried to disable them by severing the control wires, but getting close enough to perform this sabotage was difficult because a soldier could be picked off by German snipers. The Goliath proved devastating in urban combat, and as Bogdan witnessed, it could topple an entire building. If he and his comrades had not run, they would have been entombed within the rubble.

Bogdan had more close calls. Once, he was standing in a ruined building and glanced through a peephole, trying to case a German redoubt across the street. Just after he stepped away from the peephole, a bullet smashed into a wall behind him. A German sharpshooter must have spied him and fixed a bead on his target. "Had I lingered at that peephole for another second," Bogdan reflected, "the bullet would have shattered my skull."

On another occasion, Bogdan accidently made a discovery that saved him from catastrophe. Within his haversack he carried a homemade grenade, which had been manufactured by Polish underground forces. Glancing at it, he noticed that its handle was in the open position, ready to be thrown and detonated. He gently took it out, holding it with his arms fully extended, and walked up the stairs to the top floor of a building. Once he got to a window, he let it go, and the grenade fell to the ground and exploded.

But the Uprising was not filled with military action every minute. As combat soldiers learn, warfare involves long lulls punctuated by terrifying battles. The Poles sometimes went days without fighting, playing cat and mouse with the Nazis, planning and strategizing as they prepared to confront them again. Bogdan's unit often met in the basement of a bank, which constituted their unofficial headquarters.

During one pause in the fighting, Bogdan and Janusz returned to their apartment at night to check on their mother. Their home was strangely quiet; Germans had not begun bombing that area of Warsaw, so Aniela was unharmed but alone. Tadeusz was trapped outside the city. Just before the Uprising started, he went to hunt for food for the family, going to a locality called Wlochy (which translates to "Italy"). Once the rebellion began, he found it impossible to enter the city, so he stayed on the outside for the next two months, watching anxiously as he saw plumes of smoke sometimes rise from the burning city.

When he was not fighting, Bogdan usually stayed in basements, but once he was on the third floor of an apartment complex and glanced out a window. It was a warm August day, and on the balcony of a nearby office building, two German soldiers lay sunbathing. As he looked at them, Bogdan wished he had a rifle with a scope. The moment conveyed an important message, because the Germans could catch their collective breath since they enjoyed such superiority in weapons. In so doing, they often let their guard down. There Bogdan was—he could have racked up two easy kills, but having no gun, he could do nothing. It was a regret that Bogdan and other resistance fighters had throughout the Uprising.

III. The Terror of the Bombs

The Uprising caught the Germans unawares, but they soon brought reinforcements, and their superior numbers and weapons doused the initial enthusiasm of the *Armia Krajowa* and Polish citizens. After the Uprising began, Hitler wanted again to punish Warsaw and its residents and send a message to people in other cities and countries that destruction awaited them, too, if they tried to resist. To stamp out the pesky resistance, the Nazis began to bring out the big guns. One terrifying German weapon was their heavy Thor howitzer, which launched shells weighing more than two tons. Another was the dreaded MG-42 machine gun, nicknamed "Hitler's Saw," which could fire more than a thousand rounds per minute.

Aerial bombings were the worst. The Luftwaffe unleashed a flurry of bombs on Warsaw, and citizens were in a constant state of terror, fearing the sight and sound of these destructive weapons. Poland's lack of air defenses was its Achilles heel, and it allowed Germany to overrun the country and terrorize citizens throughout the war. Almost every day Bogdan watched Stuka dive bombers plunge toward the city—especially toward its Old Town section—and release their deadly payload. The bombs wailed as they hurtled downward, followed by huge explosions. Buildings crashed to the ground and spilled their contents over a wide area, choking off entire roadways.

Everything was vulnerable to the bombs. Hospitals, which bore visible Red Cross markings and flags, were supposed to be off-limits for military targeting, but the Luftwaffe bombed them. Poles were witnessing prolific evil. Even the dead were not safe: German bombers hit cemeteries, creating enormous craters that ripped open caskets and exposed the remains within.

Because of the bombing threat, Warsaw civilians got used to living in basements, giving rise to what some observers called "two Warsaws"—one on earth, the other below. Residents bore large holes through underground walls to connect cellars of different houses, creating a subterranean network that allowed residents to move great distances through tunnels. When Bogdan walked through this tenebrous system, he noticed people huddled together within large basements and along tunnel walls, fearing the next bombing raid. It was a dark, dank existence, where humans shared space with rats and mice. As the weeks went by, a visible weariness took hold of people who were forced to live this way.

At street level, conditions were worse. Buildings burned from the bombings, and dousing all the fires became impossible, especially with the skeletal firefighting forces that remained. Bogdan often saw a red haze in the air from the flames. The summer heat made the fires even more unbearable, and the stench of burning bodies sometimes wafted through the city. Once, Bogdan stood in the shell of a burnt-out building, and he wearily leaned against the remains of a brick wall. As he did so, he could feel heat still pulsing out of the building's foundation, even though the fire had been extinguished. Bogdan put his hand on the bricks; they were warm, almost hot, to the touch.

After one bombing onslaught, Bogdan saw a man lying in the street, dying from burns he had sustained during the attack. He was face down, but he wore a firefighter's belt similar to the kind that Bogdan's brother Janusz had, and he looked like Janusz, with the same height and physique.

German bombs sparked fires throughout Warsaw, which raged uncontrollably, exacerbated by water shortages and decimated fire departments (from the collections of the Warsaw Rising Museum).

Gripped by fear, he ran toward him and said, "Janusz?" The man gave no response, but as Bogdan approached, he saw that the victim was a stranger, and a wave of relief swept over him. Bogdan could tell that he was in bad shape, with life draining out of him. Moments later, the man died.

Nearby, other corpses lay in the street, some burned beyond recognition. Because they feared more bombs at any instant, Bogdan and other Polish soldiers ripped out chunks of the sidewalk, hastily dug a hole, deposited the bodies, and then covered them up with earth. It was an undignified burial, but they did their best to honor the dead. All over Warsaw, such scenes replayed themselves with numbing regularity. Nobody could bury the dead properly in graveyards. The threat of bombing was too great to allow funeral processions, and the hobbled transportation network prevented much movement, especially of the dead. So Warsaw residents buried corpses inside building courtyards, where tiny forests of crosses appeared to mark graves.

To make matters worse, when bombs sparked fires, there was little water to douse the flames. German bombing ruptured water mains, disrupting the flow of water in the city, and it became scarce, even for drinking. As if the elements conspired against Warsaw residents, the summer of 1944 was a dry one, seldom seeing rain. People tried to dig wells in city lots, burrowing down until they hit spring water, but German bombs often destroyed the wells or killed anyone engaging in such efforts. In Bogdan's apartment, the family seldom had running water after the Uprising started. Water rationing became peremptory, and people stood in long lines to get it for daily living. Remaining stationary out in the open like that was dangerous, and Bogdan learned of a German bomb wiping out an entire queue of people waiting for water.

As the people of Warsaw set their collective jaw to fight the Nazis, civilians proved stout-hearted and dedicated, but they were also scared, and Bogdan understood their feelings. Once, he asked a civilian for help in building a street barricade, and he came over to lend a hand. But a burst of German gunfire thundered through the air, and when Bogdan turned around, the man had disappeared. While he needed the man's help, Bogdan resisted the impulse to try to find him and make him work against his will. On another occasion, Bogdan's company commander got irritated at a civilian whom he felt was working too slowly, and he delivered a swift and angry kick to his rear end. That commander was hot-tempered and often irrational, and Bogdan felt that his butt-kicking was an indecent way to treat a citizen who was trying to help.

Everyone was suffering. Withering under bombs and ground artillery, Warsaw became even more of an empty shell. The Germans pulverized a quarter of its buildings, adding to the destruction they had already

Warsaw, a beautiful city known as "the Paris of the East," was left in ruins by German occupation and bombing during the Uprising (from the collections of the Warsaw Rising Museum).

wrought during the 1939 invasion and the 1943 Ghetto Uprising. Bombs fell on the city like a heavy, explosive rain that residents could not defend against or stop. Bogdan hoped that his family could avoid a destructive hit. His mother, in particular, was concerned about the bombs, and with her deep Catholic faith unshaken, she prayed daily for protection against them.

IV. Bravery

Amidst the chaos and dangers of war, the most important goal was to beat the Nazis, so everything else became secondary, even daily routines. Bathing was unheard of. While the Vistula River lay before Warsaw residents, tempting them to take a cleansing dip during warmer months, they knew that Germans occupied positions across the river, so anyone indulging in a swim or bath could be shot. Bogdan grew a beard, which he tried to keep manageable by trimming it with a dull straight razor, but each time he used it, he had to spend several minutes just sharpening the blade. Wherever they lived, rebels wolfed down meager meals, barely gaining the sustenance they needed to keep fighting. During the worst hours of depravity, Bogdan heard that some Warsaw residents ate meat from dogs, cats, and pigeons that they cooked. For all of them—whatever they ate to stay alive—the meals provided a short break from constant vigilance against the Germans.

Women and girls were the most vulnerable segment of the Warsaw citizenry. German soldiers even invaded hospitals and raped victims there. To disguise their gender, females cut their hair short and wore men's clothing. Bogdan saw women who smeared their faces and hands with crimson-colored iodine to telegraph the idea that they had lethal communicative diseases. Trying to go undetected and just surviving on a daily basis, the women of Poland showed great bravery.

The Americans tried to help the Poles. At night Bogdan saw U.S. B-17 Flying Fortresses, the bomber that dropped more tons of bombs than any other plane in the war, flying above the city. But rather than unleashing bombs, they came to assist the rebels, debarking from England and airdropping supplies over Warsaw. The Nazis, though, grabbed the preponderance of these provisions, so the Polish fighters never got most of the aid intended for them. Bogdan felt grateful for the Allied assistance and for the pilots, who showed bravery in risking their lives to fly over dangerous airspace. Never once did Bogdan see any fighter escorts accompanying the bombers; many of these pilots flew their planes alone, vulnerable yet courageous. He later found out that some of the pilots were Poles who had fled the country and wanted to continue to help their countrymen back home.

After the war, though, Poles were disappointed to find that British and American allies sometimes turned down requests to fly aid to help the AK units, saying that Poland was too deep in Europe and the flights were risky. Instead, they assumed that the Soviets—their allies, who occupied Poland's eastern half—would provide assistance. The Soviets never did.

Left largely on their own, resistance fighters showed a strong incredible fighting spirit. Poles in the East, trapped under Soviet control, risked their lives by traveling to Warsaw and crossing the Vistula at night to join rebels and fight for the city. Polish warriors showed bravery that was stunning to behold. Bogdan remembered one battle with the Germans when, overwhelmed by superior firepower, he and his comrades had to withdraw. One fellow fighter had been hit by the Germans, and Bogdan carried him, fireman-style over his shoulder, to safety. The man was so severely wounded that he was unable to walk on his own, and he bled profusely from a neck wound, which weakened him further. Night had fallen, and it was difficult to see the enemy. Exhaustion paralyzed all of them. What few weapons they had were low on ammunition. Despite all this adversity, this wounded Pole wanted to go back to continue fighting.

That kind of bravery, Bogdan thought, would bring them victory.

— 6 —

"That morning devastated us"

I. Yasuko

In Japan, amid conditions that grew harsher by the month, the most haunting specter was disease. It stalked the land, and everyone lacked medical supplies, so families had to rely on traditional remedies like herbs, which were crude and ineffective. Under these circumstances, even minor illnesses or incidents could spell disaster. One of Seiko's friends was mending army clothing, and she accidentally pierced her middle finger with a needle. Her hand became infected with gangrene, and medical care was so poor that she almost lost her entire hand.

One evening in spring 1943, Seiko's older sister Yasuko, who was then a senior in high school, finished dinner and then said quietly, "I don't feel well." Weak and tired, she went to bed early. Over the coming days, she felt drained of energy and suffered from a high fever. She coughed constantly. The family thought that Yasuko had a bad, long-lasting cold, but her extreme fatigue persisted. She went to the family physician, Dr. Minoru Oata, who was an experienced and first-rate internal specialist and a friend of Hiroshi's, so he paid special attention to the Kawakami family. Dr. Oata made a grim diagnosis. Yasuko had tuberculosis.

The family was stunned, but on another level, they might have guessed. The infectious disease, caused by a bacterium, thrived in unsanitary conditions, which were prevalent in wartime Japan. People knew how easily it could spread through a cough or sneeze. Even when a TB victim spoke, that could spell trouble for anyone nearby. The worldwide scourge hit even modernized countries; in the early 1900s, tuberculosis had been the number-one killer in the U.S. In its ubiquity, tuberculosis was like heart disease or cancer today—everyone knew somebody who was felled by tuberculosis, just as those modern scourges strike family, friends, and acquaintances. (Even into the twenty-first century, tuberculosis claimed more than a million lives annually, and an estimated one-quarter of the world's population carried the disease.) By the late 1940s, the introduction of antibiotics reduced its danger, but in wartime Japan, tuberculosis was common and deadly, while medicine to combat it was scarce. Victims suffered a racking cough, fever, and crippling weakness, just as Yasuko had.

Because many children contracted tuberculosis, Seiko's school conducted screening tests, during which a physician examined students. They had to take off their shirts, and the doctor listened to their breathing using a stethoscope, with the teacher standing next to him. Sometimes, the teacher recited the family history to the doctor in front of the whole class, indicating whether the boy or girl had a relative with tuberculosis. Students found the procedure an invasion of privacy and a humiliation. One of Seiko's friends, Hiroko Nakamichi, said that her teacher practically announced before the class that Hiroko's sister had succumbed to the disease. Feeling embarrassed and ashamed, Hiroko simmered with anger toward her teacher, and she worried that friends at school would ostracize her.

The Kawakamis thought that Yasuko likely got exposed to tuberculosis at school, since some of her classmates had the disease. After her diagnosis, doctors advised her to avoid school because she could risk exposing other children to the bacterium. But Yasuko was determined to finish her studies, and in late March 1944, the traditional graduation time in Japan, she graduated from high school.

That act of sheer willpower was just like Yasuko. She was well-motivated and extremely kind, possessing a magic mix of diffidence and determination. To Seiko, she was the model older sister. Once, she told Seiko that another teacher looked at her sternly. It was just a glance, and it probably meant nothing. But she asked Seiko, "Do you think I did something wrong?" A sensitive girl, Yasuko always was concerned about how others perceived her and worried about how they felt.

Yasuko was a fine athlete, too, who enjoyed skiing during Otaru winters and running during warmer weather. She showed interest in Japanese traditions like tea ceremonies and flower arrangements. She brimmed

Yasuko Kawakami. Seiko's older sister, born in 1927. She died of tuberculosis in 1944, just after graduating from high school.

6. "That morning devastated us"

with generosity. Yasuko wanted to do activities with Seiko and shared food, clothes, and gifts, even if it meant sacrificing herself. When they cooked pumpkins as snacks, she shared her portions with Seiko unstintingly. Seiko felt very close to her sister. Yasuko was only two years older; they shared a bedroom, and Yasuko always made Seiko a part of her life.

Hiroshi and Echi tried to conceal the seriousness of Yasuko's illness from the rest of the family. They wanted to avoid causing alarm, but at the same time they worried that the other children could catch tuberculosis from her, and they could lose their entire family. In the spring of 1944, they made the painful decision to move Yasuko to a sanitarium outside Otaru, hoping that she would regain her strength. Sanitariums allowed patients the chance to breathe fresh air, soak in sunshine, engage in light recreation, and lead lives away from the general populace, with staff carefully regimenting their activities.

When they packed up Yasuko's belongings to move her, Seiko's parents could no longer hide how gravely ill their eldest daughter was. Once Yasuko was at the sanitarium, the summer of 1944 became the first season Seiko had to spend without her older sister, and she felt an emotional barrenness that she had never experienced before.

The sanitarium was five miles from their home, and Seiko visited it only once. In early September 1944, she and her family walked all the way there. It was a sunny, late summer day, and the air was calm and quiet as they trundled along. As they walked, Seiko wondered how Yasuko was doing, how she looked, and how she was managing in her new environment.

When they arrived, just as Seiko was about to go into Yasuko's room, her mother pulled her aside. Echi then said something that Seiko found unbelievable. Yasuko's life, she said, would soon end. Seiko began to cry uncontrollably, and she dared not talk to Yasuko, because she knew her sad face and tears would devastate her sister. Standing just at the threshold to her room, Seiko glanced inside. Yasuko lay in bed, thin, pale, and motionless. She had lost more weight since Seiko had last seen her. Seiko wanted to go in and talk to her, but she could not stop sobbing.

So Seiko left. She regretted it immediately, because she wanted to talk to Yasuko, who—sensitive as she was—would surely have wondered why her younger sister failed to visit her. During the walk home, Seiko hoped that they could visit again soon, and she would have a long conversation with Yasuko to make up for this lost opportunity. The whole visit seemed surreal, as if the two sisters had stood on opposite precipices, close to making contact but ultimately failing. Seiko wished her mother had not spoken those words to her, but in retrospect, she understood. The hospital staff had likely told her mother some bad news. Echi had to absorb what they said to her, and she needed to confide in someone, even a teenager like Seiko, to prepare the family for the worst.

Indeed, Echi had special burdens to bear. Yasuko's illness took a heavy toll on Seiko's mother, because medical care and resources were stretched thin during the war, and the household matron had to care for family members who fell ill. Echi devoted most of her waking hours to looking after Yasuko. Whenever she could, she went to the sanitarium to deliver meals and help her to eat. If Yasuko wanted something special to eat, Echi shopped for it, and she gathered medicinal herbs and traditional remedies to dispense to her. During the late summer, sensing that Yasuko's condition grew more grave, Echi decided to stay at the sanitarium to provide round-the-clock care for her daughter.

Despite Echi's efforts, the disease ravaged Yasuko. Tuberculosis was called "consumption," and Yasuko indeed wasted away, even while trying to convalesce at the sanitarium. Today, the medical profession casts doubt on whether sanitariums benefited tuberculosis patients, especially because statistics showed that they died at the same rate as those who were not in sanitariums. But the sanitarium was the prescribed treatment of the era, and Seiko and her family remained optimistic, hopeful that Yasuko would recover, and they were prepared to sacrifice anything to make her better.

On September 23, 1944, in the early morning hours, a neighbor knocked on the door of the Kawakamis' house, awakening everyone. Since the family had no telephone, Echi had made an emergency call from the sanitarium to a neighbor who owned a phone. Echi said that Yasuko's condition had deteriorated markedly. The family had no car, so despite the darkness outside, Seiko's father jumped on his bicycle and pedaled the five miles to the sanitarium. A mile from the facility, a tire blew out, and Hiroshi pushed his bike the rest of the way. Arriving exhausted, he rushed to Yasuko's bedside and looked down at her. She was too weak to open her eyes but moved her head faintly when he spoke.

"Can you see me?" Hiroshi asked. Yasuko shook her head.

"It's your father. Do you recognize my voice?" he asked. She nodded.

Minutes later, her shallow breathing stopped. She died at age seventeen. Hiroshi went to a house near the sanitarium, borrowed a phone, and called home to say that Yasuko was gone. She died at 5:45 a.m. Just forty-five minutes later, the front door to the Kawakami house creaked open and then slammed shut. Seiko's older brother Suguru walked out, trudged up the long hill to Otaru's railroad station, and boarded a train that would take him to Hakodate. He was reporting to a Japanese naval base on Honshu to begin training as a kamikaze pilot.

"That morning devastated us," Seiko recalled. "We lost my sister and likely my brother, too."

II. A Family's Painful Price of War

After Yasuko died, Seiko's family was awash in grief. Even though Yasuko had been away from home for months, they could not believe that she would never come back. Every family member cried so hard, so often, that the pain began to feel more physical than emotional, a despondency so overwhelming that it seemed to have no end. "The sadness lingered," Seiko recalled. "It just did not go away." It was like a heavy cloud that henceforth scudded along their lives, and no amount of sunshine could dispel it. The sadness was also ineffable; they could have talked about Yasuko, but it was better to be silent and just think about her. Because Seiko never got to have a final conversation with Yasuko, her emptiness felt even deeper. She recalled that the constant wartime hunger that everyone felt exacerbated the melancholy. "When you are hungry all the time," Seiko reflected, "you feel every bit of loneliness and sadness that much more."

What kept Seiko motivated to continue living despite Yasuko's death was a simple will to survive. She grasped this driving force on a daily basis, concentrating first on getting sufficient nutrients amidst all the food shortages. Her family grew a vegetable garden, where Seiko looked after potatoes, pumpkins, and a few other crops. Tending to the garden every day, reaping its modest harvest, and thinking of how to sustain herself and her family every day allowed Seiko to channel her grief over Yasuko in a life-sustaining direction.

For most of Yasuko's illness, even after she entered the sanitarium and spent several weeks there, the family had thought that she would rally, get over the tuberculosis, and come home. In retrospect, they were in denial, because all evidence pointed to the contrary. After Yasuko's death, friends told them that they could clearly see that she was deteriorating, even when she still lived at home. These were observations that only outsiders could perceive, because as family members, the Kawakamis saw her decline more gradually, and they refused to accept the reality that she was fading.

They got to see Yasuko once more. A few days after she died, the Kawakami family—except for Suguru, who was now at the naval base—took a taxi to the sanitarium so that they could assist in transporting her body to a crematorium in Otaru. Once there, they went to the sanitarium's morgue to retrieve her body. The mortician led them to a room with a number of caskets, and he pulled out one of them and checked the name on it. His manner was mechanical and matter-of-fact, even though the family was enduring an emotionally wrought experience. "Yes," he simply nodded to Hiroshi and Echi after reading the nametag. "This is your daughter." They approached, carefully opened the casket lid, and looked inside.

There was Yasuko. As soon as they saw her, they began sobbing. She looked peaceful, lying in the quiet repose of death, and for the family, their first impulse was to shake her awake and try to get her out of there. They each told her how much they loved her and would miss her. Then they did the painful task of closing the coffin lid, and they left the room. The sanitarium staff placed Yasuko's casket onto a taxi, which acted as a hearse, and they boarded another taxi that followed it back to Otaru for cremation. In Japan, that was the traditional means of treating the bodies of departed souls, partly because it was more practical in a country whose severe space limitations made large graveyards impossible.

At the crematorium, the Kawakamis had to let go of Yasuko's body. They had already said their good-byes at the morgue, so they stepped outside the crematorium and waited. After several minutes, they began to see clouds puff out of the building's chimney. The wisps of smoke trailed upward, framed against the sapphire September sky, reaching heavenward and disappearing. The family knew what was happening, but nobody said anything. Yasuko's body was burning, and the smoke they saw was the physical sign that she was leaving the earth.

Even after her sister was gone, Seiko still experienced a period of denial. She continued to think that somehow she would get to have that last conversation. But there was one moment when she realized that Yasuko was truly gone. Seiko and her family were preparing for a memorial service at their home, and the family was organizing their living room to accept guests. A beautiful floral arrangement arrived, and Seiko wondered where to put it. Her first impulse was to ask Yasuko for an idea on where and how to set up the bouquet. She was so accustomed to turning to her older sister for advice that she still thought she could. In that instant, Seiko realized that she could never talk to Yasuko again.

Although Seiko's parents had done everything they could for Yasuko, Echi felt pangs of guilt. One matter especially troubled her. Every spring, she engaged in a tradition of setting up *hina* dolls in the house, a miniature display of a royal court from the late 1700s, which originated when the emperor's daughters had no playmates and the *hina* set became a way for the girls to entertain themselves. The display consisted of the emperor, empress, and their attendants—including musicians and royal guards—totaling about fifteen figures. The small figurines, each about three inches tall, sat in kneeling positions on three different levels, with the emperor and the empress alone at the top. Their loyal attendants occupied the two lower levels and had musical instruments, *o-gi* (folding fans, also known as *sensu*), rice cakes, and libations—all to serve the emperor. The dolls wore colorful robes, and the entire court sat on a bright red carpet. It was a cheerful and animated display, and over the centuries, the *hina* festival assumed special symbolism, representing parents' hope for their daughters' welfare and happiness. By setting up the dolls each year in a corner of her bedroom, Echi welcomed spring and a time of rebirth.

That season in 1944, though, Yasuko's illness put such demands on Echi that she never had time to set up the *hina* dolls. Like many Japanese, Echi had her superstitions, and she put much faith in rituals and ceremonies. She never escaped the nagging belief that her failure to observe the *hina* doll tradition had something to do with Yasuko's death. Every year thereafter, for the rest of her life, Echi faithfully set up the *hina* display (and Seiko continued that ritual).

Yasuko's passing was the Kawakami family's personal tragedy set against the national tragedy of war. Strictly speaking, she was not a wartime casualty. She did not perish on any battlefield, but wartime conditions—especially the lack of food and medicine—contributed to her death. For Seiko and her family, the loss of Yasuko became the most painful price of war.

— 7 —

Death Hits Home

I. "I Can't Lie Here and Die!"

In Poland, the Warsaw Uprising continued, but after a month of fighting, Bogdan and his confrères in the *Armia Krajowa* felt like they had hit a wall. German bombing forced them to abandon the city power station, which deprived them of the electricity they needed for daily activities. The situation in Old Town was especially grim. The area received a vicious pounding from German artillery and Stuka dive bombers, and centuries-old buildings, already ground down during the September 1939 invasion, got pulverized more. Observing from the center of Warsaw, Bogdan saw Stukas plunging toward Old Town, and he knew that precious area was receiving yet another attack. The Germans were devastating the city yet again, and by targeting Old Town, they were destroying Polish history.

Even ostensible victories turned into defeats, emphasizing how dire the situation was. Bogdan learned that in Old Town, a group of rebels seized a German explosives carrier, and people came to celebrate its capture. But it was a trap. The Nazis had used the tank as tainted bait, filling it with dynamite. As citizens gathered around to fete their good fortune, the tank exploded, killing a large number of Poles.

In late August 1944, the Polish command decided to abandon Old Town, which by then was mostly rubble. While the resistance could not save the district, rebel fighters managed to free some Polish soldiers who were trapped there. The Home Army rescued them by leading them through sewers and evacuated others through street fighting against the Germans. Some escapees who had navigated through the sewers came to Bogdan's unit, and they used what little water they had to wash off the gunk that encrusted them.

On September 2, 1944, Bogdan thought he and the members of his unit would all be killed. They were selected specially for an assignment, and they felt a deep sense of purpose, but it would be dangerous. They

7. Death Hits Home

planned an offensive to allow trapped comrades to escape from Old Town, where Nazis pinned them down. Bogdan's unit had just seven soldiers, armed only with hand grenades. He feared the Germans would slaughter them. Grimly, he thought, "This mission is suicide." But they had to try to extricate their brothers-in-arms.

A ten-foot-high brick wall ran through Old Town, creating a barrier between them and the Germans. Bogdan knew that the Nazis controlled the area on the other side, but he had no clear idea of where they were or how much of the Old Town they controlled. The foggy concept of where the enemy lay revealed how chaotic conditions were. But one thing was sure: his unit needed to penetrate the wall and rescue their fellow fighters who were—somewhere—beyond it.

In the mid-afternoon, two sappers (combat engineers) hurried to a section of the wall. From a safe distance across the street, Bogdan crouched for cover amidst building ruins and watched the engineers place a satchel of dynamite atop two legs, leaning it against the wall. After lighting the fuse, they ran back across the street. Seconds later, a deafening explosion thundered through the air, and an enormous dust cloud rose.

That was the signal to move. Gripping a grenade in his right hand, Bogdan got up and began to sprint. Through the dust and haze, he could see the dynamite had blasted a hole in the wall, and he raced toward the opening. The plan was to occupy a targeted building inside Old Town, use it as a staging area, fight off any Germans they encountered, and then find and rescue the resistance fighters. Bogdan and his unit made it through the dynamited hole, and through the haze he could see the building they needed to reach.

Rat-tat-tat-tat-tat! Bogdan heard the roar of a machine gun as it opened fire. Amidst this raging sound, his right arm jerked violently. Bullets turned pieces of the wall into projectiles, and fragments sprayed onto him. He felt brick chunks penetrate his upper thigh, turning his legs to jelly. Bogdan fell to the ground and looked at his hand.

His right thumb was gone.

Blood gushed from the wound and spilled onto the earth. Where Bogdan's thumb had been, only a flap of skin remained, loosely hanging in place. Excruciating pain wracked his legs, which felt like daggers were stabbing them. He turned his head and looked down to see dark splotches of blood pockmarking the back of his pants, where shrapnel had pierced his hamstrings. The grenade that Bogdan was carrying in his right hand was gone, and he worried that wherever it was now, it would detonate if a bullet struck it.

"*I can't lie here and die!*" Bogdan thought. His first impulse was to look for his missing thumb, but his situation was more desperate than that.

Prostrate as he was, Bogdan made an easy target, and another bullet could have finished him off. He needed medical help to staunch the bleeding, and he knew that he could no longer fight. The scene was sheer chaos. The cacophony of machine gun fire continued, and the air was clogged with thick dust from pulverized brick and concrete.

Automatically, Bogdan's wanted to get up and run, but survival instincts kicked in. He told himself to lie motionless and pretend he was dead. In powerful, sustained bursts, the machine gun still swept the area, and he dared not move or get up while it was still firing. The wait took great patience; pain gnawed at him, and he needed to stop the blood loss. Bogdan lay his head on the ground, grimaced, and suppressed the urge to move.

The machine gun bursts stopped. Bogdan thought that the gunner was changing the ammunition belt, so he decided to make a break for it. Using his left arm, he rose to a crouching position and then began to retreat, hunched over, limping back toward the dynamited wall. As soon as he got there and went back through the hole, he felt safer, escaping the line of sight of the German machine gunner. The smoke and noise subsided; Bogdan crossed the street, and with each step, pain shot through his legs. "*I might not make it*," he thought. "*I'm going to collapse.*"

Bogdan hobbled to a first aid station half a block away. There, he got immediate care because his injuries were so severe. Upon seeing his condition, a nurse led him to a treatment area. The bleeding had trailed off, which was surprising; at first, Bogdan worried he might die from blood loss. The nurse used the flap of skin that dangled from his hand and sewed it over the stump of his thumb, covering the bone. She bandaged the wound and then turned her attention toward his legs. Even in this moment of high stress, Bogdan felt modest about pulling down his pants, but he dropped his trousers, and the nurse treated his shrapnel wounds with antiseptic and then applied dressing to both legs. She instructed him to go immediately to a nearby hospital to get more advanced care. (After the war, when Bogdan was visiting Warsaw, he had a chance encounter with the nurse, and he jokingly told her that the medical treatment did not work because his thumb never grew back. She laughed.)

Bogdan's thumb area hurt worse than anything he had ever experienced. No painkillers were available, so he was in agony. He left the first aid station and, keeping his hand elevated, he hobbled four blocks to a makeshift hospital to get follow-up care. The hospital was in the basement of the eighteen-story Prudential Building, Warsaw's tallest skyscraper and the third highest in Europe, which had been damaged by a German artillery shells. Soldiers who saw Bogdan, bandaged and limping badly, offered to carry him there, but he insisted on walking, if nothing else than to prove to himself that he could do it under his own steam.

7. Death Hits Home

Once Bogdan arrived, a surgeon tried to even out his thumb bone, which jutted out above the surrounding flesh, and then stitched his cuts and sewed the skin more neatly around the area to allow it to heal into a stub. He also worked on Bogdan's legs, pulling out shrapnel from his hamstrings and calves. Bogdan had trouble seeing the backs of his legs, but perhaps that was just as well; he was reluctant to view the damage, and without anesthetics, he could feel every piece that the surgeon pulled out. The doctor said that he sewed up the wounds in such a way that the leg muscles would have integrity, but he added that everything would take time to heal. Bogdan's first impulse was to ask him to speed up the recuperation so that he could go back to fighting, but he kept quiet about that. The surgeon was doing admirable work, perhaps without any remuneration at all, and Bogdan deeply appreciated his effort. Doctors there—and everywhere in the city—operated under horrendous conditions, with minimal medicine and often with only flashlights or candles for light. This hospital was dark and crowded, and anguished groans filled the air.

When the surgeon finished tidying up the wounds, Bogdan left. He had to get out of that environment, and there was no room for him anyway. He had no way to keep track of time—his father had sold all family timepieces to buy food—but the medical care had taken hours. He had entered the hospital in the late afternoon; when he left, it was dark. Bogdan limped all the way home, each step agonizing. Although he hated to leave his comrades, he needed to recuperate. For the time being, he conceded that his fighting was over. Worse, he would spend the rest of his life without a thumb. He worried about how his hand would look and what he would no longer be able to do without it.

But Bogdan was lucky. Had the bullet hit his head or torso, the outcome would have been deadly. He also had been carrying a Soviet-made grenade, which had a special cranking mechanism that required him to twirl his arm in order to activate it. When he was shot, the grenade fell to the ground, inert. Had it been a Polish-manufactured grenade, that drop might have triggered its more sensitive activation mechanism, with catastrophic results.

Bogdan returned home, climbed slowly up the stairs to his family's apartment, and hobbled inside. When he showed his mother what had happened, she was shocked but expressed relief, because the injury could have been much worse. She also knew that he would have to stay home now, safe from the fighting, which eased her mind. Over the next several days, Bogdan rested at his family's apartment, relishing the company of his mother and brother Janusz and trying to gain strength to rejoin the fight. He was lucky, he reflected, to have his mother to comfort and take care of him at a time like this, when he needed her.

After a few days, the bandages on Bogdan's hand grew stale, and he went back to the makeshift hospital to get a new surgical dressing. The blood on the old one had congealed to form a dark, hard mass. The doctor peeled everything off, which opened the wound up again, exposing raw flesh and allowing blood to run out. The pain was so severe that Bogdan almost passed out. The physician performed the procedure while they were both standing, and Bogdan felt himself fainting from the pain. His knees began to buckle.

"Bogdan…. Bogdan…. Bogdan," the doctor said, repeating his name. With one hand, he started gently slapping Bogdan's cheek, all to stimulate blood flow to the brain and keep him conscious and upright. The patient cooperated, and the surgeon finished applying new bandages. Bogdan limped home, wondering when he should see the doctor again.

Days later, in a jarring reminder of Nazi air power, a German bomb destroyed the hospital. That facility saved many lives, and now it was gone, blocking off one avenue for Bogdan's recovery and piling more adversity against the military efforts of the *Armia Krajowa*.

II. In a Pool of Fresh Blood

On September 18, just two weeks after getting injured, Bogdan was in the living room of his apartment with his mother and a friend, Antek Maryanski, who had been a *komplety* classmate and was active in the underground resistance. A grenade had wounded Antek in the leg, and he was using crutches. That afternoon, the three of them heard aircraft overhead and saw U.S. planes drop supplies over the city. The Americans were trying to help Poland, but Bogdan felt crestfallen about it. Most of their aid, he knew, would fall into German hands.

The apartment living room faced the street, and the impact of constant bombardment had blown out all the windows in their building. Luckily, it was still summer, so the nights were warm enough that they kept comfortable and avoided freezing. But they were exposed, and they could hear outside noises clearly. As the three of them sat in the living room, they began to hear a sound they knew and feared—the shrill whistle of a mortar falling from the skies. Each second, the sound grew louder. They froze, not knowing whether to run for cover or shelter in place.

Boom! Although they expected an explosion after the long whistle, the huge noise shocked them. Their building shuddered, and small pieces of masonry, wood, and glass sprayed into their apartment through the open windows. Aniela and Antek jumped up and fled the room, Antek leaving quickly even without his crutches. The briskness of their movements surprised Bogdan, who was less mobile because of his leg wounds, and he followed them. As he did, he glanced outside toward the four-story building across the street.

It was gone. The Germans had scored a direct hit. The sight and sound of destruction once again rattled Bogdan, and he knew that he, Aniela, and Antek had escaped death by the width of a street. They ran down to the basement and waited there for this wave of danger to subside.

That night, Bogdan was resting in the basement of their building, which was darkened by the lack of electricity. He had decided to seek shelter there rather than stay in their third-floor apartment, since it was vulnerable to bombing.

But he could not sleep because of the pain. He lay there, thinking about the street battles, wondering when he could rejoin the fighting, hoping his body could heal quickly, questioning how long they could press the initiative against the Germans. Bogdan's mind tussled with the bleak possibility of continued German occupation if the Uprising failed. He scoured his mind for some way forward, even beyond military victory or defeat.

A loud explosion jolted him. Instantly, Bogdan knew that Nazi bombs were attacking again. The whole building shook and trembled as the assault continued. By this point in the war, bombings had become so frequent that Bogdan became numb to them. He tried to ignore the sounds of destruction and continued to lie there in the darkness, thinking that in the basement, he was in the safest possible place.

Minutes later, Bogdan's younger brother Janusz rushed into the room. "Our mother," he cried, "has just been killed!"

No! Bogdan bolted up and ran out of the room. There had to be some mistake, he thought, as he felt panic overwhelm him. He raced across the courtyard to the other side of the building, and he noticed a large hole in one wall that a bomb had created. He got to the far side of the building and saw that several people had gathered around a first-floor room. As soon as Bogdan got past the small crowd, he looked inside the room. There, in a pool of fresh blood, lay his mother.

Aniela and a neighbor had been standing just outside the entrance to the basement, getting a breath of the mild, late summer night air, when the bomb struck. Shrapnel entered her back and pierced her heart. Her friend was also hit; both women died instantly.

After getting struck, Aniela had fallen down a flight of stairs. Friends carried her body up to the building's first level, which housed a dentist's office, and they laid her on the floor. Bogdan crouched down, looking at her, and he cleaned the blood off her face. Her front showed no wounds, but shrapnel had gouged a deep hole in her back.

Bogdan could not believe it. His mother was really gone, and if he needed any more proof, he was holding her lifeless body in his hands. He was so used to seeing her speaking and moving—he had spoken to her just hours earlier. But now she was still, frozen in the clutch of death.

Bogdan and Janusz sobbed for most of the night. They stayed next to their mother's body, trying to keep close to her physical presence, still feeling an unbreakable bond with her even though she was gone. They agonized over how their father and older brother Zbigniew would take this catastrophe. But for weeks, no one could locate Zbigniew, and they wondered if he had even survived the Nazi occupation. Tadeusz was still trapped outside the city; Bogdan had not seen him for weeks. Tadeusz never got to see or talk to his wife one final time. Perhaps it was for the better, since the image of her dead body was haunting. Near dawn, exhausted and emotionally spent, Bogdan finally drifted into a fitful sleep.

In the morning, almost miraculously, Zbigniew joined Bogdan and Janusz. Somehow, someone had found him and told him what had happened, which bore testimony to how effective the informal grapevine of communication was in occupied Warsaw. Now reunited, the three brothers knew what they had to do next. They made a simple coffin out of untreated boards, hammering them together, and they gently placed their

During the Uprising, makeshift cemeteries proliferated in apartment courtyards such as this one. In one such plot, Bogdan and his brothers buried their mother Aniela after she was killed during a German bomb attack (from the collections of the Warsaw Rising Museum).

mother's body in it. In the courtyard of a nearby apartment complex, they dug a simple burial plot. Bogdan's right hand was still useless because of his thumb wound, so he used only his left arm to dig. Slowly and carefully, they then lowered the makeshift casket into the earth and shoveled soil on top of it, sobbing softly the entire time. "I threw down a couple of handfuls of soil, and that was the way we said good-bye to the closest person in our lives," Bogdan remembered. He and his brothers then put a simple cross and a homemade marker with her name to designate her resting place.

"Our mother deserved," Bogdan thought, "a far better burial than this—a hasty ceremony that we could only cobble together." Amidst the constant danger of bombing and destruction, though, they had done their utmost. Tears and anguish were the best dignity they could bestow upon the ceremony, and they told themselves that Aniela would have been grateful. (In early 1945, after the Soviets gained control of Warsaw, Tadeusz and other family members exhumed Aniela's body and reinterred her in a family plot in the city.)

Aniela was 49 years old. She was still youthful despite the hardship of war, and she was so active and caring that she remained the focus of the family. Bogdan had always seen her as their matriarch, and now that she was gone, he felt numb. *"How,"* he asked himself, "can I go on?"

III. Surrender and Postmortem

The *Armia Krajowa* soldiered on, valiantly but vainly, and Bogdan's emotional emptiness grew worse as the rebellion faltered. "The rest of the Uprising," he later recalled, "passed for me like a bad dream." The Nazis tightened their noose around Warsaw, occupying more territory every week, while the AK's areas of safety shrank. Meanwhile, the resistance and the citizenry became war-weary and bedraggled. People were sick and starving, confined to cellars, afraid of venturing out. The citizens of Warsaw, including the brave rebels, were reaching the liminal point of their effort; they had nothing more to give.

On October 2, 1944, they surrendered. The Uprising had lasted 63 days. The marvel was that it stretched that long, because it involved ragtag fighters, armed with more willpower than firepower, confronting a monstrous German military machine.

The death toll was frightful. During the Uprising, 200,000 Polish civilians and 15,000 resistance fighters perished (some estimates pushed the number of civilian deaths far above 200,000). Twenty-five percent of Warsaw's population had died. Estimates of German deaths were around 10,000. That meant more than 3,000 Poles died every day of the Uprising, many of them young freedom fighters. It was like watching a small town's entire population get killed every day for two months.

The Uprising had faced long odds. Resistance movements during the war all failed (with the exception of Yugoslavia, where Marshal Josef Tito beat the Germans), although they succeeded in tying up German resources and frustrating them, as in France. But the Polish insurgents would never have undertaken the Uprising if they deemed it doomed to fail. The chances of success, they thought, were decent. With the D-Day invasion occurring three months earlier, they hoped that the Allies would smash the Germans to their west, and they would pummel the Nazis on their home soil.

Guerrilla warfare often succeeds against formidable odds, as Americans experienced during the Revolution against the British or later, less fortuitously, as they learned when they fought in Vietnam. But cities posed special problems. Urban fighting was much trickier than combat in the sprawling forests of colonial America or the dense jungles of Vietnam. The Poles had fewer places to hide or find shelter, so they were always more vulnerable to superior German firepower.

Throughout the Uprising, the insurgents had to rely on a decentralized command structure to plan and effect their activities. While it helped to avoid detection, it also proved chaotic. Even the Germans fell victim to the entropy. After Bogdan was wounded, he learned that a Nazi soldier absent-mindedly walked out of the Old Town section by using the hole that the Polish engineers had dynamited. Perhaps he was lost; maybe he was exploring; he might have been simply confused. Whatever the case, it was a fatal mistake. Moments after appearing on the Polish side, he was gunned down.

The Germans had all the assets—experience in warfare, better strategy, weapons, and means. As Bogdan found, Molotov cocktails cut no ice against tanks, and Poles had no defense against dive bombers. Those sixty-three days seemed much longer than that, and the sea change in the Polish fighters' emotions and outlook was dramatic. Initially, they brimmed with enthusiasm, but death, injury, and strategic setbacks blighted their hopes and wore them down.

As Poles conducted postmortems on their defeat, they concluded that another factor played a role. Soviet Premier Joseph Stalin had deliberately dealt crushing blows to their efforts. Stalin had no love for Poland—in fact, he had despised the country for a long time. In his memoir, Soviet Red Army General Georgy Zhukov, who had an intimate understanding of Stalin's personality, quotes the dictator as making disparaging remarks about the Polish "bourgeoisie." Stalin and the Soviet leadership had done their best to sabotage the Warsaw Uprising from the start. At first, they

7. Death Hits Home

encouraged the Polish resistance to undertake the Uprising. In fact, the operation began when the AK heard Soviet guns across the Vistula River, giving them hope that the Russians would help. Then the Soviets did nothing. The rebels expected Soviet aid in repelling the Germans and, indeed, they needed it.

But once the Uprising started, Stalin displayed his contempt for Poles and his ambitions for the postwar world. Until almost the end, he refused permission for U.S. and British planes to use Soviet bases, where they could have refueled. Instead, he waited passively while the Uprising faltered. As the Soviet air force held back, German bombers unleashed their attacks on Warsaw.

Since the U.S.S.R. had stoked the Polish ambition to revolt, the rebels expected the Red Army to cross the Vistula and help to expel the Germans. They would have accepted Soviet assistance, even though the U.S.S.R. had invaded and bisected Poland along with Germany. Instead, the Russian army remained fixed on the east bank of the Vistula, unwilling to budge, leaving Poles at the mercy of German soldiers, who were determined to make them pay for the rebellion.

One difference helped to account for the Russians' idle behavior during the Uprising: the Home Army represented Poland's government-in-exile in London, not the Soviet-sponsored Lublin government. Stanislaw Mikolawjczyk, who in 1943 became prime minister of the London Polish government-in-exile, had repeatedly entreated Stalin for aid, and in early August 1944, he even met with Stalin in Moscow to ask for assistance. Stalin vacillated, then agreed, then did nothing.

There was more. Stalin's actions fueled speculation within Poland that the Soviets, while ostensibly supporting the Poles, wanted the Germans to annihilate them. Although the Russians were nominal allies, Bogdan and other Poles suspected that they wanted to see high casualties among both Poles and Germans, enfeebling these countries and clearing the way for postwar Soviet domination of both. In the end, his calculus proved accurate. The Poles lost; eventually, the Germans did, too. Stalin emerged the winner.

For now, though, the Polish people were defeated combatants, and the Germans recognized them as such, promising humane treatment under Geneva Convention terms. Bogdan had a hunch that the Germans would allow them to live—although anything could happen. Some resistance fighters slipped away from the Germans by using the sewers, but Bogdan's injuries made walking difficult, and he lacked the mobility to escape.

Even after the *Armia Krajowa* surrendered, Hitler ordered that his troops continue to sack Warsaw, utterly destroying it. A deranged man to begin with, by the time of the Uprising, Hitler was even more unhinged.

On July 20, 1944, in Rastenburg, a cabal of conspirators made an attempt on his life. They were disgruntled army officers, eager to end the war and angry especially with the Führer's incompetent management of the Eastern front. The key conspirator, Colonel Claus von Stauffenberg, placed an explosive briefcase under a table at a conference meeting with Hitler.

But Stauffenberg put the briefcase next to a table leg, which absorbed the bomb's blast. Hitler survived, although injured, and he walked with a limp thereafter, dragging his right foot. He relied increasingly on medicine, popping dozens of pills daily, and his thinking grew more gauzy. When Bogdan and other rebels heard about the assassination attempt, they saw it as a hopeful sign that Hitler's regime was imploding. Consumed with rage at the assassination attempt, Hitler turned his wrath on his conspirators, ordering their deaths. Bogdan learned that the executions were gruesome, with some guilty men being hanged on meat hooks.

In all, Hitler executed an estimated five thousand men after the assassination attempt, and he grew more mulish about having his way. He distrusted and blamed his generals for military defeats. He brooked no resistance, and Poles bore the brunt of his fury. He was especially incensed that Poles were trying to regain a country that he had invaded and controlled as part of his quest for *Lebensraum*. To him, the matter was settled, and he resented the resistance.

An irony that pained Bogdan and his countrymen was that while the Allies made gains elsewhere, liberating Paris and Rome, Poles suffered defeat. Warsaw was still in German hands. Hitler and Heinrich Himmler, an inveterate racist who was in charge of implementing the Final Solution and who ran concentration camps with ruthless efficiency, issued the Order for Warsaw, decreeing that the city be leveled and its people slaughtered. They specifically ruled out taking prisoners; they would kill all and provide what they called a "terrifying example" to any city in Europe that tried to resist the Reich. Hitler's determination to raze Warsaw testified to his ruthlessness as well as his blind rage, because the action had no military value and diverted German resources from more meaningful wartime strategy. But Hitler was beyond reason. Warsaw, he determined, should no longer exist. After looting and plundering the city, the Nazis tried to erase it from existence using bulldozers, dynamite, and fire. By war's end, the Nazis had destroyed eighty-five percent of Warsaw.

But in defeat, Bogdan and his compatriots recognized that their efforts still had a significant impact. In war, historical turning points can be spectacular and can happen in just a few days, such as D-Day. The Warsaw Uprising was a slow turning point. It took place over nine weeks, and while it ended in failure, it succeeded in distracting German attention from its wars to the West and East, diverting manpower and resources to stamp out this Polish uprising. Far worse than just an irritant to the Nazis, it claimed enough of their soldiers to damage the Nazis' war machine and rattle them into realizing that Poles would not submit to them, forcing them to devote even more energy to subduing Poland. In this respect, the Uprising accelerated Germany on the path to defeat. Less than a year after the Uprising ended, the Germans surrendered to the Allies.

Although the Nazis continued to ravage Warsaw until January 1945, when the Soviets gained control of it, Bogdan did not stay to witness the destruction. He was now a captive, and he waited for the Germans to transport him and other POWs out of Warsaw. He had left Bydgoszcz, and now he was to leave Warsaw, his home for the past five years.

IV. Under German Control

These were the darkest days of Bogdan's life. His mother was gone, his father was missing, his body was permanently disfigured, and the Germans had vanquished him and his fellow fighters. Decades later, when asked what motivated him to keep going, he gave a remarkably similar response to Seiko's characterization of her own struggle after her sister Yasuko died. It was just the will to survive. *Survive*, Bogdan urged himself constantly. That challenge was a short-term, day-by-day battle. He could not think beyond the horizon of each day, because war brought changes of fortune every moment. But Bogdan saw war as a fight for the simple gifts that people normally take for granted—family, friends, food, shelter, and survival.

And freedom. War robs a person of freedom; Bogdan learned that lesson from the moment the conflict began in 1939, when his family lost their possessions and their way of life in Bydgoszcz—his father relinquishing, among many things, his home and construction empire. The cruelest blow of all comes when war takes human life, as it did Aniela's. Even if a person is lucky enough to survive the war, he or she endures a steady process of giving up more liberty. In Warsaw, Bogdan and all other residents lived under German rule, subject to searches and many other infringements on their freedoms. Now that he was a POW, Bogdan entered yet another phase of war, which meant losing even more control. His captors possessed him, holding his fate in their hands.

Bogdan could have tried to evade the Germans by blending into the civilian population, and internally, he debated that idea. For a brief period after the Uprising ended, his brothers tried to maintain a low profile among city residents. Zbigniew stayed in Warsaw, and Janusz eventually fled to a mountain region near Krakow. For Bogdan, though, the

Destruction on Marszalkowska Street in Warsaw. When the Uprising ended, the Mieczkowski family abandoned their apartment near Marszalkowska Street, never to return there (from the collections of the Warsaw Rising Museum).

more persuasive argument was to surrender. Residents were leaving the ruined city, with the exodus totaling a quarter million people, and those who remained became more conspicuous.

Bogdan would have stood out. He walked with a limp, and one look at his thumb wound showed that it was caused by a bullet. The Nazis, who were conducting searches throughout the city, would have easily identified him as a former resistance officer. Bogdan would end up in a POW camp even if he tried to avoid it. In the end, he resigned himself to his fate. He would join the fifteen thousand former resistance fighters who became internees.

Another inducement to surrender was that Bogdan expected a humane situation would await him. As he saw it, the treatment of Polish resistance fighters came in two basic stages. In the first, during the fighting, Germans regarded Polish soldiers as insurrectionist bandits, showing them no mercy. They killed them in battle; they executed them upon capture. Once the Uprising ended, a second stage took hold, during which the Germans recognized the rebels as combatants and sent these new captives to POW camps scattered throughout Germany rather than executing them. The Nazis promised to observe the Third Geneva Convention of 1929, by which signatory nations agreed to treat humanely soldiers who

7. Death Hits Home

surrendered, housing and feeding them and providing medical help. Bogdan now entered this second phase of treatment, lucky to have avoided the first. Would the Germans shoot him? He worried they might. Everything was a gamble, and he could only hope that they would keep their word and act like civilized human beings.

Captivity, Bogdan hoped, might even bring better conditions. If the Germans housed and fed him, perhaps even administered medical care, they might improve his current state and appearance. By this point, Bogdan recalled, "I was a sight—wounded, dirty, emaciated, and unshaven. I had worn the same clothes for weeks, and I looked bedraggled. But that was how we all were when the Uprising ended."

And their future under German control was unknown.

— 8 —

Doing Something Strange with Seaweed

I. Seiko's Schooling

In Japan, the war dragged on, giving people no respite while going badly for the country. In July 1944, when Allied forces gained control of Saipan, one of the Marianas Islands, Americans were shocked to see Japanese citizens jumping off cliffs to their deaths rather than surrender. The island brought Japan's home islands within range for American B-29 bombers. Following Saipan's surrender, Prime Minister Hideki Tojo resigned. He had suffered a tumultuous tenure in office, leading the war effort while trying to squelch rivalries between the army and navy and marshal the country's limited resources to produce goods on a war footing. By mid-1944, he had no choice but to relinquish the reins of government. The new prime minister, General Kuniaki Koiso, fared just as badly as Tojo had and would resign in April 1945.

In Otaru, Seiko and other residents continued to see how war's hardships blighted their lives. Before going off to the front lines, soldiers streamed into the city from smaller hamlets and towns, staying in schools or wealthy homes temporarily, after which they boarded transport ships that would take them to their destinations. Otaru residents knew they were headed to places like Sakhalin, Manchuria, or the Aleutian Islands, and they feared for the young men's lives because of the hazards ahead. Even before soldiers reached the frontlines, Seiko and her friends heard, some fell overboard or entire transport ships sunk, so they knew battle itself was only one threat that could kill Japanese troops.

The calls to sacrifice grew more demanding and reached more of the Japanese population. In late August 1944, when the school year should have started, students got the stunning news that all classes were canceled. With the need for labor acute, children went to work instead of school, trying to compensate for the labor shortage. To ensure that they could fill in any labor gaps, Seiko and her classmates took field trips to designated places and learned new skills. They walked to one of the two hospitals in Otaru, where doctors instructed them in cleansing and treating wounds. They took a train to a farm, where the owners taught them how to plant crops. The students never had to put these skills to use, but the exercises showed how the government was willing to subordinate their schooling to whatever it deemed necessary to fight the war.

To infringe on schooling was no small move for the Japanese; education was a proud core of their lives. Seiko's mother continued to teach at her elementary school, since the students there were too young to enlist in the war effort. But her father's teaching duties were suspended, and the government transferred him to a municipal office for administrative work. Because Hiroshi and Echi still had an income stream, their family was better off than most families in Otaru, where pockets of poverty existed everywhere. Despite the hardship, everyone was expected to contribute to the war effort, regardless of the disruption or sacrifice entailed.

Seiko's turn to pitch in came as well. She would continue her schooling, but in a radically different way than she ever imagined.

II. Seaweed, Gas Masks, and a Chemistry Lesson

In Hitler's Germany, young girls and women were often exempt from factory labor, mostly to preserve their roles as mothers. That was not the case in Japan, where the country practiced total mobilization of the population. In the fall of 1944, Seiko was fifteen years old, and she and her female classmates began factory life, working in a government plant in Asari, a small town twenty minutes south of Otaru by train. Every morning, Seiko's entire class—about thirty-five students in total—walked from their homes, met at the Otaru railroad station, and boarded an 8:15 train. The government covered the train fare, so they never had to buy tickets. The process became as routine as going to school itself, and the teenagers relied on their own initiative and discipline to be on time for their commute. Their school teachers came to the station as well, and the entire group took the trip to Asari without any special treatment or designation. In that respect, it was a normal train ride, in which they grabbed seats where they were available, and stood if all the seats were taken.

Once they arrived at the Asari station, the teachers assembled them after they exited the train and called roll, making note of any absences. They then led the class on a twenty-minute walk along a dirt road to the remote area where the factory stood. Everyone usually trudged along in silence, especially during winter, when they just concentrated on keeping warm and forging a path through the snow.

During normal school days, the pupils were required to wear a uniform, called a *seeraafuku* [a Japanization of the word "sailor" plus "fuku," meaning clothes], which resembled a sailor's outfit. This requirement was relaxed for their factory work, but many students continued to wear uniforms, while others wore casual clothes, including sweaters and coats during winter. Once Seiko and her classmates got to the factory, they went straight to a changing room, where they donned boots, rubber gloves, and big black aprons with a rubber coating, similar to a raincoat. The aprons stretched from their necks to below the knees, covering their entire front area. Once wearing the appointed garb, they were ready to work.

The word "factory" conjures up the image of a massive, multi-story concrete building bustling with trucks delivering raw material and ferrying away finished products. This plant was nothing like that. It was a crude, one-story wooden structure, with bare walls and an austere appearance. Far from being the hub of activity, it sat in an isolated, rural setting, and horse-drawn wagons transported material into and out of it. Nothing indicated that this was a production center for war materiel. Inside, not even a clock graced the walls to keep track of working hours. But there Seiko and the others toiled daily until 5:00 p.m. They worked seven days a week, with no vacation time. The students called their week "Monday, Monday, Tuesday, Wednesday, Thursday, Friday, Friday."

Their task was to do something strange with seaweed. In Hokkaido as through much of Japan, seaweed was part of the daily diet. It frequently accompanied rice dishes and was a wrap for sushi and other dishes. The Japanese also used a thicker variety, boiling it to make a dish called *konbu*. But the seaweed at the factory was different from these kinds and was especially unlike the paper-thin, soft, supple fare normally associated with sushi rolls. Rather, these were thick, tough, brown-green strands resembling rope—they were closer to kelp than actual seaweed—harvested from Cape Erimo off southern Hokkaido. The factory wanted to transform this special seaweed into tubes connecting gas masks to portable air canisters. Japanese soldiers would then use them in battle.

At the plant, the seaweed arrived in cubed bundles, three feet on each side. The Japanese used a unit of weight called *kan*, which meant 3.75 kilograms, and the seaweed bundles weighed about four *kan*, or fifteen kilograms (thirty-three pounds). To the teenage girls, the packages looked heavy, and Seiko watched men muscle them around the factory from the receiving area to the first stage of processing. Workers boiled the seaweed with a caustic soda, breaking it down so that it was more malleable. Then they took the seaweed remnants out, and an electrical machine used stones to hammer the seaweed, which had become more flexible, so that it could

8. Doing Something Strange with Seaweed   115

bend like rubber tubing. They put the treated seaweed onto a five-foot wide conveyor belt so that it could get to the girls' work stations.

The next step was up to Seiko and her classmates. The conveyor belt snaked around the factory for about fifty feet, much like modern-day luggage belts at airports, making twists and turns so that they could pull the seaweed off at various points. The young students were stationed at one of five different pools of water, each a yard wide and seven feet long, which sat on the factory's concrete floor. They grabbed the seaweed off the conveyor belt, brought it to the pools, and dropped it inside. The water was warm, and they stood alongside the pools, washing the seaweed by hand. The process removed impurities and bleached the seaweed from its brownish-greenish hue to a lighter color, which was supposed to reflect greater strength. All the girls wore primitive rubber gloves and thin boots that always leaked. Beneath their feet, they felt the cold factory floor, especially during winter, but when they stood before the water pools they stepped onto crude low benches so that they could stand taller and reach into the water more easily. When they were on the benches, they could also avoid contact with the cold floor.

Once the seaweed strands seemed clean, another team of girls took them outside—they were dripping wet—and draped them on clotheslines to dry. The individual seaweed ribbons varied in length from just a foot to as much as three feet in length, and hundreds of them hung there on twelve different clotheslines, just like clothes drying outside in the open air. After the seaweed strands dried, the students walked them to the warehouse portion of the factory, where workers packed them into bundles for shipment. Seiko's class was divided into teams tasked with specific chores, and Seiko usually worked on the factory floor dunking the seaweed into the water, although on some days she hung the seaweed on the clotheslines.

It was a primitive, arcane process, and envisioning the seaweed as part of a functioning apparatus was difficult. Seiko and her classmates once approached a factor worker who lived outside Otaru and asked him to give them more insight into the manufacturing system and the product that would result. Like them, though, he knew little about it, and instead he accepted his factory role and dutifully performed it, just as the girls did.

Regardless of what task any girl was assigned, it was tough, time-consuming work. Like most factory labor, theirs had a repetitive quality to it—picking up the seaweed, dropping it into the pools, washing and then hanging it. That cycle repeated itself for an entire workday.

Seiko and her classmates found ways to break up the monotony. They were teenage girls, young and exuberant, and they created an energetic, pleasant atmosphere inside the factory. They talked to one another and sang as they worked. Of course, they would have much preferred to be in a school classroom learning normal lessons, but they tried to make the situation as palatable as possible.

Three daily breaks broke up the day's monotony and allowed the young students to sit down and get a respite from standing or walking during their shifts. After working in the early morning, the girls got a fifteen-minute break at 10:00. At noon, they had an hour to eat lunch. Because Echi was teaching in the evening, Seiko prepared her own lunch the night before, which was usually two potatoes, although if she were lucky she could make fish and rice, and she stuck everything in a knapsack that she carried on the commute to the factory. The girls ate lunch in the same area where they changed clothes and took their other breaks because it had a long table and several chairs. Resuming work after lunch, they got a fifteen-minute respite at 3:00. That was the routine, and they left each day feeling like spent rockets, utterly exhausted. Their teachers walked them back to the Asari station, where they got their prepaid tickets and took an evening train back to Otaru.

Perhaps the most singular aspect of their new lives was that Seiko and her classmates never gave up on learning. They wedged in schooling: teachers were with the students at all times, and over the din of factory machinery, they carried out lessons as everyone worked. Their music instructor told them about sonatas; while she had no piano or instruments, she described the music and engaged them in song. Another teacher gave poetry lessons, and they recited poems together and composed poems themselves, which the teacher read aloud. Seiko remembered most starkly her chemistry teacher's revelation during a lesson in early 1945. As a way to reify concepts, he tried to keep the students updated on the scientific progress of Japan's wartime enemies. The Americans, he said, were developing a tiny bomb with great destructive strength. The weapon was "just a few cubic centimeters," he claimed, as he gesticulated with his fingers, "the size of a matchbox." While he never used the word "atomic," he described this new device as so powerful that it could obliterate a large city. It seemed like science fiction, yet his young listeners believed him. How the teacher got this information, Seiko never knew.

III. A Clever Chimera

The gas mask filters—which military planners somewhere had conceived—reflected the ingenuity of Japanese engineering. Seaweed was bountiful in the seas surrounding Japan, and divers could let it grow and reap harvests without the tedious care and maintenance that farmers had

8. Doing Something Strange with Seaweed

to employ for land crops. It was there for the taking, and many varieties existed. But this kind of seaweed was inedible, so if anyone were to use it, it had to be for a function other than food. The seaweed tubes were a clever contraption, and in theory, they were supposed to help to absorb any poisonous gases and keep soldiers safe when they breathed through them. Seiko had no idea if they worked as planned, but if they did, the seaweed tubes were an ingenious use of an available resource.

They also reflected a sad crudeness. Japan tried to exploit its limited resources, and the government and engineers labored to create the illusion that the country could invent and manufacture devices that could propel it to victory. In a sense, the seaweed breathing tubes were a chimera, allowing Japanese to indulge in the fantasy that they would work and that the country would win this war.

The factory experimented with other seaweed products, constructing the prototype of a seaweed jacket that soldiers could wear. To advertise it, an official wore the suit every day at the factory. It was a spectacularly unattractive garment—imagine a brown jacket made of seaweed—but even worse, it failed to provide any warmth, which was supposed to be its purpose. Just looking at the man clad in the jacket during winter made Seiko feel cold.

It was also incongruous. The truth was that World War II was a conflict that has been dubbed the "gross national product war"; countries that could churn out the most goods and services would prevail. Seiko and her classmates were too young to sense it, and they performed their duties without question, but the industry in which they worked telegraphed Japan's desperation. If the primitive Asari factory had more automation, machines could have performed the work the students were doing. Instead, it depended on human labor, and that effort kept them out of school and stunted their learning and potential. Seiko's father ruefully joked with friends that she was supposed to get an education in one of the best schools in Otaru, and instead she was studying how to box up material for shipment to the military. The waste of human productive potential was maddening.

Ultimately, even the most fanatical devotion to the cause failed to translate to victory against the Allies' superior resources and production. The Japanese government expected a quick victory in the war against the U.S., but as the conflict dragged on for four years, the country's resources and manufacturing fell behind the demands. The war's duration and high cost not only prostrated Japan's economy; it threatened to mortgage the country's future, including the education of its young.

The Japanese people were bearing witness to how their government's plans unraveled. Japan had captured an empire for raw materials in

Southeast Asia, including the Philippines, Dutch East Indies, and Burma, but the conquests did little good. The resources from these areas never came, and the Japanese sought help closer to home, including resources right off the Hokkaido coast. The government had placed an illusory faith in the power of colonies. American submarines preyed on Japanese merchant vessels, confining them to ports, so the home islands had little access to resources from these regions. The economic chokehold subjected Japan to slow strangulation.

IV. Bad Omens

Japan's military campaign also faltered. In October 1944, U.S. and Japanese naval and air forces fought in the Battle of Leyte Gulf. It became the greatest clash in naval history, lasting three days and encompassing an enormous area of the Philippine Islands. For Japan, it was a disaster. The navy lost four carriers, plus destroyers, cruisers, battleships, and five hundred planes. Thousands of Japanese men perished. Seiko learned that one Japanese fighter pilot said that he took off from his carrier, looked back, and saw that his ship was gone. (He landed the plane on an island and managed to survive.) Once again, though, in reporting on Leyte Gulf, the government minimized the extent of Japan's losses, making it seem like it was a victory.

The battle marked the first time the U.S. experienced kamikaze attacks. The kamikaze warrior stepped out of the pages of Japanese mythology to become very real. The government portrayed these pilots as heroes; sacrificing one's life for country and emperor was ennobling. "Kami" meant divine, and "kaze" denoted wind, and the story of the "divine wind" originated in the thirteenth century when the Mongols tried to invade Kyushu, Japan's southernmost island. They had conquered China and next set their sights on Japan, which appeared vulnerable. The Mongols' military operation took place in autumn, and just as their powerful army and navy were poised to launch their attack, a typhoon destroyed their ships and foiled the attempted invasion. The Japanese maintained that a divine power had created that wind and saved their country. They hoped the kamikaze pilots of World War II would have divine power, too, and would use it to destroy their targets. In reality, the kamikaze attacks were yet another sign of Japan's limited resources and desperation.

Japan found its options narrowing. The sea was the country's source of strength, but it also became a weakness. The Allies used the waters surrounding Japan to cut it off from outside trade and provisions. The strategy was dubbed "Operation Starvation," and Admiral Chester Nimitz,

8. Doing Something Strange with Seaweed

the commander-in-chief of the U.S. Pacific Fleet, used both sea and air resources to choke off Japan. Seiko recalled that when the Japanese learned of Nimitz's role, they pointed out that he was of German descent, noting the strange irony—even hypocrisy—of the Americans. Here the U.S. was using a German-American to fight them—while America was also battling Germany! (After the war, Japanese people were even more aggrieved to learn of the relocation of Japanese Americans to internment camps, treatment that German Americans generally did not suffer.)

By early 1945, bad omens appeared constantly. The Allies launched a bombing campaign over key Japanese cities, including Tokyo, Nagoya, and Osaka. In a magazine, Seiko read about the devastating firebombing of Tokyo, which took place in March of 1945. A teenage girl recounted her experience, saying that from the sky plunged black, rain-like projectiles—which was napalm, a jelly-like incendiary that sticks to objects—spreading flames as soon as they touched any object or person. The girl wrote that she picked up small children around her, grabbing them by the hand and running to escape the flames and unbearable heat, which became so intense that water in canals boiled.

The attack on Tokyo dovetailed with the "island hopping" campaign, during which Allied forces gained control of Japan's Pacific islands, approaching the home islands to prepare for an invasion. In February, the Allies seized control of Iwo Jima, the conquest of which produced the iconic photograph of six U.S. Marine Corps servicemen raising the American flag atop Mount Suribachi. Iwo Jima was just 760 miles from Tokyo.

One Sunday in the spring of 1945, Seiko was at home in Otaru, enjoying a brief respite from factory work. She was outside, and she saw something she had never seen before during the war: an American airplane was flying overhead, infringing on Japanese airspace. That sight was hard enough to believe, but then, she saw the airplane dropping projectiles, which emitted a dribbling sound, like gravel falling down a dirt road, followed by a loud explosion.

Just as Seiko saw this scene, an air raid siren began to wail, piercing through the placid Otaru community. This was no practice drill. Seiko and about two dozen neighbors ran to a forest near their homes, reaching it in ten minutes. Everyone was quiet, as a combination of shock and fear gripped them. After several minutes of quiet waiting, the group sensed that the plane would not return, and the danger was over. Everyone emerged from the forest and, slightly rattled, they walked home. Other than the bomb whistle and the loud boom, Seiko had no idea what had happened.

The next day, she learned. As Seiko and her classmates walked from the Asari train station to the factory, they came across a huge crater, more than a hundred feet in diameter, which a bomb had blasted into the earth. It had struck farmland, ravaging a field, destroying a barn, and killing a horse. No humans were injured, and a half-mile away, the factory stood unharmed.

This incident, Seiko concluded, revealed how keen U.S. intelligence was. The bomber had clearly targeted the Asari factory, even though it had missed. The odds were astounding: Asari was a small hamlet in a remote corner of Hokkaido. How did the Americans learn that a war production factory operated there? They came all the way to the western side of Hokkaido to destroy it, which showed that the work of this forlorn factory must have been important for them to stop. Amazingly, Seiko reflected, the Americans had the insight and fortitude to strike close to the factory. That bomb also revealed a larger problem—the weakness of Japan's air defenses. As the Tokyo firebombings showed, enemy bombers could penetrate Japan's airspace at will, and later that year, the problem would prove devastating.

Seiko soon found out that after dropping the bomb over Asari, the plane suffered mechanical failure and crashed into the water break at a port. A nineteen-year-old American pilot was flying it alone, and when military personnel retrieved his body, they found a sheath of paper matches inside his flight suit. By this time, the people of Otaru despaired for favorable omens so much that they interpreted this small item as an augury of good fortune. Instead of using wooden matches, the Americans had to resort to paper, so Otaru residents thought they must be getting poorer and more desperate. They still indulged in the futile hope that they could beat the U.S. Many community members privately and quietly expressed sympathy for the young serviceman, who had sacrificed his life on a parlous but futile mission to Hokkaido, although they dared not utter such sentiments openly.

In May 1945 news hit Otaru that Germany had surrendered. By June the Allies reached Okinawa, which sat less than six hundred miles from Kyushu's southern tip. With this news came the grim realization in Otaru and elsewhere that Japan could lose this war and risk complete destruction. Seiko, her family, and friends tried to avoid these thoughts, but they knew the tide was turning. They could feel Hokkaido becoming more isolated, too. To travel to Honshu, a Hokkaido resident relied on a ferry that crossed the Tsugaru Strait, which separated the two large islands, but service became much less regular and often stopped altogether. (Today, the 33-mile Seikan train tunnel connects Hokkaido and Honshu.) People feared that U.S. submarines could destroy the ferries, and besides, they could scarcely afford the fare during the war. Moreover, precious fuel got shunted to the military instead of using it for ferry service.

8. Doing Something Strange with Seaweed 121

In July 1945, U.S. bombers struck Hakodate, the port city at the southern tip of Hokkaido. The attack sunk several ferries and military ships, including a destroyer. The link between Seiko's island and Honshu was now gone. Now, it seemed that Hokkaido became more of an outpost, left on its own to struggle through the war. Whether people worked in factories or fields, they were more isolated and now had to toil that much harder to ensure their survival.

V. New Worries

On the morning of August 6, 1945, Seiko was at the Asari factory, as usual. But what seemed an ordinary workday suddenly changed when a teacher announced that the Americans had destroyed Hiroshima, an industrial city in southern Honshu. They had deployed a massive bomb, he said, a weapon so devastating that it could have leveled a larger metropolis, like Tokyo. Immediately, Seiko and her classmates realized that this was the device that their chemistry teacher had mentioned months earlier.

Three days later came the news that a second bomb had obliterated Nagasaki, a city in northern Kyushu, about five hundred miles from Tokyo. This time Seiko was not surprised, and she and her friends believed that the Americans might drop more of these weapons. The war's verdict seemed inexorable, yet for them, the immediate instinct was to keep fighting, much as the government and their teachers had been imploring them to do for years. These exhortations had their desired effect on the high school girls. Despite the news from Hiroshima and Nagasaki, they were determined to continue working at the factory.

In Hokkaido, though, people worried. On August 8, the day before the Nagasaki bomb, the Soviet Union declared war on Japan. Otaru residents realized this event would change the whole conflict. All along, they dreaded that war would hit home—that Allied troops would invade Japan. For most of the war, this meant American soldiers, whom they feared the most, because the government and schools depicted them as devils. But now their trepidation was magnified.

Russia had been Japan's traditional enemy for centuries. The tortuous spiral of war, though, had transformed feelings, so that among the three major Allied powers arrayed against Japan, the Japanese people had seen the Soviet Union as the mildest, the country that had not yet declared war against Japan. Seiko later learned that in 1945, the Japanese government even approached the Soviets about acting as intermediaries to seek peace with the Allies.

Stalin's declaration of war changed everything. Otaru residents now thought the Russians would invade Hokkaido, enter their city, and slaughter everyone. Their island would face Soviet invaders from the north and American attackers from the south. Where could they go? They had nowhere to flee, and while they were determined to repel the enemies even with bamboo sticks and bare hands, they would be staring death head-on.

Moreover, the Yalta Accords, signed in February 1945, seared a deep impression on many Hokkaido residents. At this meeting of the Allied "Big Three"—President Franklin Roosevelt, Prime Minister Winston Churchill, and Premier Josef Stalin—Roosevelt and Churchill had yielded to Stalin's demands, surrendering Eastern Europe to his steely grip and giving up resources that he demanded. Hokkaido was next, the rumor ran; Otaru residents believed that Stalin would demand the island—and he would get it. Seiko reflected, "Our freedom—our very lives—are in peril."

VI. *Hearing the Voice of a God*

On August 14, amidst the churn of conflicting emotions, Seiko received unusual news. She learned that the following day, the emperor would speak to the nation for the first time. Nobody knew what he might say, but it had to be important.

The next day, Seiko and her fellow students went to the factory to work, despite what had happened at Hiroshima and Nagasaki. At noon, they gathered outside the manager's office, which was located in the central area of the factory, and they listened eagerly for the emperor's voice on the radio. The radio was of shabby quality, but when the announcement aired, the normally busy factory ground to a halt. Everyone grew quiet.

A voice crackled over the radio. *It was really he*—the emperor, speaking to them directly for the first time. This moment represented a radical break with tradition, but these were extraordinary times. The Japanese people were hearing the voice of a god, although they could not even be sure it was the emperor himself, since they had no idea what his voice sounded like.

The radio's sound quality was poor, but there was another problem. In his recorded message, Emperor Hirohito spoke in a peculiar manner, using a formal dialect, with ornate words encrusting his phrases. He relied on old-fashioned Chinese terms, a stilted Japanese that seemed almost like a foreign language to listeners. His delivery compounded the problem. Clearly, this was someone who needed communications coaching. Here Hirohito's cloistered existence had worked to his disadvantage. Although he was a leader, he had no practice in public speaking. His voice was feeble, his cadence uneven and hesitant. Seiko's teachers had difficulty understanding him, although no one dared criticize a god. When the emperor finished speaking, even the factory head had no inkling of what he had said, so he instructed everyone to go back to their stations and work. They were, after all, showing their dedication and performing their duty for the country.

The emperor's words remained cloaked in mystery until later that afternoon, around three o'clock, when one student broke the stunning news that the war was finished. No one could believe it. Did Japan really give up? "We thought we would never surrender, not even on our dying day," Seiko believed. It was as if a giant cloud had suddenly enveloped them, and everything now was unclear. A teacher ended the uncertainty. As they were finishing their workday, she said that she had deciphered the emperor's message and told them emphatically what he had said.

Japan was surrendering.

Surrender? "Are you sure?" the students chorused in disbelief.

Yes, came her reply.

The teachers told the students that it was unsafe to take the train anymore, so when the workday ended, they walked all the way back to Otaru. The girls were tired from work and had eaten little all day. The four-mile walk took more than an hour and added to their exhaustion.

Once Seiko got home, her parents greeted her by confirming that the war was over, and Japan had lost. They had heard the emperor's announcement, and Echi said that the neighbors—none of whom owned a radio—came to their house to listen to the radio. Hiroshi turned up the volume so that everyone in his living room could hear, and despite the emperor's quirky dialect, Hiroshi understood what he was saying. He heard Hirohito say the word "end" almost as soon as he began speaking, so Hiroshi turned to Echi and told her that the war was finished.

Normally, Hiroshi was the tetchy partner in the marriage, but this time Echi chided him. "Don't say it so loudly," she admonished, fearing that the neighbors would get angry at him. Surrender practically did not exist in the Japanese vocabulary, a word never to be uttered aloud. So the neighbors continued to listen in a bewildered silence. Then, when the emperor was finished, Seiko's father spoke words that revealed what weighed most heavily on his mind. "This means," he said, "that Suguru will come home."

He spoke quietly and slowly, chiseling the words into the silence. While the neighbors might have been stunned, surrender spared Seiko's family from more tragedy and tears, and they looked forward to seeing Suguru again. Because he had a college degree, the navy granted him the rank of second lieutenant, so he had some stature in the military. Perhaps he would regale the family with stories of training in the navy. Most of all, he could resume a normal life and begin his post-graduate career.

On September 2, 1945, General Douglas MacArthur accepted Japan's surrender aboard the battleship U.S.S. *Missouri* (symbolically significant because President Harry Truman hailed from that state), anchored in Tokyo Bay. Japanese Foreign Minister Mamoru Shigemitsu was the first to sign the surrender document on behalf of the emperor, followed by General Yoshijiro Umezu, who signed for the Japanese Army. After nearly four years of war against the U.S., the entire surrender ceremony took about twenty minutes.

The country had fallen far from its imperial zenith. The people thought Japan had no breaking point, but now its defeat was official. Families were spared more suffering. The war was finally over. Seiko had no idea what to expect next.

Part III

Determined to Bounce Back

— 9 —

From Soldier to Prisoner

I. Constant Movement

Bogdan found himself in a dark, putrid railroad car. As a POW, he was now under German control, and his captors began the complicated process of moving their prisoners. Immediately after surrendering, he and other wounded *Armia Krajowa* veterans stayed in a makeshift hospital in Warsaw, housed in a former girls' school about a block from his family's apartment. During this waiting period, Bogdan twice visited the apartment, once encountering German soldiers who had just finished plundering it. What had been Bogdan's wartime home now seemed empty and lifeless.

Within two weeks, horse-drawn wagons took Bogdan and other patients to a railroad station, where the next phase of the transport process took place, with the vanquished soldiers boarding freight cars bound for POW camps. As they did so, a palpable sense of defeat and exhaustion hung in the air.

Before the war, Bogdan had traveled in railroad cars, riding in comfort, always seeing it as an adventure. When his family went on ski vacations in Zakopane, they took well-appointed trains, and some cars even had sleeping berths similar to those in the luxurious Pullman Palace cars in the U.S. This experience was completely different, giving Bogdan a new and unwelcome look at railroad transportation. These were cattle cars, with no seats, just two separate levels, consisting of the floor and an elevated shelf. Bogdan sat on the latter.

Perhaps thousands of POWs were aboard the chain of railroad cars. About fifty men shoehorned themselves into Bogdan's car, which stunk of livestock and human odor. Because water was scarce in Warsaw, Bogdan had not taken a bath or shower since the Uprising began, and most residents of the city had the same foul experience. Amidst the German occupation and Uprising, they shared everything—devastation, loss, even stench—and now the defeated insurgents they continued to do so, in closer quarters.

Aboard the car, embers of resistance still glowed. German soldiers were notorious for enjoying alcohol, and some jaunty Polish prisoners plied the German guard on the train car with enough vodka to make him drunk. The guard, who was an older man showing little aptitude for his work, became barely conscious of his surroundings, and he looked like he had passed out. As the nighttime train slipped through Warsaw suburbs, Bogdan watched passengers open the large, clunky car door and bail out. Nearly half of the POWs aboard took the leap and tasted freedom again.

Bogdan could not join them. Even though the train was moving slowly, his injuries were too severe, and his shrapnel-pocked legs would have buckled from the jump. Were he to survive the fall, he still would be unable to walk or run to stay on the lam. Resigned to sleeping on the floor, Bogdan settled in for the night and the long trip ahead, as the train rattled along. Every bump in the tracks translated up through the wooden floor, shaking his emaciated body as he tried to rest. At least, he thought, the car was less crowded after those prisoners had jumped out.

Ironically, Bogdan now worried about the Allies as much as the Germans, because Allied bombs sometimes destroyed German railroad cars, causing the unintentional deaths of POWs aboard. Even though the Uprising had ended, they were still in peril, this time from friendly fire.

During this phase, Bogdan felt fortunate that the Germans never subjected him to forced labor. On his first train ride out of Warsaw, his company commander happened to be present, and he vouched for Bogdan's status as an officer, which spared him from such work. But he did witness it. Near Hamburg, a British air raid dropped a bomb just fifty yards from his train, creating an enormous crater. (At that moment, Bogdan again felt lucky to survive unscathed, and the incident showed the danger of friendly fire.) The Germans forced POWs from a nearby camp to fill the chasm and guards watched over them with guns and dogs.

The train traveled two days and stopped at Zeithain, a POW camp located directly south of Berlin, between Leipzig and Dresden. All the passengers disembarked, and the Germans processed their charges, making them formal prisoners of war, with individual numbers and metal identification disks. They took warm showers—the only one Bogdan had as a POW—which were wonderful, making them feel human again. It was the first time Bogdan had bathed in months. It would be months before he did it again.

Bogdan now faced a different fight to survive. The rumor snaking through the camp was that nearby were buried 50,000 Soviets, most of whom had starved to death, and Bogdan worried their fate would be the same. Bogdan reflected on the irony that just weeks earlier he was targeting Germans to kill and eliminate them from Warsaw, but now he depended on them to let him survive.

9. From Soldier to Prisoner

If they were not executed first, Bogdan reflected only half-jokingly, he was convinced their diet could kill them. Food—or lack of it—was a defining aspect of any captivity experience, and so it was with Bogdan's. The POWs received only a small daily food ration, which consisted of two slices of dough-like food. It resembled bread, but it had the consistency of soft clay and practically assaulted Bogdan's tastebuds. Though the food was barely edible, each prisoner had to guard his portion carefully because of theft. Meanwhile, Bogdan's thumb wound still ached, especially when he touched anything with it, and he learned to adjust to eating, writing, and performing other tasks with a stump where his right thumb used to be.

Bogdan resigned himself to POW life, and it proved peripatetic. Fortunately, his leg wounds had healed enough that he could amble along at a slow pace. In early December 1944, the Germans marched everyone to a nearby camp called Muehlberg. The march there took several hours, and Bogdan found the camp well organized, even offering concerts to the POWs.

But after just two nights at Muehlberg, the Germans sent Bogdan and other officer POWs aboard a passenger train—the only time he rode in such comfort during his entire POW experience—to Bergen-Belsen, a POW camp in northern Germany holding about 500 Polish officers, located next to the infamous concentration camp of the same name. Adjacent to Bergen-Belsen, a German tank brigade stood as a control measure, allowing the Germans to exert discipline over prisoners in case of trouble. They experienced no difficulty in controlling the prisoners, including Bogdan. Bergen-Belsen evoked apprehension in him—as in other POWs—because it was a site where the Nazis executed humans en masse. (Although Bergen-Belsen was in Germany, the Nazis used Poland as a staging ground for its most notorious concentration camps, including Auschwitz, Majdanek, and Treblinka. In effect, they turned the country into a massive slaughterhouse.) One evening, the POWs sang an inspirational religious song, hoping that their voices would carry into the concentration camp and give inmates encouragement.

After two weeks, the Germans moved the POWs to Fallingbostel, in northwestern Germany, about a hundred miles from the border with the Netherlands. They were close enough to the larger city of Hanover that Bogdan witnessed British air raids, including the unnerving sight of a British bomber, lit up by nighttime searchlights, getting hit and falling to the ground.

After only a few days in Fallingbostel, the Germans loaded their prisoners onto cold freight cars and sent them to Grossborn, located in northern Poland. This became Bogdan's fifth POW camp. But the stay here lasted only two days, and the POWs had to walk to the next camp.

The constant movement of prisoners showed how improvised the Germans' thinking was. The lack of efficiency was uncharacteristic of Germans, who normally ran operations meticulously, but their problems revealed that they lacked proper planning for this wartime humanitarian emergency. The sad result was that the POWs suffered far more than they should have. Moreover, the war raged on, and the Soviet offensive forced the Germans to keep moving the prisoners westward, beyond reach of the invaders from the East. The advancing Russian army provided another, more urgent explanation for why the Germans moved the POWs around constantly; they were trying to stay one step ahead of the Soviets.

Bogdan felt lucky that he had few personal belongings—everything he owned, including precious family photos, fit into a military knapsack—so he could pick up and go whenever the Germans ordered them to do so, especially if they had to march. The shrapnel wounds hobbled his gait, but he had always liked to walk fast, so even at reduced speed he could keep pace with other prisoners. As they walked, armed German guards stayed alongside them, ever vigilant. The POW columns had gaps and clusters instead of forming a continuous stream, and at intervals, they stopped and waited for others to catch up. The lacunae also formed because of POWs who died; Bogdan passed one man who expired at the side of the road, his body just lying there.

Bogdan was hungry, cold, and exhausted. Since becoming a POW, he had done considerable walking, and his journey was just beginning.

II. New Enemies

Normally, under adverse conditions, the human condition cries out for friendship, taking comfort in kindred spirits. But in the maze of POW camps, true friendship proved impossible. One morning, Bogdan heard a familiar voice and recognized it as that of a Bydgoszcz teacher who had taught Latin to his brother Zbigniew. Bogdan was gregarious and made friends easily, but as a POW he was so perennially exhausted that he lacked the energy to find the former teacher and introduce himself. The constant movement also kept Bogdan from forging friendships. It was like passing through a turnstile and seeing new faces all the time. These conditions bred a sense of detachment and anomie, and Bogdan grew accustomed to only simple conversations and long periods in silence.

He could not communicate with his family, either. Through the crude POW mail system, Bogdan had gotten word to them that he was in a German prisoners' camp, but that was the extent of his contact with them. It was as if he had been swallowed up in a giant black hole—one that moved

9. From Soldier to Prisoner

constantly—where he became impossible to find. Only after the experience ended could he tell them precisely where he had been and what had happened.

Besides the will to survive, another emotion kept Bogdan going. He feared the Soviets. They were the new enemy, encroaching from the east, and he heard that they were arresting former Polish resistance fighters and sending them to Siberia. Some POWs decided to stay put and declare their allegiance to the Soviets, saying that they were Communists, and Bogdan later learned that the Russians ended up hustling them off to the Gulag regardless of those pledges. German propaganda hammered home the truth that Soviets had committed the murders in the Katyn Forest, and that atrocity reminded Bogdan of what would happen if they captured him. By staying with the Germans, he thought he could gain a measure of protection.

It was, once again, the strange alchemy of war. Bogdan now had to pick between two unpalatable choices, this time reversing his calculus to side with his erstwhile enemy. Earlier he had thought the Soviets would be allies, but as they continued to approach from the east and control more territory, Poles recognized that they—not the Germans—had become the real enemy. (This view anticipated the future, even though Poles had no way of knowing at the time that Russian control would endure for the next four decades.)

Another enemy was the cold. As autumn slipped away, Bogdan felt the harsh lash of the Eastern European winter, with low temperatures dipping below freezing overnight and the highs barely climbing into the 30s Fahrenheit. No prisoner had blankets for nighttime sleep, and each day, Bogdan and the others endured counts during which they stood outside for long periods, sometimes hours, wearing only light jackets. The Germans did these roll calls at least once a day, barking out the prisoner numbers. Prisoners shivered violently, their whole bodies shaking, and Bogdan learned that some older POWs grew ill and died of exposure.

It was now January 1945. Since Bogdan's capture in October, he had fought numbness and frostbite while riding in cold freight cars or trudging in the snow. The frostbite was so severe that his toes had turned a chalky white color, and the nails fell off, exposing the delicate nailbeds. "I grew scared," Bogdan remembered, "because I was losing feeling in my feet and toes, and I feared they would sustain permanent damage—or perhaps be amputated."

On the second day of the march to the new camp, the POWs were housed in a barn. In the morning, while the column of POWs fell out and began walking, Bogdan hid under a thatch of straw. When he emerged, he found that several other POWs had also waited, and they formed their own small group that ambulated at their own tempo. They learned that a group of Polish laborers, who engaged in compulsory labor in Germany, lived on the outskirts of town, and they found this settlement. Their kitchen was warm, and Bogdan took off his shoes and socks to inspect the condition of his feet. Seeing their frightful condition, the Polish hosts brought hot water that they had used to boil potatoes, and Bogdan bathed his feet with it. The warmth restored some circulation, and he thought their kindness might have kept him from losing his toes.

At that moment, separated from the other POWs, Bogdan considered escaping by simply staying where he was. But he concluded the gambit was impossible. Germans were everywhere, and Bogdan could barely walk, let alone run. Moreover, Germany neighbors threatened to call the police after seeing the POWs. Bogdan resigned himself to rejoining the POWs for the next march, and they eventually caught up with the main formation of prisoners. The march led to a small POW camp, near Stettin, which today is the city of Szczecin, just inside Poland's western border, near the Baltic Sea. There Bogdan found a pair of tennis sneakers that he began using, since they were in better condition than his beat-up shoes.

But the stay near Stettin lasted only three nights. When the Germans announced that they were leaving for the next camp, Bogdan found he could barely walk. He peeled away from his column and trudged behind a horse-drawn cart to try to get to a railroad station and look for medical help. But a German guard spotted him and, delivering blows, forced him to rejoin the others. When they got to a barn that night, Bogdan collapsed on the straw, even refusing the ration of boiled potatoes that the Germans served late at night.

The next day, in a show of mercy, Bogdan's captors let him climb aboard a horse-drawn buggy, where he met Serbs who were fleeing the Soviets, and he took a slow ride to the next barn where they would lodge for the night. For the next days, Bogdan endured more walking, until they boarded freight trains for the remainder of the journey. Eventually, they got to what would be Bogdan's seventh POW camp, Sandbostel, located between Hamburg and Bremen, port cities in northern Germany. (His previous POW camps, in order, were Zeithain, Muehlberg, Bergen-Belsen, Fallingbostel, Grossborn, and Stettin.) After reaching the Sandbostel rail station, Bogdan and the other prisoners walked nearly ten miles to get to the camp.

All told, they moved about 500 miles, much of it by foot, zigzagging through Germany in a frenetic attempt to stay away from the Soviets. The whole effort tested the POWs' stamina, will to live, and ability to fight off new enemies like the approaching Russians and the debilitating winter cold. Bogdan now wondered how long they would stay in the latest camp—and when the Germans would march them to a new location.

III. Shriveled Souls

The Germans used the term *Stalag* for their POW camps, and the one at Sandbostel was Stalag XB, located in Military District X (or ten), in a zone labeled "B." Authorities selected this site for a camp because the land expanse was large, flat, and mostly barren. They could thus build a large detention facility there where they could easily watch over POWs, who could be spotted if they tried to escape.

The camp held POWs from many countries, and Bogdan was part of the last wave of Polish POWs to arrive there. The first group came immediately after Germany's 1939 invasion of Poland, and another large influx came when the Uprising ended. Bogdan joined the tail end of that movement, arriving in the winter of 1945. When he got there, the camp held about twenty thousand inmates total, including POWs and concentration camp inmates, and sprawled over considerable territory, comprising more than a hundred buildings, many of them rickety and crude.

This was Bogdan's new home, and since Stalag XB was more developed than previous camps where he had stayed, he received slightly better

Yanek Mieczkowski at the old POW camp in Sandbostel, Germany. On this site—perhaps within these very structures—Bogdan was held during the final weeks of World War II. While the camp comprised more than one hundred buildings during the war, only two dozen of the original structures remain.

treatment. Swiss Red Cross representatives distributed care packages from the U.S. and Canada. For the emaciated POWs, getting one of these was like striking gold. The food they contained—typically dried fruit, jam, and cocoa—was a nutritional treasure, and it braced up their wavering spirits. The American parcels were especially coveted because they contained cigarettes, which some prisoners smoked while others used for barter. To add to this good fortune, a special surprise came when Bogdan received a mail parcel from a Polish acquaintance near Warsaw. Bogdan had written to him earlier, asking for onions, thinking they would stave off beriberi and give the vitamins he needed to keep his teeth and nails intact. Bogdan opened the package and was delighted to see several onions, old enough to be sprouting small shoots, yet unspoiled and in reasonably good shape. Bogdan ate them raw, munching on them like they were apples.

Still, Bogdan had to adjust to Sandbostel's crowded, harsh conditions, with no hygiene or privacy. The central hallway in POW barracks and the rooms were dreary, unpainted, and cold. They had no heating and the Germans provided no sheets, bedding, or blankets—not even straw. Prisoners were emaciated and exhausted, like shriveled souls, and although they got a respite from the long march, some cracked under the strain of camp life. They staggered about disoriented, while others lay on the floor most of the time, just sleeping and trying to conserve morsels of energy. At night, moans filled the air, coming from POWs who were in too much pain to fall asleep.

The camp's perimeter had the usual barbed wire and guard towers. Grey-clad German guards took counts of the prisoners, walking among them with German shepherds, who were trained to sniff out prisoners who might have been hiding, a task that must have been easy for their keen olfactory senses. After all, the POWS marinated in their smell, grime, and bedraggled clothes.

What further dulled them was diet. Once again, the food was rancid. The provisions were the familiar doughy mass supplemented by what Bogdan could only describe as a stinking soup, which was watered down and reeked of cow feed. It had a turnip base, and Bogdan recalled that during World War I, Germans dubbed the cold months of 1917–18 the "winter of the turnip," because that vegetable seemed the only food left in their country. In 1945, the POWs were enduring another turnip winter.

The American POW William Ash, who piloted British Spitfire planes and became celebrated for escaping from Nazi prisons, wisecracked that while the food in German camps was atrocious, he could not argue with the price. That might have been true, Bogdan mused, but he would have gladly paid for palatable fare—and more of it. He estimated that he was eating only a few hundred calories of food daily, and while he had no way to measure it, he guessed his weight was down to 120 pounds, about forty pounds less than normal. Like all POWs, he was a skeletal vestige of his old self.

What detracted further from the eating experience was that the camp had no area designated for it, like a dining hall. Normally, that kind of arrangement prepares and enhances the gustatory senses, as if signaling to the body and palate that they can sit down and enjoy the cuisine. But in the POW camp, the prisoners ate where they slept. The Germans wheeled a large kettle down the hallway, ladled out soup into each prisoner's bowl, and gave them each a piece of bread. They had no utensils, so Bogdan just sat on his bed and used the bowl and his hands to eat. If they suffered stomach upset, no medicine was available, so they just had to wait until the problem passed—literally.

The food was so sparse that most prisoners seldom had to use the bathroom, but when nature called, a primitive bathroom lay at the end of the barrack building. It was a large, open area with a hole dug into the ground. Above it was a wooden board that stretched across the chasm. Prisoners had to climb onto the board, do their business while balancing carefully, and then climb off. No toilet paper was available, but there was newspaper. Once again, the stench was horrific, but everyone adapted.

Sleep was perhaps the only aspect of POW life that made the captives feel normal. They had three-tiered wooden beds, without mattresses, pillows, or any accouterments, so everyone slept on hardwood. Many of the slats in the bunk beds were missing because the Germans had used them as firewood, a common practice as their war situation grew more desperate in 1944 and 1945. Lacking sheets, blankets, or nightwear, the POWs slept in their daytime clothes. But for all these inconveniences, Bogdan slept soundly. After all, he was twenty years old, a stage in life when deep sleep comes easily, and slumber also provided a time when he could escape from gnawing hunger. That hunger plus constant fatigue and weakness made him appreciate the comfort that sleep gave.

Amazingly, Bogdan's mind could still focus, and he retained a determination to learn even within the POW camp. He studied foreign languages. He spoke to Italian POWs and began to pick up their language; luckily, he had studied Latin in Polish schools and in the *komplety* classes, which helped him to pick up their language easily. Even more important was his study of English. There was a Polish pilot who had been shot down, and he knew some English, and he taught small, informal classes to about five or six POWs, focusing especially on vocabulary acquisition. The clientele was small because most prisoners just concentrated on surviving, and the utility of learning English was uncertain since most of them had no idea where their future would be. But Bogdan had an intuitive sense that

English would be valuable to him, envisioning the possibility of a career that would need it. It was remarkable that prisoners could transcend the miserable circumstances and continue their education, without the benefit of chairs, desks, pens, or paper. They relied solely on their minds and ability to remember information.

One aspect of the Sandbostel camp's physical arrangement was striking: it was next to a concentration camp, with a barbed wire fence separating the two camps. The concentration camp prisoners awaited a fate far worse than that of POWs, and Bogdan could see how badly they were treated. Inside the adjacent concentration camp, so-called *kapos*—prisoners whom the Germans picked as a kind of internal police—enforced discipline and order. This system allowed the Germans to conserve their own troops and resources, and it maintained a crude order among the prisoners. Some concentration camp prisoners had no strength and could not even walk a straight line, and the *kapos* targeted them for bullying. One big *kapo* was obviously better fed than the other prisoners, "with rosy cheeks contrasting with the ash-pale pallor of other prisoners," Bogdan recalled. He walked with a swagger in his step, and Bogdan saw him savagely hit other prisoners with a large club.

Bogdan witnessed an ominous scene that involved the concentration camp. One day, the Germans singled out a Polish Army colonel who had led one of the largest units in the Uprising. Two guards marched him through the POW camp to the exit, leading him to the neighboring concentration camp. The scene was striking. The Polish colonel, despite the depravity of a POW camp, looked tall, lean, and proud. He drew quite a contrast walking next to his jackbooted German guards, looking more robust than his captors. Although the Germans had access to better food, by this time of the war, the German Army had depleted manpower, and the soldiers who got guard duty were often lowly runts, many of them elderly. Bogdan watched the Polish colonel walk through the camp, toward the grimmer one next door, where he faced the prospect of a short life. Yet he had an air of pride and resistance to him. (Luckily, he survived to the end of the war and was liberated from the camp.)

As weeks passed, any sense of time ebbed away. Besides better food, what POWs craved the most was news from the outside world. Isolated, they chewed on any morsel of news they could gather. At most, Bogdan could find an occasional old newspaper that would get him caught up on wartime events. Bogdan sometimes received news by word of mouth. For example, a friend of his was liberated from his camp, and Bogdan learned of it through the prison grapevine.

The ordeal of the war and POW life had left Bogdan physically spent, but worse, his frostbitten feet made walking excruciating. After leading such an active life, Bogdan was now bedridden, and that was tough to accept. He passed hours either on the floor or, whenever he could climb up to it, in the top bunk of a three-tiered bed. He got no exercise, and he could see his muscles atrophying. The POWs had no medical care, so the best Bogdan could do to rehabilitate himself was to lie down and let his body rest. While he loved to read, he had no books, and he ruefully observed that POW camps weren't exactly known for great libraries. The informal English and Italian language lessons were really the only mental exercise he got as a POW.

For his survival in the POW camp, Bogdan felt grateful to his father. Tadeusz had urged the boys to read, keeping a large bookcase in the living room and encouraging them to stay focused on their studies. He also wanted his boys to engage in sports, and following his father's guidance, Bogdan practiced a gamut of exercises—he swam, bicycled, played tennis, skied, ice skated, played soccer, and partook in school excursions. The mental and physical acuity that Bogdan developed helped him to endure the POW ordeal, and Tadeusz was the one who had prodded him and his brothers to nurture these skills.

The human body reacts to stress unpredictably, and Bogdan had one experience that he could never explain. Before the war, he suffered sinus problems that caused pounding, debilitating headaches. The pain began in his forehead, and it would get so excruciating that he had a specific spot in the Bydgoszcz house where he would recline on a wicker sofa and just lie there, miserable and unable to move. Once the war began, the sinus pain disappeared. Bogdan thought his body just subsumed the pain so that it could concentrate on survival. (After the war ended, the sinus headaches returned, but they were never as severe.)

To adapt to the austere circumstances, Bogdan's metabolism slowed down. His hair was a little longer, but it grew more slowly, so he barely ever needed a haircut. While Bogdan had a razor, he seldom shaved because his facial hair grew at a slow pace as well, so he never developed much of a beard.

For all the suffering he experienced in the war, Bogdan witnessed reminders that other prisoners endured worse fates. At one point, the Germans moved their prisoners from one section of the camp to another in order to make more space for the concentration camp area, accommodating more captives. They were evacuating prisoners from the Stutthoff concentration camp near Gdansk so as to keep the prisoners, once again, away from advancing Soviet troops. These prisoners had to walk from that camp all the way to Sandbostel, and many of them died along the route or shortly after their arrival. In a shower area, Bogdan saw bodies in a heap, like a stack of twisted branches. It was unclear how they died, but it was one of the most arresting scenes in a horrible war—senseless, wanton human death, piled up on a shower floor.

IV. The Sweetest Sight of the War

By late April 1945, Bogdan had been in Sandbostel for more than one month. At night, he heard a hopeful sound—distant gunfire rumbling in the West, which meant that the Allies were advancing on the Germans. As the days passed, the thunder of guns grew louder, and soon Bogdan heard tank engines. The British were coming—and with them, freedom.

On April 29, Bogdan was looking out past the perimeter of the camp, peering into a forest whose border began three hundred yards away. Something moved. It was quick and incongruous, a flash that broke up the forest's color scheme of earthy brown and emerging springtime green. It did not belong there.

Or maybe it did. For a moment, Bogdan looked hard at the movement in the forest and tried to discern what was out there. Then he felt a rush of hope and excitement. This was the sweetest sight of the entire war. They were soldiers, clad in military brown, dodging from tree-to-tree. These were liberators—advancing British troops, preparing to free the POWs from their captors.

Crack! Crack! Crack! The Brits began to exchange gunfire with the Germans. One German soldier fell, wounded, and his fellow guards helped him up and led him away. Realizing their impending fate, the Germans decided to flee. Bogdan saw black military vehicles carrying Nazi officers speed off, and the POWs no longer saw soldiers manning the guard towers. Soon, word spread that all Germans had evacuated the premises.

Bogdan's ordeal in German POW camps was over. It had lasted seven months, and when freedom came, it seemed almost anticlimactic, especially because the British had advanced at a glacial pace and worked slowly even after arriving. For what seemed an eternity, Scottish bagpipers walked around the camp, playing tunes. The delay made the prisoners impatient, since they were starving and aching to be released. Inside, Bogdan raged, "Why don't they give us some bread instead of playing this silly music?" The ceremony was agonizing and pointless in equal measure.

Bogdan hated to be querulous, but when he got the chance, he vented against British General Bernard Montgomery, who had been slow in advancing to free them. American General George Patton, who had proved his daring and discipline during the North African and Sicilian campaigns, was much faster. Patton exercised his own form of *blitzkrieg*, moving with such celerity eastward after D-Day that he had to take special precautions to ensure that his vehicles had enough fuel, dedicating a team to furnish gasoline. Bogdan discovered that some of his friends who were in Patton's path were liberated as much as one month ahead of his camp.

Still, they were finally free, and that was the important point. Once they broke into the camp, the British first detained the POWs, delousing them with DDT. They sprayed everyone with a hose, and the DDT puffed out as a dust. Bogdan closed his eyes, held his breath, and they applied the chemical, asking him to turn around and bend over as they applied the material to the skin beneath his clothes. Although DDT was a potent, dangerous agent—and as doctors found later, a carcinogen, which prompted its ban in many countries—Bogdan was grateful for the delousing, because it meant that he would no longer have to worry about lice or fleas. Some POWs who had arms or legs in casts had developed lice under these, and the itching tortured them. Once Bogdan finished the procedure, he dipped his fingers in a special brown liquid, which was the Brits' way of identifying who had undergone the delousing.

Confronting a mass of weathered human scarecrows who lacked papers, the British attempted to establish an identification process. The procedure took time, but the freedom was real: on May 2, Bogdan emerged from processing and was free. He and another former prisoner took a long, limping walk, exploring the countryside and finding their legs again. They ambled along mostly in silence, trying to soak in their newfound liberty, and they saw a British jeep damaged by a road mine and the body of a prisoner killed by an anti-personnel mine. Both sights warned them to be careful where they stepped, and when they saw the body, they cautiously withdrew from that area and went back to the road.

Bogdan's physical wounds were as painful as his emotional ones. He needed new bandages for his thumb, his hamstrings still ached as the flesh healed, and his feet hurt with every step hurt. But he was free to move about now, so he left Sandbostel by a military truck and went to Verden, a small city in northern Germany, where he stayed at a former German military barracks. He found a Polish doctor at a first aid station for recently liberated Polish soldiers, and he performed an operation on one of Bogdan's toes to ameliorate the effects of frostbite. One of the toenails was too damaged to repair, so he applied local anesthetic and then removed it. He changed the dressing on Bogdan's thumb, which was still slow to heal, with a mass of blood coagulating around it. Although in rough shape, Bogdan felt like he was becoming whole again.

In Verden, Bogdan awaited resolution of his situation. There was an outdoor swimming pool, the original purpose of which was to preserve water to use in case of fire, and he swam there. It was a sport he had always enjoyed, but this was the first time he had swum in seven years. Bogdan also took small excursions to the port town of Bremen and to Kassel, riding back from the latter on a locomotive, clinging to the engine and hoping that the noise would do no permanent damage to his hearing and the exhaust no harm to his lungs.

Bogdan's English was limited, although he was learning more every day. One Polish woman who was liberated from the POW camps was being taken by ambulance to a hospital, and the medics asked him to accompany her to act as a translator. Bogdan felt flattered by their request—although he was a poor translator. What helped him to learn English was contact with British troops. He befriended some British soldiers, and he felt grateful to them because they had freed him. They cursed constantly, not to show ill temper but out of habit, using the word "fuck" and its derivatives as an organic part of every sentence. Some of their cursing creations were comical, and in his mind, Bogdan gave these soldiers an apt nickname—he called them "fuckers." But these were the marvelous fuckers who had set him free.

Bogdan also received his first substantial meals in years. The Red Cross distributed parcels among the former POWs, and although the food was cold, canned fare, it tasted good. Bogdan found he still was not getting enough nutrition, so he sold the cigarettes in his Red Cross parcels and used the money to buy dried figs.

Everyone needed clothes; they had been wearing the same threads for months. Perhaps most of all, Bogdan worn-out tennis sneakers provided no walking comfort and almost no protection from the cold. He would finally get new shoes when he moved to Italy, but that would have to wait until after the war in Europe concluded.

That came soon—on May 8, 1945. The previous day, General Alfred Jodl signed surrender documents for Germany at General Dwight D. Eisenhower's headquarters in Reims, France. V-E Day touched off massive celebrations in Western Europe, as crowds gathered at London's Trafalgar Square and the Arc de Triomphe in Paris. But for Poles, V-E Day lacked the meaning it carried for the rest of the Allies. They could not celebrate victory until their country was free. Hopes of a new Poland kindled their desire to return home and build an independent nation. In his mind, Bogdan had visions of the Polish flag, its red and white colors flying freely, and perhaps of his return to Bydgoszcz and the family home there.

That explained what Bogdan did next. He decided to re-register as a soldier and become a member of the Polish forces under British command. The army would provide a means and support system. It would give him sustenance—food and clothes, both of which he had barely enjoyed for years, and he relished the thought of a new fighting uniform.

The army would also give him a way to resist the Russians and continue to fight for Polish independence. The anti–Soviet sentiment among the freed POWS was strong, and they wanted to provide an independent alternative to Russian rule over Poland, which they could not abide. Since the Soviets had invaded their country and left their Uprising to its own fate, Polish soldiers harbored deep animus toward the Kremlin. Bogdan distrusted and feared the Soviets, and he resolved that he would fight them to keep Poland free.

Most of all, the army gave Bogdan a goal. What people called the "entering-Poland-on-a-white-horse syndrome" gripped him, and he entertained the almost idyllic image of returning to his country, freeing it after it had suffered for years, and allowing Poles to resume the lives they had enjoyed before the German and Soviet invasions. He would help to make Poland an independent nation-state again. That was the most worthy objective of all, and it gave Bogdan a sense of purpose. The lure of Polish liberty impelled him forward.

V. Officers School

As part of Bogdan's new goal, he took the bandages off his right hand. Although he was right-handed, the loss of his thumb forced him to get skilled at using his left hand, and people complimented him on how adept he was at redressing the wound using only his left hand. But now, there would be no more bandages. Bogdan wanted to avoid appearing that he was wounded or needed help, because he was determined that nothing would block his reenlistment.

Bogdan tried to join the Polish Armed Division, headquartered in the German border town of Meppen, but that group was at full strength and turned away newcomers. Bogdan decided to go to Italy and join the Polish forces there. He hitched rides through Germany on military trucks, which the Polish forces in Italy had sent for fellow fighters. While in southern Germany en route to Italy, in the town of Murnau am Staffelsee, Bogdan found a Polish priest. Before he celebrated mass, he asked the priest to perform mass for his mother, which salved some of Bogdan's emotional wounds. But he still grieved deeply over her death.

In early August, as he traveled through southern Germany, Bogdan learned that the U.S. exploded an atomic bomb over Hiroshima, Japan. That news made him think that the war would end soon. Still, his patriotic feelings toward the Allies were so strong that he was willing to fight in the Pacific theater if the war dragged on. First, though, he had to help Poland.

Reaching the Italian border, Bogdan made his way southward to the heel of the Italian boot, marveling at the country's beauty as he traveled—the mountains, valleys, and a sky so bright that he described it as "white-blue." In the town of Massafra, located on the arch of Italy's "heel," he formally registered as a member of the Second Polish Corps in Italy, which had helped to liberate Monte Cassino, the ancient Benedictine monastery in the Italian mountains. The Germans had turned it into a redoubt that they fiercely defended, but in May 1944, a multinational Allied force—comprising many Polish soldiers—captured Monte Cassino, after the Germans repulsed an initial offensive. For Polish soldiers, it was one of their finest hours. About four thousand Poles died in that battle, but when the survivors reached the top of the mountain, they raised a Polish flag. Bogdan felt proud now to count veterans of this battle as his colleagues.

In the southern Italian town of Matera, located in the province of Lucania, Bogdan began attending an officers school. One highlight of his stay there was a visit from General Wladyslaw Anders, a leader in the Polish resistance movement. He and several other officers arrived in an armored personnel carrier, and he climbed onto a speaker's platform and gave an emotional speech about Polish independence. As Bogdan listened, he felt a jolt of inspiration surge through him, and Anders' uplifting words confirmed that he had made the right decision—despite its dangers—to continue the fight for Poland.

The officers school had a tank division and two infantry divisions, and Bogdan joined one of the latter. This training, he found, was far more sophisticated than the schooling for the Warsaw Uprising. Bogdan and his Polish classmates were more ready for it, too. They were now combat veterans who had faced the enemy and tasted battle, and they could draw upon that experience. They used regular classrooms, where they sat at desks and studied the theory and tactics of warfare, trawling through military manuals and practicing with actual machine guns and anti-tank weapons. Their exercises included advancing by foot while facing enemy fire, and they took turns inside American-made Sherman tanks. When Bogdan finished at the school, he graduated as a cadet officer with the rank of sergeant, which gave him a sense of achievement and prestige. (Later, when Bogdan was in the U.S., he received a promotion to second lieutenant.) One dividend of the new schooling was that the officers had a notification of their Warsaw *komplety* degrees, which meant that a college could accept them as having the legitimate equivalent of a high school diploma.

In total, the Second Polish Corps numbered a hundred and fifty thousand soldiers, and many of them had participated in the Warsaw underground resistance. Bogdan even recognized one comrade, who had specialized in artillery during the Uprising. Some members of the corps had been released from Soviet labor camps. They seethed with anger against their mistreatment there, and they had a special drive to return to Poland and wrest their country from Soviet control.

After completing officers school, Bogdan and his new cohort of military alumni went by train to Naples, where they boarded a ship. By then, though, Bogdan had contracted jaundice, with his skin turning an eerie yellow, and he had to spend the voyage in the ship's hospital ward. He was uncertain what caused the jaundice, but he believed the military diet might have exacerbated it because the soldiers ate plenty of pickles, whose salt might have put additional strain on the liver. The ship sailed to Glasgow, Scotland and then Bogdan went immediately to Great Britain's Lake District, a beautiful, mountainous area on the west coast, north of Manchester and Liverpool. After debarking, he checked into a hospital. A special diet

Bogdan in his army uniform after the war, prepared to fight again for Poland.

speeded his recovery, and after two weeks the jaundice disappeared completely. He felt healthy, well fed, and well schooled—a sensation that he had not experienced in six years.

As autumn's coolness descended on Europe in 1945, Bogdan was ready to fight again for his country.

VI. *Disillusionment and a New Goal*

By that time, though, Poland's fate was clear. Japan had surrendered, and World War II was over. Across both oceans, combatants had laid down arms, and new national boundaries bespoke a vastly different geopolitical situation. In February 1945, President Franklin Roosevelt, Prime Minister Winston Churchill, and Premier Josef Stalin—the so-called "Big Three"—held their second and final summit conference at Yalta, a city on the Crimean Peninsula bordering the Black Sea. No representatives of Poland had a seat or voice at the conference, and it became clear that Roosevelt and Churchill—the latter despite his reputation as an ardent anti-Communist—wanted to retain Stalin's cooperation even if it meant sacrificing Polish rights to self-government.

Later, American historians defended Roosevelt's Yalta concessions as recognizing the "realities" of the situation at war's end, with the Soviets occupying Poland. The "realities" that Poles faced were seared into Bogdan's consciousness, and he had physical wounds as a reminder as well. Poles made gigantic contributions to and sacrifices for the war effort. Their underground resistance against the Nazis proved to be one of the most effective in wartime Europe, conducting sabotage against German communication and supply lines and killing Nazi soldiers, which crippled Germany's ability to fight a two-front war and hastened the Nazis toward defeat. It was Polish ciphers who built a duplicate of the German Enigma code machine, which marked the first step in Project Ultra's achievement of breaking the code. (One mathematician who made decisive contributions to Ultra was Marian Rejewski, a Bydgoszcz native.) Polish soldiers and sailors fought for the Allies after fleeing their country. Poles fought hard for their country, lost family and friends, property and possessions. They had seen evil at work, invading and destroying their country.

Bogdan and other Poles had battled with the expectation that Roosevelt and Churchill would honor the principle of self-government that they avowed in their 1941 Atlantic Charter. Indeed, Roosevelt speechwriter Robert Sherwood commented about the Atlantic Charter that when a president promulgated a moral principle, he was bound by it. Moreover, the war started in 1939 as a fight to preserve Poland's independence. Ironically, by 1945 the Allied leaders had all but forgotten it.

We had not, Bogdan thought. After struggling so mightily, Poles had earned representation at Yalta. They deserved no less, yet they received much less. "'Betrayal' is a strong word, but the West betrayed us at Yalta," Bogdan believed, "leaving us at Stalin's mercy." Yalta had haunting echoes of the disastrous Munich Conference of 1938, which Czechs viewed as a betrayal of their country, protesting that it was "about the Czechs, without the Czechs." No Czech representatives had a seat at the table when British Prime Minister Neville Chamberlain agreed to let Adolf Hitler seize Czechoslovakia's borderland regions.

The Yalta Conference had no Polish representatives, and none of the Big Three discussed the supreme sacrifices that Poles made during the occupation and Uprising. In the end, what mattered most to Roosevelt and Churchill was continued Soviet help to crush Germany, Soviet cooperation in defeating Japan, and Soviet participation in the new United Nations, the last constituting FDR's supreme goal, which he saw as his enduring legacy.

They were willing to compromise on—in fact, sacrifice—Polish independence to secure their objectives. They adjusted national borders in such a way that Poland's territory was reduced by almost one third. They recognized Stalin's phony puppet government in Lublin, which Poles despised. In taking these measures, the Big Three overlooked a cardinal rule of diplomatic negotiations, that no nation's liberty should ever be thrown down as a bargaining chip.

As historian Thomas Fleming wrote in his critically acclaimed book, *The New Dealers' War: FDR and the War Within World War II*, Roosevelt tried too hard to win Stalin's favor, even disparaging the British as a way to triangulate better with the Soviet leader. But by bending himself too far in Stalin's direction, FDR weakened his position, and "the Russians negotiated the British and Americans down to something very close to zero," Fleming observed. U.S. Secretary of State Edward Stettinius "was dismayed by such flabby negotiating" that he witnessed Roosevelt and Churchill engage in, Fleming wrote.

The president was out of his depth—a "dying president" at the time of Yalta, as historian Robert Ferrell characterized him; indeed, Roosevelt died just two months after Yalta, on April 12. On January 20, 1945, when he was sworn in for an unprecedented fourth term, he gave the second-shortest inaugural address in history, delivering it from the White House's South Portico rather than going to the Capitol. He was too feeble to participate in the reception that followed.

Weeks later, Roosevelt made the grueling trip to Yalta. Pictures of him at Yalta showed a tired, vacant gaze on his face, which marked a contrast with his more animated appearance at the Teheran Conference a year and a half earlier. By early 1945, FDR's body was failing, a state that had concomitant mental degradation. The president had trouble following the trend of conversations, and when aides gave him thick briefing books to study before the conference, he "barely looked at a single page," as Fleming described it. Roosevelt was in no condition to stand up to Stalin at Yalta, Poles regretted, and the results were disastrous for Poland, Eastern Europe and, in fact, the world.

Another calamitous letdown for Poles was that the Allies gave only lukewarm support to the Polish government-in-exile, led by General Wladyslaw Sikorski in London, which Poles recognized as legitimate. This backing was so tepid that Bogdan later remembered that many Poles believed that Sikorski's death during a 1943 plane crash was no accident. His B-24 Liberator bomber, a plane that was a mainstay of America's bombing fleet, was taking off from Gibraltar to fly to England, Bogdan learned, and when it was airborne, it suddenly dove into the water. Later, Poles heard that one cable was blocked in such a way that its vertical altitude was impossible to maintain. A rumor floated around Poland that Sikorski had become a nuisance to the Allies because he demanded an investigation into the Soviet massacre of Polish officers at Katyn, an incident that nettled the alliance.

These thoughts might have been hard to understand for Americans and Brits, because the Soviets were their allies during the war. They were not Polish allies. The brittle triangular alliance with the U.S.S.R. was a source of angst for Polish patriots because of Soviet treachery, especially their invasion of Poland. Poles felt that the alliance, over the long term, would degrade and redound to the West's disadvantage. They had already felt its deleterious effects, because Stalin clutched the eastern half of their country in his fist. Now he had all of it.

Just as World War II began in Bogdan's country, in a real sense, the Cold War began there, too. In Poland, Stalin's cruel postwar ambitions became stark, bringing him into almost immediate conflict with his allies. Stalin's policy was to eliminate Polish independence and autonomy, a plan that he had already telegraphed by failing to support the Uprising.

Sadly, Bogdan and his fellow officers had to face these "realities." By the fall of 1945, they knew that fighting for their country would be hopeless, and the Polish Second Corps demobilized. In essence, they became a resettlement corps, knowing that their priority now was to find a country that they could call home.

"My disappointment was deep and extreme," Bogdan recalled. His new goal was gone, and feelings of disillusionment welled up inside of him. What deepened these psychic wounds was the sense that the Allies abandoned his country. In Britain, Bogdan detected traces of condescension, even animus, toward Poland. Later, in 1946, British Prime Minister Clement Atlee's Labour government organized a London parade that celebrated the Allied victory, honoring veterans from various countries. It failed to ask any Poles to march. Bogdan remembered a Polish airman who had participated in the 1940 Battle of Britain—with Polish pilots contributing mightily to the victory over Germany—standing on the sidelines as he watched the parade. Tears streamed down his face.

Bogdan suspected that the Soviet influence—and the nature of the wartime alliance—accounted for these anti–Polish sentiments, as unwelcome as they were for him to witness. After France surrendered in June of 1940, Brits hoped that Germany and the Soviet Union would break their Non-Aggression Pact and get ensnared in bloody conflict, which would give Britain a greater chance to survive. The German invasion of the Soviet Union answered British prayers. Thereafter, Britain depended on the Soviets to fight the Nazis and thus take pressure off the Allies to the West. As it turned out, two thirds of the fighting in World War II took place on that eastern front, and the Russians absorbed massive casualties. Soviet blood helped the British, so the latter did what they could to support Russia. Since the Soviets had an adversarial relationship with Poles and created further animosity by invading Poland, Bogdan reflected, the British must have felt some obligation to respect Russian feelings.

The anti–Polish sentiment that Bogdan sensed in Britain disillusioned him so much that he flirted with the idea of leaving the country and returning to Poland. Some colleagues did go back. Others adopted the label of "displaced persons," which became common in the years immediately after the war. The term referred to Europeans—especially those in the eastern and central parts of the continent, like Poland—who had lost their homes. Domiciles were destroyed, or if they still stood, residents found the thought of living under Soviet rule so distasteful that they refused to return.

Bogdan in London, 1946. Although he had to abandon plans to fight for Poland's postwar freedom, Bogdan was still fiercely proud of his country and its military, donning his uniform for this photograph.

Bogdan never considered himself a displaced person. He was a soldier. For the past year and a half, it had been his full-time occupation and the core of his existence. But now, he had to find a new role in life. His thoughts gravitated toward education. Among many things, war had destroyed Polish institutions of learning. It was six years since Bogdan had been inside a real classroom. His parents had always emphasized the importance of schooling, and his father stood as a living embodiment of its value. Tadeusz's drive to study, learn, and improve had led him to the U.S., and the bachelor's degree he earned there created many opportunities, opening doors for him in business and government. Although Aniela was gone and Bogdan's contact with his father was limited, he knew that his parents would want him to continue studying, and Bogdan felt a yearning inside him.

He wanted to go back to school.

—10—

The Tough Transition

I. An Inversion of Feelings

After Japan surrendered and the war concluded, Seiko never went back to Asari. Although the town was just twenty minutes away from her home, and the train stopped there whenever she traveled south from Otaru, she had no reason to return. She heard that the townspeople dismantled the factory shortly after Japan surrendered. It was a miserable looking building to begin with, but now it reminded everyone of the war. They could do little else but raze it.

Never again did Seiko work in a factory, not in the war's immediate aftermath nor in her later career. When the war ended, radio broadcasts and word-of-mouth informed students that school would resume immediately. Seiko was supposed to be in tenth grade now, and she was eager to go back to the classroom.

The war's abrupt end spared her older brother. On August 16, Suguru was scheduled to fly a kamikaze mission. While the atomic bombs created unimaginable death and destruction, ironically, they saved Suguru, and he returned safely to Otaru just two days after the emperor's radio address. Family and friends wanted to hear about what military life was like, but Suguru had other ideas. For the rest of his life, he remained silent about his kamikaze training, never discussing what the experience entailed. That was not unusual for Japanese veterans; their survival brought shame to them, for they had failed to sacrifice their lives for their country. Others felt embarrassed that they represented Japan's wartime fanaticism, which had wrought so much devastation. One of the only mementos of Suguru's military service was a silk parachute that he brought back with him, which he was supposed to use in case his plane was hit by enemy strafing before he could strike his target.

Historians will debate for eternity whether dropping the atomic bombs was proper. They were horrific weapons. They brought death and devastation. But the war's end saved Suguru's life and also spared the

10. The Tough Transition

Japanese people—and American soldiers—more suffering. As Yasuko's death attested, disease stalked the land, and scourges would have continued to claim lives at frightful rates. The war's sudden conclusion eased the suffering and helped the Japanese to resume normal conditions of public health and medical care.

In Otaru, people talked little about the atomic bombs. Partly, they felt helpless to aid the victims in Hiroshima and Nagasaki, and discussing the destruction would have worsened their feelings of guilt and powerlessness. Otaru residents also had their own survival to contend with every day, and that struggle dominated their thoughts and conversations. Another factor that constrained them from discussing the bomb was the U.S. Occupation of Japan. If they talked about the bomb in a critical way, that would telegraph resistance to the Occupation or ill will toward Americans, and they wanted to avoid that. Instead, they wished to show the Occupation forces how cooperative they could be.

On Hokkaido, people were relatively lucky because they were spared from bombings and attacks. In this respect, being something of a remote, rustic outpost—which sometimes brought scorn or bewilderment from the more populated islands—worked to Hokkaido's favor. On Kyushu, Shikoku, and especially Honshu, returning veterans fared much worse when they came back to pick up the shattered shards of their lives. Many soldiers expected to walk back into their homes in Tokyo and other Honshu cities but found them gone—destroyed by the Allied firebombing campaigns. They were like Confederate war veterans after the U.S. Civil War who repaired to their homes in Georgia or South Carolina only to find them obliterated by the Union's campaign of "total war," which destroyed the South's infrastructure and will to fight.

Throughout Japan, many soldiers never returned at all. The country suffered more than two million combat deaths during the war. Soldiers committed suicide, too, because to surrender and be taken as a prisoner of war was not only dishonorable—it was punishable by death. Rather than risk opprobrium and execution, soldiers took their own lives. The senseless policy of making POW status illegal only compounded Japan's national tragedy of war.

Those veterans who returned to Hokkaido found their homes intact, but they still suffered from poverty, depression, and various forms of what today would be diagnosed as post-traumatic stress disorder, the psychological trauma that afflicts war veterans. Yet Otaru residents were kind, and though veterans might have felt that they had failed in their wartime mission, townspeople embraced them, regarding them with honor and sympathy. Typically, citizens wished that they could do more to help veterans, but most people had little to offer them—not even essentials like money, food, shelter, or clothing. Whereas America's GI Bill of 1944 offered U.S. veterans college educations, Japan had no equivalent legislation, even though the country placed a high premium on education. Japan had no tradition of social welfare or governmental assistance. In Otaru, war veterans sat around the train station, begging for spare change or food. To make matters worse, once the U.S. Occupation forces arrived in Japan, they discouraged citizens from giving alms to such veterans.

The Kawakami family had a number of friends who were returning veterans, and among them, two themes emerged: financial hardship and disillusionment with the government. One friend who was an army captain came home destitute. His military salary was gone, and he was unable to support his family. Another of Hiroshi's colleagues came back from the war and had little means to sustain himself. He decided to sell books on the street. He took a door from his home, laid it out over two boxes, and displayed his books for sale daily. But Otaru weather limited the months he could do this street vending, and people had little money to spend on books. Seiko's father said that his friend, maundering through subsistence living, was bitterly disappointed with the government—for driving the country to war, fumbling toward a conclusion, failing to help veterans, and ruining lives.

Over the years, Seiko encountered tough survivors, too. Decades after the war, she was living in Ithaca, New York, and she met a woman who was a small child in Hiroshima when the atomic bomb dropped. She persevered, got married, started a family—and suffered no cancer, radiation poisoning, or other ill effects traceable to the bomb. When she looked back at her good fortune, she recalled that she had eaten plenty of figs while growing up, and she believed that the fruit must have powerful anti-cancer properties. She added that radiation sickness carried an enormous social stigma. People who survived the atom bombs tried to hide their experience, refusing to disclose that they were at Hiroshima or Nagasaki at the time because of the widespread belief that radiation disease was contagious. On top of the physical suffering it inflicted, radiation sickness could turn people into pariahs.

For all young people, school once again became the center of life. Lessons resumed with an air of normality, although on the first day back in the classroom, students still lacked food and proper clothes, so Seiko's homeroom teacher told the class to go home and rest for a few days. Once everyone returned to a rhythm of classes, the teachers focused on academic subjects, avoiding discussion of the war. World War II became the classic elephant in the room. The teachers were unsure of what to say, Seiko conjectured, but they also were reluctant to blame the government so quickly after years of unquestioning loyalty. They were public officials,

10. The Tough Transition

too, and they wanted to show respect for their employer and for the soldiers who had sacrificed so much.

Feelings toward the Americans began to change after Japan's surrender, and ironically, school helped this process. Seiko's years in public school were tumultuous, beset with wartime interruptions. In looking back on her education in Japan, Seiko realized that her schooling comprised three distinct phases. Prior to the war against the Allies, school inculcated a cautious respect for the U.S., and teachers tended to be non-judgmental. During the war, the classroom became more active in molding young people's thoughts about Americans, always in a caustic cast. Now, a third phase of Seiko's schooling began, where the classroom became a crucible to forge different ideas about Americans. Teachers began giving English language lessons, which had been verboten for the past three years. Students learned that Japan would be under a U.S. Occupation. They would not die after defeat, and they would be spared from a Russian invasion. They would have to accept American directives, but everyone would be safe. Their former enemies now served as protectors.

Students started hearing a new word, too. Their homeroom teacher told them that the Occupation forces would implement *minshushugi*—"democracy." This word and concept now entered the Japanese lexicon, and everyone in Otaru and elsewhere seemed to use it. Seiko recalled, "We went from a mentality of 'fight, fight, fight' to 'democracy, democracy, democracy,' and the switch came suddenly." Seiko's parents even joked about how commonplace the term *minshushugi* became. But the change also showed how willingly the Japanese embraced the Americans and the ideas and mores they tried to transplant to the land of the rising sun.

Within weeks after Japan's surrender, two hundred thousand U.S. Occupation troops arrived in the country. Many American GIs were stationed in Hokkaido, and some of them came to the island by first debarking in Otaru. The city's only college, a school of economics and commerce, functioned as their headquarters, where soldiers stayed in dormitories and offices. They soon left, moving mostly to Sapporo, Hokkaido's capital. (A generation later, Sapporo garnered world attention when it hosted the 1972 Winter Olympics, symbolizing Japan's resurgence as a world economic power.)

The reversal of feelings that took hold in Japan, Seiko observed, was quick and nearly universal. For years, as the Japanese fought against the Allied enemies, they trusted the government and devoted their lives to the war effort. Now that trust tasted like ashes, and they felt deep disillusionment with the government that had led them down the road to devastation and defeat. In experiencing defeat, the Japanese people as a whole—not just veterans—lost faith in their government. Leaders proved that they could not protect Japanese citizens. Worse, they had ignored the public weal and created a national calamity. People still believed in their religion and other verities, including the benign nature of the emperor. But the war shattered the people's belief in their system of government, because everything that they had fought for had collapsed.

Other incidents battered confidence in Japan's government. As the Allies rounded up more leaders and put them on trial in Tokyo, eventually executing Hideki Tojo and others, the Japanese realized how badly officials had misguided them. Seiko and other Otaru residents heard stories, too. They still had to scrimp and save, yet they learned that Japanese soldiers, in abandoning their outposts, dumped sugar and other food into the ocean to prevent Australians and Americans from getting them. Seiko thought, what on earth? While we sacrificed, our soldiers could so easily throw away precious food? Japanese citizens could barely stomach hearing about such waste. Seiko read that Fleet Admiral Isoroku Yamamoto, whom the government had lionized as a great hero—and martyr, too, after American fighters shot down his plane in April 1943—was living a lifestyle marbled with fat, dining on scrumptious Western food that included French delicacies, and enjoying the company of a mistress. Then they learned that Japanese authorities treated the American occupiers with lavish food. They began to wonder how severe, truly, the shortages were during the war. Instead of feeding us the nourishment we needed, Seiko and others asked, had our leaders fed us tales while they lived well?

The Soviet Union's behavior accelerated the change in Japan's world view. During the war, Japan's traditional adversary, Russia, had seemed the least objectionable opponent among the Axis Powers. In April 1941, Japan signed a non-aggression pact with that country, so that it fought against the U.S. and Britain but not against the Soviet Union. But the Soviet Union ended up as Japan's true enemy. It denounced the pact in April 1945 and declared war against Japan four months later. In late August and early September, with Japan still reeling after the atomic bomb drops, Russia invaded and captured what Japan called its "Northern Territories," four islands just north of Hokkaido: Etorofu, Habomai, Kunashiri, and Shitokan. These islands were rich in fishing resources, and one of Habomai's many small islets sat just two miles from Hokkaido. The Soviets forced the islands' 17,000 Japanese residents to leave, and Japan protested the Russian takeover of its territory. Because of the Soviet action, Japan refused to sign a peace treaty with the Soviet Union after the war, and to this day, the issue remains unresolved between Japan and Russia.

In the new Cold War that polarized the world, it became easy for the Japanese to pick sides. Their wartime enmity toward the enemy turned into respect, and they now trusted the Americans to guide them toward reconstruction and a peaceful future. This inversion of feelings marked the start of a great transformation in Japan that would continue throughout the Cold War and into the twenty-first century.

II. The God Is Human

General Douglas MacArthur knew little about Japan before he lived there, but from his headquarters in Tokyo, he now supervised the U.S. Occupation. Under his leadership, the U.S. implemented reforms to democratize Japan, making its government more responsive to popular will and endowing the citizenry with more rights. Japan drafted a new constitution, and a key component was Article 9, which renounced war and made the country's military "self-defense forces" so that Japan would remain a nation committed to peace, never again venturing down the road to imperialism and war.

A dramatic postwar reform involved Emperor Hirohito. The Japanese heard all kinds of rumors about what would happen to him, ranging from severe punishment, even execution, to lenient treatment, and they were unsure what to believe. The U.S. made the wise choice to spare Hirohito from prosecution as a war criminal, instead allowing him to retain the throne as a constitutional monarch, similar to the British royal family's ceremonial role in the United Kingdom. That move alone helped to make Japan's transition to the postwar world smoother. Had the emperor been arrested or tried—let alone executed—the Japanese people would have fought that decision and perhaps revolted against the Occupation forces, because their affection for and loyalty to him were still profound.

Three steps helped to destroy Hirohito's divine image and bring him down to earth. The first was when the Japanese people heard his quirky, halting voice announcing the country's surrender. The second came on September 27, 1945. On that day, Hirohito visited MacArthur at his Tokyo residence. That in itself disappointed the Japanese—Hirohito paid a visit to MacArthur, and not the other way around, showing that the emperor deferred to the general. Initially, Hirohito was nervous about the meeting—he even worried that he would be arrested—but he grew more comfortable with the general as they spent more time talking.

A photo of their meeting showed MacArthur looking casual, with his shirt collar unbuttoned, while the emperor looked stiff and formal in a business suit. The six-foot-tall MacArthur towered over the five-foot five-inch Hirohito. The general looked older (at sixty-five, he was twenty-one years Hirohito's senior) and more authoritative and powerful. The contrast was an insult to the quondam god; Japanese authorities wanted to suppress the picture. But the Americans insisted that it be disseminated to the media, who printed it, breaking another taboo, because taking photos of the emperor had been forbidden.

This image marked a second turning point in the Japanese people's relationship with Hirohito. Whereas the emperor was supposed to be a sun god, MacArthur made him look small. Hirohito could just as well have been kneeling or bowing before MacArthur. The blow to Japanese dignity was monumental. "We felt ashamed," Seiko recalled, "almost like the American authorities had slapped us across the face." Yet the photographic evidence of Hirohito's short stature was there to see, and the Japanese had to accept it.

Then came the third step. New Year's Day is the most important holiday in the Japanese calendar, and on January 1, 1946—the first New Year's after the war ended—Emperor Hirohito issued an Imperial Rescript in which he renounced his divinity, calling it a "false conception" rooted in myth. He denied that the Japanese people were superior to other races and destined to rule the world. This was Hirohito's first message since he announced Japan's surrender, and this one destroyed the edifice of Japanese superiority that had been the cornerstone of the entire war. For Hirohito himself, the address also removed the wall that separated him from the people. He declared himself human, and that brought him close to the citizenry.

The U.S. media described the Japanese people as being stunned by the imperial rescript. The *New York Times*, for example, called it a "shattering" event and compared it to Commodore Matthew Perry's arrival in 1853, which opened up Japan to the Western world. Seiko and her family had a more subdued reaction; they wondered why the declaration was even necessary. After all, the Occupation forces had already reduced Hirohito to human status. They still respected him, and their affection for him was unchanged.

What had changed was the nature of the Japanese people's relationship with their emperor. Now, they saw him through a different lens. "We still felt a tug of loyalty to him," Seiko recalled, "but it was imbued with sympathy for him." Japanese citizens felt that the emperor had tried to save the country, and he had fought government militarists. The irony was that although Hirohito was the emperor and supreme ruler, he had no real power. In essence, he rubber-stamped decisions that the government made, endowing them with great legitimacy. Thus, the Japanese tried to avoid blaming him for the calamity of war, and instead, they wanted to cooperate with him to rebuild Japan.

Seiko saw Hirohito in person when he and his wife took a goodwill tour during the Occupation and visited Otaru. They were inside an odd-colored Rolls-Royce, a luxury car that bespoke of their continuing privilege at a time when the country could barely make civilian automobiles (Seiko saw some Japanese cars that were so crude they burned wood or coal as fuel). He was wearing glasses and a business suit, no longer adorned in imperial robes, making him look more like a politician than an emperor. He doffed his hat; he seemed cloth-tongued, shy, and awkward. He was not a sun god anymore but a human.

In a sense, this diffident, bespectacled man in mufti was a metaphor for the new Japan, a country willing to divorce itself from old traditions and embrace the modern world. The emperor's transformation reinforced the reality that Japan had lost the war, as hard as it was for citizens to believe when they heard him announce it in that unforgettable radio broadcast. Now, they could see the reality of it in Hirohito himself—not a god, but an ordinary man.

III. Curious about an Erstwhile Enemy

The Occupation did allow the Japanese to experience improvements in living standards. Although scarcity still crimped their lives, and they had no new clothes for years after the war ended, they did notice an almost immediate change in food supplies. They received salt, which they barely encountered during the war, and Seiko and her family used it for cooking and even for melting snow during winter. To the Kawakamis' delight, cocoa was available again, and they resumed their routine of drinking hot chocolate during winter—although milk was still expensive. Otaru residents got canned food, especially American pork and beans. This combination was new to Japan, and some people felt insulted by it because they thought it was pig feed from U.S. farms. Some Japanese even contemptuously threw the cans away. (A decade later, though, when Seiko came to the U.S., she was amazed to find canned pork and beans in grocery stores. She wrote to family and friends in Japan to report, "Remember those cans of pork and beans that we scoffed at? Well, Americans actually eat this stuff!")

Other American foods inspired awe. While working for an Occupation interpreter, Suguru obtained chewing gum, which he brought home and gave to the rest of the family. It had been years since Seiko tasted gum. On another occasion, a young Japanese man who worked as a carpenter and factotum for the Americans came to the Kawakami house to do repairs. He offered a Hershey chocolate bar that he had gotten from American GIs, gushing about how delicious it was. It was so good, he raved, that he could be hit on the head and feel nothing at all—as long as he was munching on that chocolate. Seiko laughed at his enthusiasm, and while he offered the chocolate as a gift, her parents insisted on paying him because they knew that candy bar was precious.

As the young handyman could attest, relations between American soldiers and Japanese civilians were congenial, which stood as a metaphor for the amity that bonded the two countries during the postwar years. Romances sometimes formed between U.S. GIs and Japanese women; in fact, one of Seiko's high school friends, Akio Sueoka, married an American serviceman, and she emigrated to the U.S., where they lived in Buffalo, New York. Harsh wartime feelings faded into a more durable tapestry of cooperation and comity.

As the wartime wounds healed, the Kawakami family gathered the broken pieces of lives and resumed a routine. Seiko's parents went back to teaching, although her father had to give up his favorite subject, chemistry, and instead began teaching social studies. It was a dramatic change for him, but it reflected the sweeping nature of educational reforms that the U.S. Occupation introduced to Japan.

Visits to the family cemetery plot now included homages to Yasuko, whose cremated remains rested there. The Japanese had a tradition of going to temple to console the spirits of family ancestors, and the Kawakamis went at least twice a year, once during the summer observance of *Obon*, which celebrates ancestors, and again during winter. They also put up Yasuko's photo in their *jinja*, a beautiful picture in which she, as a high school senior, was dressed in her *seerafuku*, a photo that captured her serene and gentle qualities. It was the last photo ever taken of Yasuko.

After returning from the navy, Suguru began to work in Otaru, while Shizuko and Kazutoshi continued their schooling. In March of 1946, Seiko graduated from high school, but opted for a year of additional classes starting in April to make up for deficiencies in her studies that the war had caused. Many students pursued this extra year, which consisted of general education classes. Plus, the building was always warm during winter, and for students whose houses were often cold, school exuded a welcoming feeling.

In 1947, the Kawakami family decided to upgrade their living quarters. Their need for a larger house had been obvious, but the war froze forward progress in people's lives, and it forestalled the Kawakamis' attempts to seek a better home. Now, they began looking for a place that they could afford. When Seiko's parents found a decent, four-bedroom home in Otaru, Hiroshi secured a personal loan from a wealthy doctor whom he knew, which enabled them to move to the new house that year. Seiko shared a room with Shizuko and Kazutoshi, while Suguru had his own room, in recognition of his status as the eldest son. Importantly, they hired

10. The Tough Transition

Seiko during an Otaru winter, near her family's home, after the war. Winter was a long and brutal season in Otaru, with freezing temperatures and heavy snow.

a plumber to install running water in the house, an amenity that made the house seem like paradise.

In the spring of 1947, Seiko was reading *Hokkaido Shinbun*, a newspaper published in Sapporo that covered news for the entire island, perusing it carefully from top to bottom and side to side (a thoroughness that was necessary because of Japanese script, which runs top to bottom, in contrast to that of Germanic and Romance languages). A small advertisement caught her eye. A two-year college for teacher training was opening at the Otaru School of Economics and Commerce, and it invited students to apply. The institution had forty-five slots in its inaugural class for future teachers, and a competitive exam would determine admission.

Seiko set her sights on this goal and studied day and night, skimping on sleep. To her delight, she was accepted, becoming just one of four females in the freshman class. Her family, though, could scarcely afford the tuition, so the institution waived these fees under an agreement that she would teach English language at an Otaru junior high school after graduating. The junior high school was also a new venture, an innovation that the Occupation created to model the Japanese education system after America's, creating a bridge between elementary and high schools and making public education follow a 6-3-3 model: six years of elementary school, three of junior high, followed by three years of high school.

That fall, Seiko enrolled at the Otaru School of Economics and Commerce, studying especially English language courses. She read classic works of American literature like Washington Irving's *Rip Van Winkle* and Nathaniel Hawthorne's *Twice-Told Tales*, and she took history classes. The curriculum was intensive and classes took place year-round, even during the summer months, so that after two-and-a-half years, Seiko earned the equivalent of a bachelor's degree in teaching. In March 1950, she graduated and was ready to enter the working world.

IV. An Amazing Exchange of Letters

In 1950, endowed with a new degree, Seiko began teaching at *Osahi ga Oka* junior high school in Otaru. Almost immediately, she sensed that this profession was her calling. Perhaps because teaching was in her bloodlines, she felt comfortable in front of the classroom, instructing and mentoring students. She had a natural facility for remembering students' names, too, so much so that her colleagues jokingly called her *koseki na kari* (registry agent) because of her mental catalogue of all students. "Some people labor at work just to earn a paycheck," Seiko reflected, "but I was lucky enough to find a job where I derived immense gratification from the moment I started."

In the teaching profession, Seiko also observed the ferment of change. At one meeting, a female colleague spoke up to say that she wanted to lobby the government to provide better treatment for teachers. In a patriarchal society like Japan, her audacity initially shocked colleagues, especially men and older teachers. But she represented the new, postwar generation who were willing to upset the norms. What Seiko's colleague did might have been a transgression against an old paradigm, but it also symbolized that Japan was undergoing rapid, fundamental transformations.

Seiko felt she was part of it. During the U.S. Occupation, Japanese women had a humorous view, laced with bitterness, of the hierarchies in society. At the top, they believed, stood American women. They watched enviously as the wives of American servicemen sunbathed during the summer while their husbands were stationed in occupied Japan. They

10. The Tough Transition

Seiko and her students in Otaru. Once the war concluded, Seiko earned her college degree and became a teacher of English in her hometown.

seemed to be living in clover, and the Japanese were obligated to cater to their needs. The Japanese often observed that American women's husbands dutifully took orders from them, and it was U.S. men who now informed Japanese companies on how to restructure and run their firms after the war. In turn, Japanese businessmen then went home and instructed their wives on what to do, and they accepted their husbands' directives and worked hard at fulfilling them. In other words, Japanese women joked that American women sat perched at the top of the world, while Japanese women groveled at the bottom.

Seiko wanted no part of this inequity, and teaching gave her more incentive to shake things up. She wished to stand with confidence in front of her students; she had no desire to languish on the lowest rung of the world's order. In Japan, students revered their instructors (calling them "sensei," an honorific term meaning "teacher"), and Seiko aspired to be worthy of that title.

But she felt she was not. Seiko thought her English was terribly inadequate, yet she had to instruct students, professing to be skilled at the language while truthfully her knowledge was not advanced. Japanese teachers had never received graduate degrees or lived in the U.S., Britain, or any other English-speaking country. In school, the English language exercises consisted of simply writing out English sentences into Japanese, with no instruction on pronunciation or the niceties of the English language. Thus, students knew English vocabulary and grammar, but their pronunciation was imprecise, which made their spoken English hard to understand.

Now that Seiko was teaching English, she resolved to improve her knowledge of it to become a better mentor, and she looked for ways to do so. She tried to listen to U.S. Occupation forces' radio broadcasts, turning the volume up loud so that she could hear and understand the English, although her parents often reproached her efforts by saying, "*Urusai!*" ("loud"). Loud or not, those broadcasts were hard for Seiko to decipher, and the difficulty she experienced underscored the need to immerse herself in an English-speaking environment. Yet she found these opportunities to improve were limited.

The best way to achieve fluency in English, Seiko realized, would be to go to the U.S. to study. Although the country had been Japan's recent adversary, Occupation forces were friendly and charitable. That behavior stamped a new impression of Americans on the Japanese people, and the wartime tensions quickly waned. Moreover, U.S. soldiers told the Japanese that America was an advanced country, in every way. They stressed that Japan should learn from the U.S., and Seiko noticed that the Japanese government started to invite Americans, including Joseph Dodge, a bank CEO from Michigan, plus university professors, to come to Japan to help the nation model itself after the U.S. and modernize.

In 1952 the American Occupation of Japan ended, but the democratic reforms had an indelible impact on the country. On a personal level, they inspired two powerful emotions in Seiko. One was continuing disillusionment with the Japanese government. The very act of accepting U.S. Occupation reforms was a concession that Japan was not so great as the government had said it was and needed guidance from another country.

The second emotion was that the U.S. was benign, a far cry from what Seiko had heard during the war. This exposure to America washed away any reservations Seiko and her peers had about the country. They could not help but admire America's industrial efficiency, which had seemed ruthless during the war but awe-inspiring afterward. The Americans had carried out the war like a business, crushing the Axis powers—across two oceans—under the sheer weight of superior production numbers, which illustrated the dynamism of their economic and political system. Seiko grew curious about the U.S., and she wanted to visit, especially to improve her English speaking skills. If she saw an opportunity to get to the U.S., she would lunge at it.

A magazine showed her the way. Seiko read an article in a Japanese women's journal, *Fujinotomo* ("Friends of Females"), featuring the diary of a Japanese woman who had traveled in the U.S. One of her stories grabbed Seiko's attention. The author described a private liberal arts college that had been founded in 1855 in Berea, Kentucky, where its one thousand students paid for their tuition, room, and board by working. "This," Seiko thought, "could be my ticket to the U.S.; it may enable me to afford study in America." Once again, she was grateful for her parents' passion for reading and their cosmopolitan outlook, because her mother's subscription to *Fujinotomo* opened a window to the world and allowed her to learn about this institution.

Seiko wrote to Berea College, explaining that she desired help to improve her English and was interested in studying at their institution. The college replied, detailing their work-study program and including a guidebook. It was an amazing exchange of letters, from Otaru, Japan, to Berea, Kentucky, and it encouraged Seiko to pursue this chance. She asked her junior high school's administration to help her to apply to the college, with the idea that she could study English there, improve her knowledge of the language, and return to Japan as a better instructor. The school agreed. Although Seiko was taking a huge gamble, her parents expressed no opposition to her plan, and actually supported it. As teachers themselves, they wanted her to acquire more knowledge to advance her classroom skills, and they saw the value of studying in the U.S.

So Seiko applied to Berea College, and in the spring of 1953, she received an acceptance letter in the mail. She was thrilled, but she had no reason to celebrate yet because of contingencies that she needed to solve. While she could earn tuition at Berea by working, she needed to find a way to pay for transportation costs. The Japanese government could provide no help, since the war had driven it to financial ruin and additionally, it discouraged young people from going abroad and diminishing the country's intellectual resources. Securing funding became a complicated process, involving considerable scrimping and saving, obtaining generous assistance from friends, and jumping over hurdles. It also involved persistence, because the process took two full years. Finally, Seiko mustered the financial wherewithal, and she informed Berea College that she was ready to enroll for the fall 1955 semester.

She was determined to pursue her studies in a new country.

—11—

New Goals, New Country

I. A Success and a Disaster

Although the war was over, Poland remained out-of-reach for Bogdan, and his family had yet to recover from the conflict's devastation. Besides being robbed of Aniela, the family was destitute, and they had no way to reclaim their home in Bydgoszcz. As if cast adrift, Bogdan had to find a new home and a way to make a living.

Bogdan's wounds reminded him of the war's physical toll. He was still adjusting to missing the thumb on his dominant hand, and the stump continued to throb. Frostbite had eaten away at his feet, making the skin tender, and using any kind of footwear was painful. The nails on his toes had hardened into small, tough stones that lay riveted in the nailbeds. These nails ceased to grow, and Bogdan seldom again had to clip them.

The war created another transformation that Bogdan had not anticipated: it broke his faith in Catholicism. His family had been devout believers, and church weaved itself seamlessly into their lives, so that from the time Bogdan was a small boy he never questioned its role. War changed that. Its cruelty made Bogdan doubt that any cosmic or divine justice guided the world. Satanic figures like Hitler and Stalin shattered his faith in moral righteousness. So many innocent people died, so wantonly and senselessly—including his mother—that he questioned why divine power had failed to help them. Bogdan stopped going to church and no longer believed; for all practical purposes, he became agnostic on matters of religion, and he remained that way for the rest of his life.

For all its destruction, war hammered home instructive lessons. It stirred up feelings of patriotism that he never realized welled within him. Paradoxically, defeat had made him even more proud of his country, because the war taught all Poles to meet hardship head-on, even when victory slipped from their grip. The horrible conditions that everyone faced made them fight for their nation rather than back down. War steeled Bogdan to adversity and gave him motivation to survive under horrendous

11. New Goals, New Country

circumstances. Amidst the German occupation, Bogdan carried on with his activities and goals, especially his education, despite the worst setbacks. Bogdan's motto became to persevere and overcome any obstacles.

Biology and evolution teach that an organism will survive only if it learns to adapt to new circumstances, and war taught Bogdan this lesson. From the moment that Germany invaded, conditions changed constantly, often deteriorating drastically, and hopeful plans—including the Uprising—lay in ruins. Bogdan's new goal of returning to secure his country's freedom was also destroyed. For four years, he had focused on only that objective, and now that it appeared irretrievable, he had to set new goals.

Bogdan later reflected that he never suffered from any kind of post-traumatic stress disorder. He thought he avoided it because he had too many urgent choices to make, keeping his brain active and dynamic, pressing him to make decisions quickly and concentrate on the next step, whether tiny or titanic. The anger he felt toward the Germans and then the Soviets, who both had taken his country and savaged its citizens and landscape, also left little room for any kind of trauma. Although bitter and disillusioned, he had to direct these energies as motivation.

Bogdan needed to decide on his future, and the prospects were unpleasant. He could return to Poland, acceding to its new status, accepting Soviet rule and a new, unfamiliar homeland. Besides being stripped of its independence, Poland had changed geographically, making it less attractive to natives like Bogdan. The eastern section of the country that the Soviets had invaded in September 1939 had been overrun by the Germans when they invaded the Soviet Union. Then, once the war was over, the Baltic states of Estonia, Latvia, and Lithuania absorbed that section of Poland. The new country of Poland was shifted westward, occupying land that used to belong to Germany. It was a geographic mess that involved ethnic cleansing and the takeover of land and homes, which compounded the war's tragedies. Poland was a country far different from the one Bogdan had known—scarred by war and realigned by outside intervention.

If Bogdan went back, he would have to be tight-lipped. Poles who had fled the country during the war and then made anti–Soviet statements were now at risk if they wished to return. He heard stories about people who returned to Poland and wound up in Siberia because they protested or let slip Soviet criticisms. Bogdan would have to self-censor and say nothing about the country's plight—difficult for a patriot and freedom fighter.

After the war, Bogdan twice wrote letters to a friend from the *komplety* classes, Wacek Kruszewski. A Warsaw native, he worked at Udycz, so they saw each other regularly during the war, and after the conflict ended he moved to Gdansk. Wacek never answered Bogdan's letters, behavior that was uncharacteristic of him, and Bogdan suspected that the Communist government intercepted his missives as a way to monitor people and gain more information on an *Armia Krajowa* veteran. Bogdan stopped reaching out to him, fearing that his communications might endanger both his friend and himself.

Bogdan wrote a letter to his old Bydgoszcz address, and his younger brother Janusz replied, telling him that the rest of the family had survived the last phases of the war. But Janusz also informed him that a Polish government official inquired about his whereabouts, which showed that the new government was trying to keep tabs on him as a former resistance fighter. The conclusion was inescapable: the government wanted Bogdan, and while no one knew what treatment awaited him if he returned, he disliked thinking about it.

This "official" interest in him strengthened Bogdan's resolve to stay away. "If my mother were still alive," he later reflected, "the pull of my homeland would have been much stronger, and I might have returned." But now, while it pained him to concede it, the option of going back to Poland was out. The more safe, logical choice was to stay abroad, which meant remaining in Britain or relocating to the United States, Australia, Canada, or perhaps Argentina, countries where Poles settled. Were he to go to one of these faraway lands, though, he might never return to Poland as a permanent citizen. That was a difficult concept to accept, because Bogdan's family was still there, and he had risked so much to save his country.

For the moment, Bogdan decided to stay in England. After quartering in a military resettlement camp for Polish veterans in the Lake District, he took a ship to London, where he was determined to begin a new chapter in his life. He received a small stipend as military pay, which came from the Polish government. The money allowed him to find lodging at a YMCA in London. Bogdan's first priority was to find a place at a university, because he believed that education would open doors for him. Using the British capital as a base, he traveled by train to various universities, going as far as Glasgow in Scotland, which was more than five hours from London by train, making inquiries about admission to study during the fall 1946 semester. Everywhere, though, he received the response that the incoming classes were full. Many veterans like him wanted to return to school, and university enrollments had mushroomed, so Bogdan felt like he had reached an impasse.

Finally, back in the capital city, Bogdan found the Polish University College [PUC]. A subsidiary of London University, this school was created especially for soldiers who had remained in the Polish Army after the war and wanted to continue their education. It offered competitive exams in various subjects for prospective students. The *komplety* classes had

11. New Goals, New Country

provided a general education on basic subjects like geography, math, and history, but something intuitive inside him told him to go for the economics and commerce exam. His bent toward this subject, he suspected, probably had a genetic basis, coming from his father, who was a businessman with an engineering background.

But there was a catch. Only sixty places were available for economics and commerce, and 360 candidates were applying. The competition would be fierce, and Bogdan took the exam, uncertain of his chances. If he passed, he would win a place in the school, and he could also get a tuition exemption, with the British government generously picking up the tab for his education. Bogdan had to have a backup plan. "If I fail," he ruminated, "I'll work in fishing or coal mining, and finance my education that way." He was ready to do that, but it would slow down his schooling, which had already suffered disastrous interruptions because of the war.

When Bogdan received the results, out of the 360 candidates who took the exam, he ranked sixth overall. He was in. He found a room on the top floor of a four-story dormitory house in London, which a German bomb had damaged during the war, and he prepared to resume his role as a student.

The PUC held classes near Sloan Square, in the Victoria District, at an adjunct campus to the University of London, which was farther north. Some classmates whom Bogdan met became lifelong friends, including Marek Rudzki. Marek was a small fellow, standing only about five feet

While the war disrupted his schooling for six years, Bogdan assumed a new role in London, as a student, working toward his undergraduate degree.

six inches, with a thick mop of jet black hair and a pipe-smoking habit. He had a sparkling wit and was great company, and during summers, Bogdan hitchhiked with him through Spain and France, enjoying the break from their studies. Bogdan also took an immediate liking to Marek's parents. His father Adam was a former cavalry officer and prewar director of the port of Gdansk, and his mother Walunia became a substitute mother for Bogdan.

During the years just after the war, Bogdan also tried to improve his English. He studied with an English dictionary within reach, and once, when he began reading a textbook on British economic history, he found about thirty words just on the first page that he had to look up (the text got better as he went along). At PUC, he took classes in English, and he went around London and visited museums, which waived entrance fees for veterans, embarking on what he called his "museum education," which expanded his mind in fields such as art and natural history while also immersing him in the English language. In his breast pocket, Bogdan kept a small notebook, jotting down new phrases and expressions whenever he could, even while he was riding on the bus. One of the most difficult adjustments he had to make was learning the "th" sound, which is common in English because of words like "the" and "with" but is absent from the Polish language, so Bogdan had to learn to pronounce it correctly. He used every opportunity to gain more English proficiency, and his growing facility with the language gave him confidence in his studies and ability to navigate through London.

While absorbing the English language and growing accustomed to British mores, Bogdan still felt that he was a Pole. A person's national identification can hardly disappear overnight, and while Bogdan sensed himself becoming a Londoner, his country tugged at him. During one class at the PUC, a professor introduced a group of Polish students—including Bogdan—as "emigres," implying that they were in England permanently. Upon hearing that word, Bogdan felt a flush of resentment, because he still regarded himself as a member of the Polish fighting forces and just a visitor to Great Britain. Over time, though, he began to think that he might never go back to Poland permanently. "It was no small realization to think that never again would I live in my native land," Bogdan remembered. "It shook me to the core."

Thus, Bogdan saw his study in England as both a success and a disaster. For the former, he was back in school, which fulfilled a yearning that gnawed at him since 1939, and he was settling into a new phase in his life, setting new goals and ambitions. For the latter, it struck a death knell to his dream of returning to Poland. Bogdan finally admitted to himself that he would never resume the life he had known there before the devastation that war wrought.

II. Decisions

A lucky student might find a teacher who exerts such a profound impact that it changes the course of his or her life. For Bogdan, that was Dr. Zbigniew Siemienski. A PUC professor, he was bespectacled, tall, lean, and dark-haired, and he spoke English with a strong French accent because he had first learned French as a foreign language while he was living in Poland. Before coming to England, he earned a Ph.D. in economics and worked in the research section of Poland's central bank. His intellect and knowledge impressed Bogdan, who considered him the brightest member of the faculty. He was a kind man who showed a welcoming attitude toward Bogdan, and his disposition gave Bogdan added interest in taking his classes. Because of Dr. Siemienski's courses and the professor's contagious enthusiasm for the discipline—Bogdan especially liked Siemienski's "Money and Banking" course—the young student made a decision that was to chart his life's trajectory: he would major in economics. When Bogdan told Siemienski of his choice, he seemed pleased; the news must have flattered him.

Although pundits joke that economics is the "dismal science," it became Bogdan's passion. He studied hard. His motivation came from his love of the subject but also from a survival instinct that the war had sharpened, only this time it sensed a different threat, transmuting his energy into an academic determination. Bogdan knew that if he underperformed—or worse, failed a course in his new major—the college would revoke his scholarship. Thus would end his aspirations to find a good career and a better life. Then, like many Poles then living in London, he might labor in a job that would bring little satisfaction, perhaps working in a physical trade. Like many immigrants, Bogdan had to rely on resourcefulness, diligence, and a drive for self-betterment. He dared not flirt with failure, so he left nothing to chance. For example, when he bought his first typewriter in London for typing term papers, he immediately enrolled in an evening typing school so that he could learn to touch-type and use that machine to its fullest efficiency.

In observing peers and evaluating his own situation, Bogdan was struck by how one habit handicapped some people while handing him and others like him an advantage. He had never taken to smoking cigarettes, and besides the health benefits accrued to nonsmokers, he witnessed other dividends. He noticed that classmates who smoked were often in financial straits and had to devote more of their vacations to working, earning money for cigarettes, which detracted from their studying hours. Because he was not spending money on cigarettes, Bogdan saved enough to buy a British-made, three-speed Hercules bicycle, which allowed him to commute to campus faster, saving precious time.

Time was vital to Bogdan because the war had taken so much of it. The war cost him years of schooling, and he had to make up for the loss. By taking the maximum allotment of courses and working furiously, Bogdan finished the program in two and a half years. In the spring of 1950, he graduated with a bachelor's degree in economics, finishing with second-class honors, upper division, in a selective group. Fewer than five percent of students graduated with this distinction, so Bogdan felt privileged.

After graduating, Bogdan worked in London. He had two jobs, one at a suburban Lyons food store and another at the celebrated Harrod's Department Store, where tourists often throng. He was becoming a British working stiff, he mused, but at the same time, he could hardly picture staying there. He had taken umbrage at the Brits' failure to appreciate Polish veterans and, moreover, British society had a patina of snobbery. For centuries, England's social hierarchy had well-defined strata, with heredity a key factor in determining status. Luckily, the war helped to democratize the country, breaking down class and gender barriers. Soldiers from all classes fought side-by-side, and women transcended traditional roles to work in factories.

Yet after the war, stratifications still existed. The upper classes seemed entrenched and closed, and the various strata calcified people into fixed social positions. Bogdan heard patronizing phrases like "You know, old boy," which reflected an exclusivity that blocked off newcomers. Bogdan pictured himself as someone who would never fit into British society. Even though he had earned a bachelor's degree, he was working in retail, and he worried that he might end up toiling in a factory; the thought of lifelong manual labor carried little appeal. Instead, the study of economics had whetted Bogdan's appetite for learning, and he wanted to pursue his education further, somewhere that he could break the shackling socioeconomic impediments that he felt in England.

Another aspect of British life held little attraction for Bogdan: the food. London featured affordable restaurants for impoverished students like him, such as the ABC—the Aerated Bread Company—which he frequented. They served fish and chips wrapped in newspaper, which seemed odd and unsanitary but was a British custom. Everywhere Bogdan went, though, the food was mediocre, and his palate hungered for something different and better, especially when recalling his youth in Poland and after suffering through POW camps.

Bogdan had a major decision to make. Averse to staying in the U.K., he needed a new country to call home, and he toyed with the possibility of going to Australia or New Zealand. But the United States attracted him the most. That nation was home to many immigrants, including Poles. It celebrated freedom—which contrasted with the pall that the Soviet Union cast over Eastern Europe—and its postwar job market burgeoned.

The most attractive feature about the U.S. was its openness. For Bogdan, "open" meant that anybody could make it if he or she had the motivation and a modicum of talent. The U.S. offered opportunities for people who came from the outside, not just for the "in" crowd, as he sensed in Britain. Wartime American Red Cross packages further stimulated his interest in the U.S.—the food had tasted good. For any POW, those aid packages proved a tremendous—and in the pages of history, underrated—advertisement for the U.S., luring newcomers to its shores. Having been deprived of sweets during the war, Bogdan especially savored and remembered the delicious cookies in those parcels. In a small sense, American Red Cross cookies helped to lure him to the U.S.

Bogdan caught a lucky break through Adam Rudzki, who was locating Polish veterans and directing them to settlement areas. Adam helped to place Bogdan on the list of people emigrating to America, and he gave a special favor of granting him high priority for obtaining a visa. Bogdan was helping the Rudzkis, too, because their whole family wanted to come to the U.S., especially Marek and his younger brother Alec, and he could function as an advance scout for them, reporting on conditions there.

Bogdan went to the U.S. embassy in London to get fingerprinted, and then he gathered up his belongings in his dorm room. He had so few items that he could cram everything into a rickety wooden suitcase. Luckily, the Polish Resettlement Corps paid for his ocean ticket to the U.S.

Bogdan was twenty-six years old, and he was about to cross an ocean for the first time and embark on an adventure. With just $72 in his pockets plus a college degree, he was going to America to start a new life.

III. Graduate School and a First Job

In December 1950, Bogdan stood at the shore of the River Mersey in Liverpool, the port city from which so many emigrants left Europe to start a new life in America and elsewhere. With the majestic Liver Building looming behind him, he boarded the 600-foot ocean liner *RMS Franconia* and sailed out of the city, leaving Europe. Aboard the ship, Bogdan shared a cramped berth with two other passengers. He tried to spend as much time as possible on the deck, reading, although it was cold. The ship made a stop in Halifax, Canada, which seemed brutally frigid to Bogdan, before proceeding to the U.S.

Bogdan's plan was to go to Chicago because he had an uncle there, Wlodzimierz (or "Walter," the Anglicized version of his name), Tadeusz's younger brother, who had come to the U.S. before World War I. Celebrated for its Polish population, Chicago was home to more Poles than Warsaw, and the climate was similar to that of the Polish capital, so Bogdan figured that he might feel at home. He had also heard encouraging reports about the job market in Chicago, which was America's second-largest city, with a population of 3.6 million. Overall, the U.S. economy was robust, especially because the country was a half-year into the Korean War, and wartime spending acted as a stimulus to shake off the jolting readjustments to peacetime footing that the country experienced after World War II.

At five o'clock in the morning, Bogdan caught first sight of America. A cold December wind battered the *Franconia*, but he stood on the deck and glimpsed the outlines of New York City's skyscrapers. As the *Franconia* sailed into New York Harbor, Bogdan got a clear view of the Statue of Liberty, the classic beacon signaling to ship passengers that they had arrived in America. But Bogdan saw something else that struck him: a necklace of headlights stretching all along Manhattan island. Here were droves of people in cars, he thought, already going to work well before daylight. But it was more than the morning commute that struck Bogdan. The huge volume of traffic spoke to the importance of automobiles in the U.S. and to the high standard of living. As Bogdan took in this sight, he and other passengers gathered in the lounge of the ship, and as soon as everyone debarked, immigration authorities processed them. After completing this procedure, Bogdan went to a YMCA to spend the night there.

On his first full day in the Big Apple, Bogdan asked a pedestrian for directions to get to a relative of Marek Rudzki. He responded, "Are you with a car?" The question stunned Bogdan. Was he kidding? There Bogdan was, with little money and fresh off the boat, and somebody assumed that he had a motor vehicle. This car culture struck a contrast with what Bogdan had endured in wartime Warsaw, where automobiles were scarce—and if a person saw one, it was likely to be of German manufacture.

After a few days in New York, Bogdan took a train to Chicago so that he could stay with Uncle Walter, whom he had never met before. He was much different from Tadeusz; he never pursued his education and led a simple life, working as a custodian at a large department store. He had saved enough to own a house in Chicago, and Bogdan was grateful that Walter and his wife, who was from the Ukraine, hosted him for a few weeks.

As always, Bogdan's first priority was work; he needed to find a way to support himself and afford his own place. His brand new bachelor's degree helped him to land a job at the National Cosmopolitan Bank in downtown Chicago, handling checks and monitoring account balances. At first, he stayed at Walter's house, but he found that the commute was too long, so he moved to a YMCA closer to work.

For four months in early 1951, Bogdan worked at the bank, but his

11. New Goals, New Country

salary was abysmal. He tried selling vacuum cleaners, but his heart was not into foisting the devices onto potential customers. He decided to switch to industry, and he found a job as a timekeeper at the Crown Can Company in South Chicago, checking workers' time cards. After one year of work in Chicago, Bogdan became eligible for subsidized, low-cost tuition at the University of Illinois. Upon passing the entrance exam, he registered as a full-time student, and he packed up his belongings in that same dilapidated wooden suitcase he brought from London and boarded a train for Urbana-Champaign. In February 1952, Bogdan began graduate study in economics at the University of Illinois.

Graduate students are notoriously impoverished and bereft of family help. Bogdan was poorer than most, and money was always a concern. In the summer of 1952, he took a job that initially seemed delightful but became torture. He worked at a donut factory, which manufactured just two basic kinds of donuts, glazed and plain. Bogdan made the donuts and cleaned the baking equipment with a heavy wire brush, which required considerable strength and elbow grease. He ate lots of donuts at this job—in fact, too many. Even though Bogdan liked pastries and cakes, for the rest of his life he avoided donuts. If it were possible to overdose on donuts, he did that summer.

He might have surfeited himself with donuts, but Bogdan still felt hungry—for self-betterment, an impulse that drove him forward. He tried to improve his English, and he registered with a speech therapy clinic at the university. They recorded his voice and played it back for him. Bogdan knew he spoke with an accent, and he expected it to be a Polish one. Instead, when he heard his voice during the tape playback—he sounded like he was from Germany! Having recently fought German soldiers, Bogdan was horrified. The linguistic quirk must have come from his years of speaking German as he grew up. But he went through speech therapy sessions to reduce his accent and improve his English.

One of the first graduate seminars Bogdan attended was for international economics. Taking a seat in the lecture hall, he struck up a conversation with a student who introduced himself as Stanley Zemelka. Stan kept one arm deep in his pants pocket at all times, and Bogdan realized that he was missing his right hand. It was a war injury, and the two students bonded because they were both injured veterans. But they had fought on opposite sides. Bogdan learned that Stan had been an officer in the German Army, a Pole who had been forced to serve there or else be killed. He had fought in the siege of Leningrad, the protracted, four-year long operation where the Germans tried to take the former Russian capital, located just two hundred miles from Finland and famous for frigid winters. In the bitter cold of Russian winter, Stan kept his machine gun in a blanket instead of on a stand. Most soldiers kept theirs on the stands, and when the time came to use them, they had frozen up. Stan's was the only one that could fire. Because of his smart thinking, he received a promotion to officer.

Friendly and loquacious, Stan became Bogdan's close friend, and they stayed in contact during their careers, both finding jobs in academia. During the war, even though he came into contact with many fellow Poles in the army and in POW camps, Bogdan made no lasting bonds with those he encountered. His ability once again to forge friendships constituted another signal that the war was indeed over.

To earn money, Bogdan spent the summer of 1953 in New York City, working on Wall Street, but he worried that without more financial support he might have to abandon graduate school. Luckily, the Department of Economics offered him an assistantship, so in the fall of 1953, Bogdan returned to Illinois and served as a teaching assistant, leading a section of the introductory survey, "Principles of Economics." It was a new experience to stand before a group and lecture, but by semester's end, Bogdan felt like he had been doing it his whole life. He was comfortable with the material, and he felt flattered when other teaching assistants came to him to ask questions about what they were supposed to teach. Apparently, the Department approved of Bogdan's work, because in the spring semester, they gave him three sections to teach in exchange for full tuition remission.

Because he was constantly cash-strapped, Bogdan had a financial incentive to finish graduate school quickly and start on a career path. He completed his master's degree in less than one year and Ph.D. in two and a half years. His doctoral dissertation was entitled *Communist Money and Banking: The Case of Poland*. In a little more than a decade, Polish currency had experienced tumultuous change. During the war, the Germans ordered a special stamp affixed to the Polish zloty. Once the war ended, the Communist government imposed its own "reform," canceling the currency's value and substituting a new, devalued zloty worth much less than the old one. By doing so, the Communist government had levied what amounted to a one-time tax. It benefited from this exchange, while consumers and businesses suffered.

This phenomenon happened throughout the Communist countries and in the Soviet Union as well. Bogdan argued that it was lousy management and a defective system for handling the zloty and other currencies. Yet at the same time, the propaganda was that Communism brought equality and a beneficial standard of living. In truth, the Communist method of managing money was bureaucratic, and it cried out for reform. (Because Bogdan had read about the Russian government's postwar monetary moves, he wrote to his family back in Poland, warning them that Communist monetary reform

11. New Goals, New Country

was arriving soon and advising them to prepare themselves for an adverse shock.)

At the end of the 1954 summer school session, Bogdan defended his dissertation and received his doctorate. When he finished graduate school, he had only $72 left. That was the exact amount he had when he arrived in the U.S., and he found it an odd coincidence. But with so little money, he needed a job, and luckily, he landed one: the University of Vermont hired him as an instructor. (Once the University of Illinois officially conferred his degree in the spring of 1955, Bogdan received a promotion to the rank of assistant professor.) Even in the land of cars, Bogdan still did not have one, so he went by train from Urbana-Champaign to Burlington.

The first years of a teacher's career are intense, because he or she has to prepare lectures and lesson plans for the first time, in addition to grading exams and papers. Bogdan worked hard, never missing a class, and he was proud of his perfect attendance. His diet improved now that he had a steady paycheck, and he began to treat himself to the cornucopia of foods that was available in the U.S. He had not had tropical fruit like bananas since his prewar years, and he could also now enjoy red meat, canned fish, and nuts. In November 1954, Bogdan got his first real introduction to the American tradition of Thanksgiving when Philipp Lohman, who chaired his department, invited him to his home for the holiday feast. There Bogdan saw a roasted turkey for the first time in more than sixteen years.

In Vermont, Bogdan bought a used 1941 Studebaker sedan, which gave him more mobility, and he got to know the U.S. better. For the first time since his family's prewar winter vacations, he skied, tackling the slopes at Mount Killington and in Lake Placid, New York, site of the 1932 Winter Olympics (and later, the 1980 Winter Olympics). The skiing in Vermont was terrific, and it reminded Bogdan of the winters in Poland before the war. In 1956, Bogdan also returned to New York City and became a naturalized citizen. The country that had gifted him with opportunities to study and work after the war was officially his home.

At the same time, Bogdan felt wanderlust—not with America, but with his current situation. Vermont was rustic but isolated, and he could feel himself slipping into a rut. He was spending all his time teaching, grading exams, and doing little else. Burlington was relatively small, and the long winters and lack of major cities added to a sense of seclusion. In his early thirties, Bogdan felt restless and starved for fresh challenges. So when an opportunity arose to go to Poland to do research on Communist money, he grabbed it, finishing his third and final year at Vermont when the 1957 spring semester ended.

Bogdan's new boss was Thad Alton, an economist at a Polish research agency in New York City, near Columbia University. His first assignment was to spend three months in Poland, conducting research, after which he would work at Alton's Manhattan office.

More than a decade had passed since the war ended. Bogdan wanted to see his father and brothers. He was eager to see his country again, and he was curious about its condition.

IV. A Different Place

In the summer of 1957, Bogdan took a ship to Rotterdam in the Netherlands, and from there went by train to Vienna and then Warsaw, where he caught a train to Bydgoszcz. There, he saw his father for the first time in twelve years. The reunion was bittersweet. Tadeusz had returned to Bydgoszcz because he considered it home and wanted to be ensconced in familiar surroundings. But life would never be the same, and reminders stood everywhere of the comforts they had once enjoyed—and everything they had lost. As if to symbolize his fall from lofty heights, Tadeusz now rented a few rooms in their old house, which he transformed into an apartment. Being there as a tenant in a house that he had built and owned might have been comforting, but it was also demoralizing.

As soon as he saw his father, Bogdan knew he was not the same man. Tadeusz had gained weight, and Bogdan's younger brother Janusz later told him that he ate honey by the spoonful, sometimes getting up during the night to indulge in it. At seventy-two years old, Tadeusz lived simply, and he was more quiet and less energetic than the father Bogdan had known. His hair had thinned and greyed, and he now had the hunched-over posture that takes over the body when youth begins to fade. These signs of aging were palpable, and while Bogdan had expected them, they were sad to see.

What troubled Bogdan the most was that Tadeusz's mental faculties had declined. "My father's once-sharp memory was slipping," he observed, "and he appeared to be operating at half-power." Tadeusz had a new wife, Sozosia, a widow whose first husband had been killed in 1939 when the Germans invaded Poland. Tadeusz perhaps remarried out of convenience, to have someone to keep him company and help him with cooking and domestic work. Sozosia, though, brought her brother (who had been wounded during the war) and sister into the new Mieczkowski household, arranging for them all to live in Tadeusz's apartment, which became crowded.

Janusz was studying law in Poznan, a city an hour southwest of Bydgoszcz, and he eventually became an attorney. Zbigniew's situation was more complicated, showing the perils of life under Communism. A

11. New Goals, New Country

common expression behind the Iron Curtain was to "choose freedom," which was a euphemism for escaping and a not-so-subtle dig against the alternative of being forced to surrender one's liberty to a Communist state. Zbigniew decided to choose freedom. On a communist-sponsored trip to Austria, he stayed there instead of returning to Poland. But as a matter of routine, anyone who refused to return to a Communist country faced prison, and Zbigniew was detained in jail.

Bogdan visited Zybigniew in a Vienna prison, where he asked guards to bring his brother to the interview room. He wanted to give him some cash, but the guard monitoring them forbade him from doing so. Luckily for Zbigniew, though, he won release after a few weeks, and he joined a scholarly community in Vienna, where he began doctoral studies. (Eventually, he earned a Ph.D. and moved to Canada, becoming a professor of geography and tourism at the University of Winnipeg.)

Bogdan's return to Poland left lasting impressions about the Communist system. Its rule cast an economic pall over Poland. Whereas the country should have rebuilt and rebounded after the war, Bogdan was surprised at how dilapidated everything was, while other countries such as West Germany modernized at a brisk pace. In 1948, when the U.S. formulated the European Recovery Program (more commonly known as the "Marshall Plan," after Secretary of State George Marshall), Western Europe eagerly accepted, and the U.S. extended the aid offer to Eastern European countries as well. At first, Poland accepted, but bowing to pressure from the Kremlin, it ultimately declined to participate. The result was that Western Europe thrived, while Eastern Europe stagnated.

Wherever Bogdan went, he saw the results. People looked demoralized and seldom smiled, as if they lived in a perennial state of anxiety and fear. When he visited the port of Gdansk on the Baltic Sea, normally a bustling hub of trade and retail commerce, it seemed dormant. Once teeming with ships, the harbor was practically empty, and the tourist trade floundered. But all of it made sense: who would want to visit a country where freedoms are trammeled and the economy was stagnant? As a tourist destination, Poland now stunk—literally. When Bogdan visited apartment buildings, the stench of urine permeated the air, which meant that maintenance crews failed to do their work properly or else were in short supply. Public ownership bred a casual indifference to property, so people felt that they could relieve themselves wherever they wanted because the government would somehow take care of it.

And the lines! During the Cold War, the long lines in Communist countries became infamous, and Bogdan saw them firsthand. Consumer goods were in short supply, and shoppers, most wearing drab clothing—indicating poor economic conditions—queued up in flea-bitten stores to obtain sales slips, make payments, and then obtain the products. To buy a can of fish, for example, a person had to go to a saleslady first, get a chit bearing the price of the can, then go to the cashier to pay. Then the customer had to line up again to obtain the can of fish. The whole process was inefficient, time consuming, and wasteful.

As research for his new job, Bogdan obtained price lists of consumer goods, which reflected the country's economic conditions and were useful in calculating national income. He peppered people with questions about pocketbook issues, and he met with professors to ask about prices, employment, consumption, production—arcane things that interest economists because they give insight into a country's condition.

Bogdan's inquisitiveness attracted the wrong kind of attention. During this trip, he had the strange feeling that someone was watching him, and friends tipped him off that he was indeed being followed. His father's second wife had two daughters who were Communist Party members, and Bogdan wondered whether they had alerted Soviet authorities to him. He hated to think it, because these girls were now part of his extended family. But in closed societies, such suspicions crept into one's mind, and family and friends fell into the penumbra of suspects. The very nature of authoritarian regimes prompted people to fear, worry, and wonder about who cooperated with the authorities.

Once, Bogdan was riding near Warsaw on a rented motorcycle when a police officer pulled him over. Bogdan thought the action was odd, since he was obeying all traffic regulations and observing the speed limit. The officer had no reason to stop Bogdan, but the incident showed how closely authorities monitored people—and perhaps him especially. When he left the country by train, guards frisked him, checking for documents. These experiences left Bogdan with an unsettled feeling about Poland, and he had little desire to remain there for long.

What made the situation more difficult for Bogdan to stomach was that the American academic and diplomatic community seemed to accept the Iron Curtain and the legacies of the Yalta Conference, showing reluctance to agitate against the Soviet Union's control of Eastern Europe. True enough, U.S. foreign policy had embraced a containment policy against Communism early in the Cold War and had taken strong stands with the Truman Doctrine, Marshall Plan, Berlin Airlift, and Korean War. But Soviet control over Eastern Europe seemed a *fait accompli*, and American resistance to the Kremlin there seemed hollow. While he was in Vienna, Bogdan met Boyden Marison, who eventually immigrated to the U.S. and worked as the senior editor of Voice of America (VOA) in Polish Services. Marison recalled that at the VOA, they were not allowed to criticize the Soviet Union; for example, they were forbidden from discussing the Katyn

11. New Goals, New Country

Forest massacre, with the result that the Soviet Union avoided blame for it until 1991, after the Cold War was over. Helping Poland seemed hopeless, and even the American diplomatic community kept its distance. That reality ratified Bogdan's decision to leave his country and made him reluctant to go back while it was a Soviet satellite.

Overall, Bogdan's return to Poland—while useful from a research standpoint—was disillusioning. His homeland was a different place. A far cry from the happy country he remembered from his childhood, it had become a repressive, somber nation behind the Iron Curtain, where people seldom smiled and everyday items like toilet paper were of poor quality and in short supply. His father was different: he was a diminished man, failing to flourish like he did before the war, living under circumstances that showed a steep decline from the energetic business titan and community leader he once was.

After three months in Poland, in the fall of 1957, Bogdan returned to New York City. For the next four years, he worked in Thad Alton's cramped office on West 116th Street, crunching numbers on national income in Poland as well as East Germany and Romania, trying to calculate their gross domestic products accurately using Western methods of measurement, which led to more precise assessments. (The Communist governments failed to incorporate the contribution of services, which included a huge category of economic activity, ranging from retail sales to restaurant work to medical treatment and more. This failure to include services led to skewed numbers.) The work at Thad Alton's agency culminated in a book that they published as a team of co-authors, *Polish National Income and Production: 1954, 1955, and 1956*, which was published in 1956.

Bogdan continued to work as a research associate in Alton's office, living in an apartment on West 111th Street. In 1958, he moved to an apartment on West 113th Street, just two blocks south of Alton's office. The walk to work was short and convenient, and Columbia University and Riverside Park were close by.

Bogdan's decision to live in that building would change the course of his life.

— 12 —

Clashing Countries to Clashing Cultures

I. *Voyaging, 1950s-style*

In August 1955, Seiko stepped out of her family's house in Otaru, walked to the train station, and caught a train out of the city. She did not know it at the time, but those steps marked the start of a journey that would take her away from Japan for good.

Next to saying good-bye to Yasuko, leaving Japan was the most difficult thing Seiko had ever done. Although she intended to be away only for a year, after which she planned to return and continue to teach English, her departure from Otaru marked the first time she would be away from her family—and she would be half a world away. With those thoughts weighing on her, she settled in for the long trek to Tokyo, which would take two full days.

The first leg of the journey, from Otaru to the port of Hakodate, was beautiful, as the train snaked along the Sea of Japan first and then along the Pacific Ocean. Seiko could see fishermen's boats and traps dotting the coast, visible signs of how many island residents made a living from the ocean. She took a ferry to Honshu, and then came the longer leg of the trip, to Tokyo. This was an era before Japan's renowned *shinkansen*, or bullet train (which began service in 1964), so train travel was relatively slow. After several hours more of travel, Seiko finally arrived in the capital city.

Seiko's ambition to study in the U.S. might have been a long shot, but her family supported it regardless. When she got to Tokyo, she stayed at one of her mother's relatives. Shizuko and Kazu came down from Otaru to join her in Tokyo, as did two of her mother's cousins, and they all went by train to Yokohama, a port city a half-hour from Tokyo.

In Yokohama, Seiko boarded the *Hikawa-maru*, the ocean liner that would take her to the U.S. When the Japanese were embarking on a trip by boat, they had a tradition of throwing the ends of paper tape rolls to

12. Clashing Countries to Clashing Cultures 179

relatives or friends, with the persons at each end holding on until it broke. Seiko had three rolls of paper tape, each a few inches wide and of a different color, and she saw Shizuko and Kazu standing on the dock. Dozens of passengers were throwing down their strings of paper to relatives and friends, and the space separating the ship from the wharf began to look like a three-dimensional Jackson Pollack painting, with multi-colored lines shooting off in different directions. Seiko focused on her siblings and threw the paper ends down, trying to send them directly to Shizuko and Kazu so that their paper lines would avoid getting mixed up with all the others. Both of them caught the lines, and Seiko looked carefully at their faces and held on to her ends of the paper.

"*Ugoi teru!*" one passenger near Seiko exclaimed, meaning, "We are moving." She was so intent on looking at the expressions on Shizuko's and Kazutoshi's faces that she was not even aware that the ship was slowly drifting away. Then the tapes finally broke, and at that moment, Seiko knew she was on her way. Strangely, though, she didn't have time to be sentimental. She was thinking more about her studies, and she was full

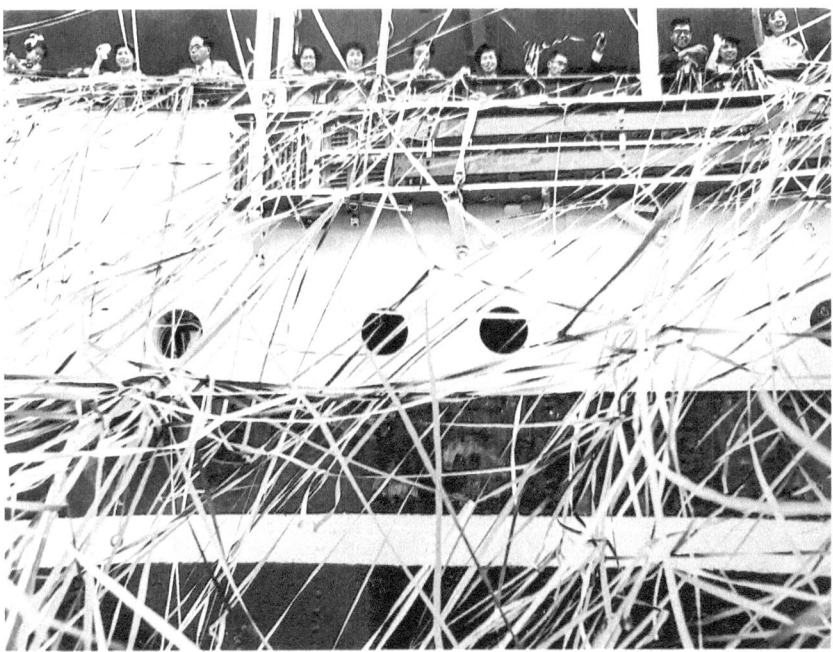

Seiko (fifth from the left) prepares to depart from Yokohoma aboard the *Hikawa-maru* ocean liner. The Japanese had a tradition whereby ship passengers held one end of a paper tape while family and friends held the other. When the ship left port, the paper eventually broke, and the voyage began.

of anxiety about whether she could succeed as a student in an American college.

The ocean voyage was rough. Seiko had a lower-deck room that sat above the engine, so noise hammered the walls at all times, and catching a solid night of sleep was difficult. Worse, she was seasick constantly. Although Seiko was young and healthy, her body was unaccustomed to being on a moving object. She had seldom been on boats or cars; her most sustained experience with travel was during her daily train commute to Asari. Throughout the whole voyage, nausea robbed her of any appetite.

Some moments of the trip were memorable. Seiko sought relief from her seasickness by going on deck to get fresh air, and when the ship cruised past the Aleutian Islands, she saw a pod of whales surfacing, shooting air through their spouts. Once, at night, she saw the lights of another large ship as it returned to Japan. It was a majestic sight to see a vessel like that passing silently in the other direction.

Seiko's journey to the U.S. symbolized classic voyaging 1950s-style, an era when sea transport still reigned over air travel. As with so many facets of life, World War II marked a dividing line. After the war, airlines became more commonplace, overtaking ship travel in low cost, convenience, and speed. But Seiko's voyage to the U.S. was stuck in the fading era of passenger liners, and on another level, her trip symbolized a journey from the slower, old-fashioned Japan that she experienced in Hokkaido to the more dynamic America.

The *Hikawa-maru* took two weeks to cross the Pacific, docking in Seattle. The magic combination of luck, thoughtful strangers, and a dollop of Seiko's gregariousness paved her path to Berea. Aboard the ship, she befriended some Japanese women who had American husbands. A few of them had married before the war, became permanent U.S. citizens, and endured life in inhumane relocation camps during the war, even though they had committed no crimes. Others had wed U.S. servicemen during the Occupation, and settled with their new husbands in America. They told Seiko about life in the U.S., and one of them introduced her to a Japanese minister and his wife who were traveling aboard the ship. Because Seiko was alone, the couple empathized with her, and after the ship docked, they invited her to join the other passenger and come to their Seattle home, where she stayed overnight.

The next morning, the minister took Seiko and their passenger friend to the train station. Since Seiko was still unfamiliar with U.S. currency, she gave him her money and he bought a Union Pacific train ticket for her. After thanking him for his generosity, she bid him farewell, and boarded the train, which traveled three quarters of the way across the continental U.S., to Chicago. Unable to afford a sleeping berth, Seiko slept in her seat.

At one point during the trip, a young man dressed in a military uniform tried to strike up a conversation with her. In her limited English, she told him that she was in the U.S. to study in college. He seemed impressed, and he gave her some of his food, which was a wonderful gift because she had nothing to eat during the train voyage. "He might have been stationed in Japan during the Occupation," Seiko surmised, "and the Japanese probably treated him kindly and reverentially, and he returned to the U.S. with warm feelings toward Japan and its people."

From Chicago, Seiko boarded another train that took her to Cincinnati, where Seiko stayed at the YWCA, and a staff member kindly took her to a Greyhound bus terminal to catch a ride to her new home—Berea, Kentucky. The bus, too, was a symbol of a new country and different era. In the 1950s, long bus trips were a popular and cost-effective way of getting around the country. The trip took about two and a half hours, and when she arrived at the Berea bus station, a college staff member picked her up and took her to her room in the Anna Smith Residence Hall, a three-story dormitory located in the heart of the campus.

Seiko was ready to begin a new phase of her education—as a student rather than a teacher, in an entirely different country.

II. Major Adjustments

In the fall of 1955, Seiko turned twenty-six years old, so she was older than the typical college freshman. But she was still young, and everything was new to her, so in that respect she was like a freshman embarking on a college career. She felt unmoored from familiar Hokkaido surroundings, and while she had read about the U.S—its history, economy, and literature—she knew little about daily life in America.

On many levels, Seiko's situation was stunning to contemplate. Just a decade earlier, America had been Japan's wartime enemy, and the two countries clashed with venom and bloodthirst. But the reconciliation was quick, and the U.S. intrigued and seemed to welcome Seiko. Certainly, she found that Berea College students and people in Kentucky were kind and friendly, which aided her transition immeasurably.

Many people helped her. Seiko made friends in the dorm and classes. The advisor for foreign students was Dr. Charlotte Ludlum, who lived with her mother in a house near campus and had a distinguished family. Her great-granduncle was Commodore Matthew Perry, whose 1853 voyage to Tokyo opened up Japan to the Western world, and her brother was the writer Robert Ludlum, author of *The Bourne Identity* (which later spawned the movie series starring actor Matt Damon). When she first met Seiko,

Seiko outside Anna Smith Hall, her dormitory at Berea College in Berea, Kentucky, where she came to study English, eventually earning her second college degree.

Ludlum exclaimed in a surprised but forthright way, "You were a teacher of English in Japan. But your English is very poor." "That's why," Seiko replied, "I came to this country—to learn English and get better at it. Otherwise, I could not return to Japan and even consider myself a true English teacher there."

The biggest hardship was, indeed, the language. Seiko had trouble communicating, and when she engaged in English conversation, she had difficulty understanding what people were saying to her. She had to work extra hard in her studies because the foreign language stood as a barrier to learning. Although she had studied and taught English in Japan, the differences between the two languages were vast, including their written scripts, phonetic combinations, and pronunciation. For example, the "l" sound did not exist Japanese, so Seiko had to learn to enunciate it and be careful in distinguishing words like "rice" and "lice" or "election" versus "erection." The Japanese had no "th" sound, yet words like "the," "this," and "that" were common in English. Not only was the sound of "the" absent in Japanese, but so were articles like "a," "an," and "the," and although these were small words, the nuance among them could make a large difference in meaning. A linguist could fill a book with all the differences: in Japanese, verbs usually came at the end of sentences, rather than in the middle,

12. Clashing Countries to Clashing Cultures   183

as in English; in Japanese, they used a special (and confusing) system of counters to designate plural nouns, but the English language denoted plurals by adding an "s." On top of the language barrier, Seiko had to learn a new system of weights and measures, because Japan used the metric system, while American still embraced the old imperial system of pounds, feet, gallons, miles, and Fahrenheit temperature.

Despite the innumerable differences, Seiko was determined to improve her English—it was the purpose of her coming to the U.S.—and she took every measure possible to practice the language in the academic year she planned spend there. She told classmates how much she wanted to learn English and how much she appreciated their teaching her new phrases and expressions. She met two students from Japan, but she explained to them that she would try to avoid socializing with them because she did not want to lapse into speaking Japanese. That was too easy and self-defeating, she explained to them; being around American students would force her to practice English, and that was the only way to get better at it. Seiko attended every class, read all the assigned books, wrote every term paper, and tried to follow each bit of English that she could, despite the difficulty.

Whereas the U.S. and Japan had clashed at war a decade earlier, on a personal level Seiko found now that the great clash was one of different cultures, and she had to make major adjustments, although she found American ways quite acceptable. She ate at Berea College's dining hall, and at mealtimes, she sat in a chair instead of kneeling on a tatami mat, discovering it was easier on her legs and back to sit in a chair. American food was new, but she liked it. Seiko had never seen fried chicken, hush puppies (fried cornmeal bread rolled into balls), or fried liver before; they were popular Kentucky foods, and they all tasted good, even the liver. Every Friday, the cafeteria served fried fish. When she approached the dining hall, the aroma of fried fish wafted through the entire area. She had never smelled anything like it; growing up next to the ocean, she ate most fish raw, sometimes broiling it, but always keeping preparation simple. Yet she grew accustomed to fried fish and learned to like it. Perhaps the only dining hall meal that was substandard came on Sundays, when dinner was a couple of slices of bologna served on a bun. It was cold and greasy; Berea students, who were usually easy-going and accommodating, complained about it, and Seiko found that she could not stomach the breaded bun.

The food item that Seiko missed the most was rice. She obtained a cooking pot from a girl who graduated and occasionally scraped up enough money to buy rice from a grocery store, preparing it by using a hot plate in her dorm. On Sundays, for example, instead of eating the sandwich bun, she would have baloney and rice, sprinkling soy sauce on top, a combination that was salty but a welcome reminder of the Japanese diet.

From her vantage point as a Japanese student in Kentucky, Seiko witnessed American customs and traditions. One was church. Berea College asked that all students attend Sunday worship services, and the institution took this ritual seriously; Seiko knew one student who was expelled from school because she intentionally skipped these meetings. The chapel was located in the center of campus, and the number of people who went there on Sundays was surprising—students as well as faculty and their families.

Another American tradition was sports. Seiko had never seen a football or basketball game, and she had no idea what they involved. But she could tell that they were popular, and the college distributed free tickets to every student before nearby University of Kentucky home football games (Berea College had no football team). These tickets were highly coveted, yet Seiko never went to any of these games because she was oblivious to what they involved and, moreover, she had to devote every minute of her time to studying or working various jobs. When classmates learned that Seiko never used the tickets, they asked her for them, which she gladly gave away.

Another uniquely American behavior Seiko witnessed was movement. During the late autumn and early winter, she watched retired travelers from the Northeast and Upper Midwest, especially New York and Michigan, stream through Berea bound for Florida, acting like migratory birds that escaped the cold for warmer climates. These human snowbirds undertook this migration with ease, which she saw as a metaphor for the fluid mobility of Americans generally, a phenomenon she did not witness in Japan. In addition, Seiko was grateful that winters in Berea were milder than Otaru's, although temperatures still dipped below freezing on some nights, and the city got several inches of snow each year.

As the fall 1955 semester ended, Seiko was reminded of the difficult adjustments she was making. During holidays like Christmas, when dormitories cleared out, she remained in an empty building, with no way to contact her relatives other than through letters. But during that time, students who remained on campus bonded and became close, and it was during her first winter break at Berea that she got to know Lee Mitchell, who became her closest friend at Berea.

Besides friendships, correspondence kept Seiko's spirits up and made her feel less isolated. One of her daily routines in Berea was to go to her mailbox to check for letters from her parents. They wrote to her each week, and while Seiko's studies and financial condition gave her little time to write or money to afford international postage, she wrote letters to her parents about twice a month. The mailbox represented Seiko's one link to her family back in Japan, and she went there each day hoping to get a letter from them.

One professor stepped in to mentor Seiko and made an enormous difference. During the spring 1956 semester, after attending a student meeting, she was walking down Berea's main street and a white-haired, professorial-looking gentleman stopped and began speaking to her. Seiko recognized him as the History and Political Science Department chair, and he introduced himself as Professor Joseph Van Hook. He asked if she were Japanese, and when she answered yes, he said he had traveled in Japan and had worked with baseball players there. He inquired about Seiko's major, and when she told him that she was studying English so that she could improve her language skills, he recommended that she take history courses. Grateful for his suggestion, she enrolled in classes with him— and got hooked, so to speak. The professor's recommendation carved the contours of Seiko's undergraduate career, because she took two to three classes with him each semester and decided to major in history and political science, which was a combined discipline at Berea, with Dr. Van Hook as her advisor.

Originally, Seiko had planned to stay just one year in America. But by April 1956, when the academic year wound down, she felt her facility with English still had far to go. As she observed seniors finishing their last courses and preparing to graduate, an aspiration tugged at her. She thought that she, too, should earn a degree from Berea, and improve her English speaking skills that much more. When Seiko mentioned the idea to Dr. Van Hook, he immediately supported it. "That's right," he said with conviction. "You are intelligent, and you should get your degree from here." Those words had an enormous impact on Seiko and her determination to achieve her goals in the U.S.

Just as with Takakura-san, her fifth-grade teacher in Otaru, Seiko was lucky to have a mentor who encouraged her in her studies. She respected Dr. Van Hook because of his scholarship as well as his pedagogy. He had begun his teaching career in a one-room schoolhouse in 1909 before he fought for the Army in World War I. After teaching at a number of institutions, he arrived at Berea College in 1948 and made it the last stop in his academic career. He had a gift for imparting information, and his cheerfulness and sense of humor made him popular among students. He authored a textbook, *The Kentucky Story*, which was a history of the Bluegrass State geared toward junior high school students and popular enough to go through four editions. The book was a tour-de-force of Kentucky history, covering native political giants like Henry Clay as well as the state's literature, arts, and economy, including its agriculture and coal mining. Dr. Van Hook was also what Seiko termed "Kentucky kind," showing a thoughtfulness and generosity characteristic of people from state. He gave Seiko desk copies of textbooks because he knew she had little money, and he even offered to proofread her papers before she submitted them. He was a true scholar and gentleman.

III. Working Her Way Through Berea

The decision to pursue a bachelor's degree at Berea was a turning point in Seiko's education and her entire life, because it meant that she was plunking down more roots in the United States, staying throughout the calendar year, witnessing all the seasons, major holidays, and the customs associated with them. During the summer of 1956, she took a job waiting tables at Boone Tavern. This hotel and restaurant had a commanding presence on Berea's main street. It resembled a gigantic white fortress, with Ionic pillars at its entrances and flowers and shrubs manicured to perfection. It seemed a combination of Fort Knox and the White House, blending bunker-like mass with artistic elegance. At the time, the restaurant also had a no-tipping policy, which reminded Seiko of the custom in Japan, where tipping is unheard of.

In fact, work was integral to life as a Berea College student, and its work-study program made the institution renowned worldwide and had first attracted Seiko to it. In a real sense, Berea made her dream of studying English in the U.S. possible. Asking her parents to send tuition money from Otaru was unthinkable, so Seiko worked at on-campus jobs to pay for tuition plus room and board. During the 1955–56 academic year, her first in the U.S., she worked as a seamstress. Beginning in the fall 1956 term, she worked as a custodian in her dormitory. This job was convenient because she lived there and could work when she wanted, reporting her hours to a supervisor. That flexibility allowed her to set aside the time she needed to study.

Through these jobs, Seiko earned her way through college. Each time she worked, she thought of this privilege she was enjoying—studying in the U.S.—and felt appreciative. Her background in wartime Japan made her accustomed to hard work, having done everything from cooking at home to laboring in the Asari factory. This disciplined routine continued at Berea, where she budgeted time for courses and jobs. Often, while cleaning the dorm, Seiko thought about classes, reviewing lessons in her mind, so the work helped to keep her mentally focused. In the 1957–58 academic year, her conscientiousness paid off when Berea awarded her a scholarship, waiving tuition and fees and allowing her to complete her studies as long as she performed her work duties on campus.

The work ethic among Berea students was a characteristic that Seiko liked and admired. Many of them came from impoverished backgrounds common in the Appalachian region, so they never took for granted the honor of going to college. They approached their studies conscientiously, worked hard at their jobs, and saved every penny they could. For example, the drab routine of laundry became an opportunity for them to save money for their families. The dorms had basement laundry rooms, and the washers and dryers charged no fees to operate. Normally, college students save up dirty laundry for home, taking it there during breaks, but at Berea, the practice was the converse. Before Berea students went home at the end of the semester, they did as much laundry as possible to avoid using their parents' water and electricity once then returned home. Likewise, upon returning to the dorms after vacations, they brought back dirty clothes from home and engaged in an orgy of washing and drying.

The financial condition of Berea students put them all in a similar situation of lacking resources and needing to scrimp constantly. They were not big spenders; students bought little outside their dormitory, and for essentials like food, they stuck to whatever the college provided on the meal plan. Constrained by similarly tight purse strings, Seiko identified with her fellow students.

IV. A Specter Haunting the South

Berea students accepted Seiko warmly, even though she was a nontraditional student in many ways—she was from abroad, she was older than most of them, and initially, she was not enrolled in a degree program but rather wanted primarily to study the English language. But the kindness that Seiko witnessed on campus clashed with one aspect of the broader societal context of the 1950s. As a Japanese woman in the South, she encountered prejudice. Once, she was traveling with international students in a car, going through West Virginia. As they passed through a town, she saw a patrol car sitting between two houses, monitoring traffic and checking for speeders. Seated in back next to a window, Seiko looked at the police vehicle and noticed two officers inside. The students' car was going slowly enough that she could see their faces. And they could see hers. Immediately, the car pulled out of the driveway and followed them, turning on its sirens and lights. The driver of the car that Seiko was in, who was from Hungary, pulled over and rolled down his window. The officer approached and began speaking. "There is an Oriental woman in this car, and she saw us," he said. "She must not have said anything to you."

It was an odd statement, not exactly menacing, but not innocuous, either. He seemed to imply that Seiko should have warned the driver to slow down. But the student driver was observing the speed limit, and she had no reason to say anything. The officer let them off without a ticket, but he had clearly singled out the "Oriental woman" after seeing her and implied that she should have had acted more responsibly to warn the driver.

It was bad enough for a law enforcement officer to put his prejudice on display, but another incident seemed to define the stereotype of the provincial South. Seiko went with her best friend Lee Mitchell to visit her home in North Carolina, and as they boarded the Greyhound bus to return to Berea, Lee let Seiko go ahead of her up the bus stairwell.

The bus driver was looking forward, his arms stretched across the large steering wheel. He glanced at Seiko and then turned his head forward again. Staring through the windshield, without making eye contact with Seiko, he said, "There are plenty of nice seats in back."

"Oh, no, don't say that!" Lee snapped, flashing an irritation rare for her.

Seiko did not understand the meaning of what the driver had said. She knew that something was wrong to make Lee—a patient, generous, soft-spoken woman—react so strongly. They took their seats without incident and Lee never pursued the matter with Seiko.

Decades later, when talking to Japanese friends at her home in Ithaca, New York, Seiko realized what had happened. They mentioned that they encountered prejudice and segregation in the U.S., and Seiko asked them what made them say that. As one example, they said that a bus driver once told them, "There are plenty of nice seats in back."

There it was. The driver had used the exact phrase that Seiko heard on her trip with Lee. Bus drivers in the South must have deployed it regularly, like a verbal stamp they reflexively hammered down whenever they saw a target. Seiko's friends went on to explain that they were traveling with an American friend, whose response was harsher than Lee's. "Shut up!" she told the driver. Only in hearing this story years later did Seiko comprehend what that North Carolina bus driver was saying to her, as well as the reason for Lee's vehement response. He was encouraging her to bow to segregation and take a seat at the rear of the bus with other allegedly lower-class citizens.

In the mid–1950s, Berea College emerged on the cusp of the burgeoning civil rights movement. The institution had always admitted black students, and after the 1954 Supreme Court decision of *Brown versus the Board of Education*, which declared school segregation unconstitutional, the school was quick to embrace full integration. During the fall 1956 semester, in fact, Seiko had an African American roommate. But in the world outside the campus, obstacles still cropped up. A group of students told her that one evening they went to a movie theater, and a female African American student was among them. When they arrived at the cinema, the manager told them that she would have to sit in a separate section, away from her classmates.

Encountering prejudice was hurtful, and it constituted a regrettable and cautionary tale. During that era, segregation was a specter that still haunted the American South, and it stretched back more than a century. In the antebellum period, Kentucky was a slave state, although once the Civil War broke out in 1861, it was one of the border states that President Abraham Lincoln desperately needed to keep loyal to the Union to scotch the secession movement and fortify his government and military. With his wry sense of humor, Lincoln commented, "I hope to have God on my side, but I must have Kentucky." He got his wish—the state stayed in the Union, and after the war the Thirteenth Amendment abolished slavery. But by the 1950s, nearly a hundred years later, the ghosts of old attitudes and discrimination had yet to be fully exorcised.

At the same time, Seiko felt lucky. Maybe she was young and idealistic, and perhaps she felt entirely consumed by her studies. But she did not sense racism restricting her or her determination to study English in the United States. Berea College helped in this regard, because the environment on campus was open and welcoming. Students, faculty, and staff embraced Seiko as a member of the community, and the same held true for other students of different races or ethnicities. In the supportive environment that Seiko found in the U.S., she was ready to reach for new goals.

V. *Working for Graduate School*

In 1958, Seiko graduated from Berea with a bachelor's degree in history and political science. Although she still aimed to return to Japan to teach English, her Kentucky college experience had inspired her to go further. She now wanted to remain in the U.S. and attend graduate school, and she was determined to achieve that objective. Tuition, though, was a huge concern. She needed to generate income and save money to afford more schooling.

Seiko enrolled in the graduate history program at the University of Kentucky. While she lived in Lexington, Berea College allowed her to leave some belongings in the basement of Anna Smith Hall, which had been her home for three years. But after one semester at Kentucky, Seiko's money ran out, and she had to stop her studies there. It was a huge disappointment, but she resolved to pick herself up and move forward. Most important was finding income, even if it meant moving out of Kentucky. Seiko mulled over her options. She thought about returning to Berea and staying with Lee Mitchell, who lived with her mother, a Berea College staff member.

But Lee Mitchell's mother came through for Seiko. She worked in an office that tried to match Berea students with restaurant jobs, and she found a Japanese restaurant in Manhattan called Suehiro, which offered Seiko work. She moved to New York City and, while waitressing at Suehiro, she met an extremely attractive Japanese woman who often became the object of attention from restaurant patrons. Men flirted with her, and she often asked Seiko to accompany her anywhere she went, acting as a kind of marshal to protect her. At one gathering, they met an employee of Mitsui Bank, who told them that the bank's Manhattan office was trying to fill a position. Seiko contacted the branch, and they immediately gave her the job. "I think they saw me as a hard-working student," Seiko reflected, "and they believed they could rely on me." So Seiko left Suehiro and began to work for Mitsui, which was located at 40 Wall Street, a 72-story skyscraper that in the 1950s was one of the tallest buildings in lower Manhattan. The job involved office errands, like photocopying papers, but it allowed her to salt away a small amount of savings for graduate school.

Seiko's first apartment in Manhattan was on West 116th Street, just across from Columbia University's main entrance. The building was old and run-down, and she looked for someplace that was a little nicer. Japanese friends told her about the Viking Apartment building at 600 West 113th Street. She went there and immediately secured a corner studio. Her new apartment was on the 14th floor, and it faced east, giving a partial view of Manhattan's East Side and the East River. Although the location had a congenial, college-town feel because of its proximity to Columbia, Seiko kept mostly to herself. She had little money for a social life, so when she was not at work, she stayed at home and continued to practice her English skills. She tried to translate a book on U.S. diplomatic history, reading it over and over, pronouncing the words and attempting to develop English correlates for them. In one of the most exciting cities in the world, hers was a simple, straightforward routine.

But in the Viking Apartment building, a new chapter of Seiko's life was about to begin.

Conclusion
The War Never Left Them

I. The Matchmaker Was an Elevator

During the 1950s, on Manhattan's Upper West Side, the fourteen-story Viking Apartments sat at 600 West 113th Street, across from the Columbia University campus and just yards from Broadway, the long avenue that wended its way southward almost the length of the island, intersecting the Theater District that most people associate with the street's name. The higher floors of this grey, solid-looking building that faced west featured spectacular views of the Hudson River. The elevator in the Viking Apartments was slow and creaky, and it seemed to take forever whenever anyone pressed the call button. For residents rushing to work in the morning, the wait was an inconvenience.

For two residents, that wait was a blessing. In 1959, Seiko Kawakami was leasing an apartment on Viking's fourteenth floor. Working at Mitsui Bank on Wall Street, she walked from her apartment building to the 116th subway station and took the local "One" train straight to Wall Street, which was about a half-hour commute. One morning, as she waited for the clunky elevator, a young man stepped out of his apartment and walked toward the elevator. He smiled at her, and she smiled back. Seiko immediately noticed that the man had bright blue eyes, which she never saw in Japan. As they exchanged greetings, she noted a European accent.

Bogdan Mieczkowski lived on Viking's fourteenth floor, and every weekday he left the building and walked three blocks to work at the Polish research agency's offices on West 116th Street. He saw a well-dressed Japanese woman waiting for the elevator, and after he smiled at her, the two struck up a conversation. Because the elevator was so slow, they began to see each other almost every morning at the same time as they left for work.

The elevator waits allowed Bogdan and Seiko time to talk, and an intellectual spark created a chemistry between them. Seiko was impressed to learn that Bogdan had earned a Ph.D. in economics. She recalled Berea College professors reflecting on the discipline and hard work that went into a doctoral program and the specialized skills and intellectual achievement that the degree represented. Moreover, during the postwar years, colleges and universities expanded, with nearly eight million veterans taking advantage of the GI Bill's generous educational provisions. Thus, the job outlook for anyone with a doctorate looked promising, and Seiko's Berea professors referred to a Ph.D. as a "meal ticket," saying that it would almost guarantee a good career.

As they chatted before work, Bogdan recognized that Seiko was extremely well read, citing economic theory and inquiring about world events. When she learned that Bogdan came from Poland, Seiko asked him about President Wladyslaw Gomulka's policies. "Do you think that President Gomulka will just be a puppet of Nikita Khrushchev?" she inquired. "After all, during the Japanese Occupation, we had to follow whatever General MacArthur told us to do. So I'm wondering if Gomulka is just doing whatever Khrushchev tells him to do, and whether the Polish people will follow as well."

In asking the question, Seiko was trying to gauge Bogdan's reaction to the possible parallel between MacArthur's leadership and Khrushchev's ironclad rule. Bogdan was impressed that Seiko knew about Gomulka and could try to draw analogies with what she lived through in Japan after the war. Both Bogdan and Seiko followed world events closely, and they considered themselves part of a cosmopolitan community living in New York City, the crossroads of the world. Like many Americans during the 1950s, both were leery of Communist encroachment in global flashpoints, including Europe and Asia.

One morning, as they stood before the elevator, Seiko confided to Bogdan that she doubted she could stay much longer in the U.S. "I want to go to graduate school here in America to get a master's degree in history," she said, since she had studied history at Berea College and enjoyed it. But she felt uncertain about affording more schooling. "With the salary I'm earning right now at Mitsui Bank," she explained, "I doubt if I'm ever going to be able to save enough money to pay for a master's degree."

Seiko's aspirations to study and attain an advanced degree impressed Bogdan, and he tried to encourage her to stick to her plan, working and saving money while living frugally. He even offered to lend her money to defray her expenses, but she told him she might have trouble paying him back. She said she might return to Japan and teach English, which had been her original plan when she enrolled at Berea College four years earlier.

"Well, if you're really serious about going back to Japan," Bogdan replied, "you should try to see some of the cultural sites that New York City has to offer. They are splendid, and you ought to take advantage of them while you are here—places like the Metropolitan Museum of Art, the Museum of Natural History, the new Guggenheim, and Carnegie Hall. They are all worth seeing." Bogdan had continued his "museum education" in the Big Apple's grand venues, and he thought that Seiko could derive benefit from visiting them, much as he had.

Seiko expressed interest in going, but she said she lacked the money, and her job restricted her free time to just weekends. Bogdan offered a solution. For the next several weekends, he took Seiko to these attractions, paying for her admission and acting as a tour guide. For a young lady from Otaru, these Manhattan museums were dazzling, and Seiko appreciated Bogdan's generosity.

Reciprocating kindness was an important principle for both Bogdan and Seiko, and to pay him back for his thoughtfulness, Seiko started to invite Bogdan to her apartment for dinner. Luckily, he did not have to travel far. His apartment was right across the hallway from hers, and when they both had their entrance doors open, Seiko could look through Bogdan's quarters and see New Jersey across the Hudson River, while Bogdan could glimpse the buildings east of Broadway out Seiko's windows. For their suppers together, Seiko cooked the Japanese dishes that she had learned to prepare while growing up—sushi, sashimi, suki-yaki, and various noodle combinations. Bogdan had almost no culinary skills; for dinner, he often just cooked macaroni or other pasta and ate it straight. So he delighted in the delicious, nutritious meals that his neighbor prepared.

As they talked over dinners and during museum visits, Bogdan and Seiko reflected on their families and respective wartime experiences. Seiko learned that her older brother Suguru was born just one week after Bogdan, on November 15, 1924. They discovered that—less than one week apart—they suffered wartime tragedies. On September 17, 1944, Bogdan's mother Aniela was killed by a German bomb, and six days later, Seiko's older sister Yasuko died of tuberculosis. Bogdan and Seiko confided in each other about how much their grief affected them, and their shared sympathy brought them closer.

They realized that World War II gave them a common adversary. Poles had historic bad blood with the Russians. The animosity intensified when the Soviet Union invaded the eastern half of Poland in September 1939, and it continued after the war, when the Kremlin kept Poland behind the Iron Curtain and stifled its independence. The Japanese never forgave the Soviets for their August 8, 1945, declaration of war, just after the Hiroshima atomic bomb, at a time when Japan was already prostrate and beaten. Then the U.S.S.R. seized the four islands of the Northern Territories. Bogdan and Seiko spoke to each other about their countries' respective struggles against a truculent neighbor.

Over the weeks that followed, Bogdan and Seiko continued see each other, and they fell in love. During the warmer months, they went to Jones Beach in Brooklyn, attended a few Broadway plays, and occasionally enjoyed a restaurant meal. But they were most comfortable at home in each other's company. Neither of them were theatergoers, and Seiko liked cooking for Bogdan, especially because he showed such gratitude for her meals. They developed nicknames for each other, too. Seiko added the honorific suffix "-san" to her boyfriend's name, calling him "Bogdan-san," and he called her "Seishi" or simply "Seish."

In part, Bogdan and Seiko were drawn to each other because they were both strangers in a new land. Neither of them had close relatives in the U.S., and they felt alone in the country. But they found each other, and they felt a bond of solidarity and kinship because they were their new family in America, soul-mates and partners whom they could mutually rely upon and trust.

The young couple delighted in each other's sense of humor, too, perhaps an unexpected aspect of their personalities, since their parents tended to be serious. World War II might have played a role; its hardships made life's other trials seem easy by comparison, and after that bitter experience, Bogdan and Seiko could more readily see the lighthearted side of any situation. The war endowed them with the wisdom to put all experiences in perspective. Once they were in the U.S., the days of German POW camps and an oppressive Japanese government seemed far away, and these survivors could feel more lighthearted in a country where residents enjoyed liberties and a cornucopia of consumer goods.

World War II shaped their personalities in other ways. It created unimaginable disruptions in their lives, forcing them to veer far from the tranquil lives they had been enjoying as school-age children. Their wartime situations forced them to endure adversities that they would have never imagined earlier in the 1930s. Life was never perfect, but from a child's eyes, everything seemed good—until the war turned it all bad. They had no choice but to adapt and survive, as any successful living being had to do, and they learned to be malleable. One of Bogdan's favorite refrains was "I am flexible," and he and Seiko showed an ability to accept tough times and persevere. Those traits were visible as both came to a new country, conformed to new mores, and pursued their educational objectives.

Bogdan and Seiko were cheerful, too. Perhaps their adult personalities would have turned out that way regardless, but surviving that brutal war gave them insight into the worst aspects of the human experience. Having lived through the darkness of war, they emerged into what was, in effect, brilliant sunshine, and Bogdan and Seiko could be optimistic about whatever lay ahead—including a future together.

II. "You're Crazy"

On Sunday, February 5, 1961, two years after they first met while waiting for that lethargic elevator, Bogdan called his friend Marek Rudzki, who lived in Forest Hills, Queens, and worked for the New York Port Authority. "Marek," he said, "Seiko and I are going to get married tomorrow. Can you come and act as our witness?" "You're crazy," Marek replied. He could not believe that his best friend was leaping into marriage on such short notice—calling him the day before the wedding—and he worried that Bogdan was acting impulsively. But Marek agreed, taking time off from work that day to help his friend.

Bogdan and Seiko had talked about marriage, but they kept the idea to themselves. They felt a strong bond, and the move made sense on a functional level as well. Seiko had a student visa in the U.S. and remained in the country on a temporary work permit. Each year, she had to report to an immigration office in Manhattan to request permission to stay another year, and Bogdan feared that an order could come at any time that would force her to leave America and return to Japan. Ever practical, Bogdan recalled that "we decided to eliminate that threat by tying the knot," and February 6 marked a favorable date for him because it was the Polish Name Day for anyone with the name "Bogdan," honoring the Catholic saint with that same name. Name Day was more important to Poles than even one's birthday, so combining it with his wedding day would make the date more memorable for Bogdan.

On Monday, February 6, the couple met Marek at Manhattan's City Hall. In a simple ceremony, Bogdan and Seiko got married, with only Marek acting as a witness. It was a frugal, no-frills wedding, but that was fitting for two immigrants from opposite sides of the globe who had come to the U.S. with no financial resources but who were both determined to make good in their new country.

As Bogdan and Seiko emerged from City Hall as newlyweds, they began walking to catch a subway. That February, the New York City weather had been brutal. Four days earlier, temperatures plunged below zero, and over the next two days, a snowstorm dumped more than a foot of snow on the city. But Bogdan and Seiko's wedding day was sunny, and the temperature rose into the low 40s, causing some of the snow to melt and shift. As they walked to the subway station, the sun glinted off the blankets of snow while Bogdan and Seiko tread carefully along salted sidewalks and melting snow.

Suddenly, a sheet of ice and snow came crashing down from a building's second story, landing just two feet in front of them. Shocked, they both jumped backward. Had it landed on them, they would have been seriously injured. It seemed an inauspicious start to their marriage, but taken another way, it was a fortuitous sign. They were lucky to have avoided disaster, even death, just as they had during the war.

It was their wedding day, but Bogdan and Seiko were remarkably unfazed by it. At work earlier that morning, both of them simply asked for a little extra time off during their lunch hour, and after their wedding, they returned to their offices. Despite its unpretentiousness, their union was remarkable. It brought together two survivors of World War II who came to the U.S. across two different oceans, with uncertain prospects, fueled only by determination and dreams of a better life. It was as if the war had come full circle.

III. Family and Careers

In 1961, after getting married, Bogdan and Seiko traveled to Japan so that Bogdan could see Seiko's native country and meet her parents. When they got to her parents' house in Tokyo, Seiko greeted her parents without great effusiveness or fanfare, and Bogdan was surprised at the relative lack of emotion. When Seiko saw her parents, rather than running to embrace them, she moved toward them and then bowed reverentially.

One almost comical quirk that came out of the trip was linguistic. The name "Bogdan," sounded much like the Japanese word for "bomb," which is pronounced "bakudan." When Seiko introduced her new husband to friends, some of them pulled her aside and asked in disbelief, "Is his name really 'Bakudan'?!"

In 1962, Bogdan and Seiko left New York and moved to Boston, where Bogdan began work as an assistant professor of economics at Boston College. There Seiko enrolled in graduate school, earning a master's degree in history in 1965. The couple started a family when their son Van was born in Boston. But the position at Boston College was an uncomfortable fit for Bogdan, and World War II played a part in that. Although raised in a devoutly Catholic home, he had abandoned Catholicism after the war. Boston College was a Catholic institution where prayer was part of the pedagogy and liturgical vestments were common on campus. These were reminders of a past that Bogdan had abandoned, and he never shook the feeling that the job there was like an ill-fitting garb.

Opportunity came knocking when Ithaca College offered Bogdan a tenured position beginning in the fall of 1965. The institution, founded in 1892 as a music conservatory, was growing, and some of its programs were gaining national recognition, including in health and physical education. Its growth was auspicious, too. In the early 1960s, the school moved its campus from a cramped location in downtown Ithaca to a more expansive, sylvan site on South Hill, surrounded by forest and overlooking the city and Cayuga Lake, one of the Finger Lakes of Central New York. The spot offered the potential to create a bigger campus, and the college's dynamism offered Bogdan the chance to expand his scholarship and pedagogy.

The couple, with their young baby Van, found an apartment in downtown Ithaca, next to Cascadilla Creek, a tributary that snaked through the city, making its way toward Cayuga Lake. As relative newcomers to the U.S., Bogdan and Seiko continued to learn about the country's customs and traditions. Some were baffling. During their first autumn in Ithaca, on October 31, they were at home in the evening when they heard a knock on their front door. Bogdan answered the door and was surprised to find a gaggle of small children dressed in costume, who yelled at him, "Trick or Treat!" He stepped back slightly, confused by the greeting and the scene in front of him. Neither he nor Seiko had any idea what was going on. The kids explained that it was Halloween, and they expected candy from them. The Mieczkowskis had none in their home, so Bogdan gave each child a dime instead, and he thanked the little ghouls and goblins for introducing him to an American tradition.

After living for a few months in the apartment, Bogdan and Seiko bought their first house together, a four-bedroom home half a mile from Ithaca College. Their house was a 1920s-era dwelling with a large front porch and detached garage, both typical of early twentieth-century homes. They eventually added a family room, bringing the house's square footage to 1,700.

In August 1965, just weeks before Bogdan was to begin his first semester in his new job, the young couple returned from Ithaca College's outdoor swimming pool, a large facility on the campus's eastern end that became a favorite watering hole for the college community. Bogdan began going through mail, and he suddenly became quiet. Seiko recognized the blue parchment of international mail and knew that he was reading a letter from Poland. It was from Bogdan's brother Janusz, relating the news that their father Tadeusz had died on August 5. He was eighty years old.

Tadeusz had attended college in the U.S. and began his working career there, but he had been unable to return to the country, even after Bogdan became a U.S. citizen. Bogdan regretted that his father never got to meet his grandchildren in the U.S. He and Seiko's family grew to three sons: Van, Yanek, and Dean. Tadeusz gave Bogdan a model for good fatherhood, working industriously at his job while providing for his family. Bogdan did the same, and he was utterly devoted to his three boys, driving them to the public library each week for books, taking them on bicycle trips through an abandoned railroad line that stretched south of Ithaca, and driving the family to Florida for multiple vacations. Bogdan continued to read constantly, both for work and leisure, but he had an ironclad rule: if any of his sons entered his study to talk to him, he would stop reading even mid-sentence to address whatever concern brought him there.

Raising three boys kept Seiko constantly busy. She never drove a car in Japan or during her first years in the U.S., but in the postwar years, the car practically became part of the American family (with the garage becoming attached to homes, symbolizing the physical as well as emotional proximity of the automobile). While in Boston, Seiko obtained her driver's license, which allowed her to run errands for her family. She continued her career, too. Whereas she began her teaching career instructing English to Japanese students, she now switched roles, teaching Japanese to American students. In 1971, she joined the East Asian Studies faculty at Eisenhower College in Seneca Falls, New York, becoming an adjunct professor of Japanese language. The small liberal arts college was founded in 1968 as a national tribute to Dwight D. Eisenhower, the five-star general and thirty-fourth president, but its enrollment struggled during the 1970s. When the college closed in 1983, Seiko next taught at Binghamton University. Her distant commutes to these schools were often difficult, since winters in Central New York brought heavy snowfall that made travel treacherous. But Seiko enjoyed college instruction and the classroom environment, and she was a popular professor among students.

What had brought Bogdan and Seiko to the U.S. was their determination to continue their education. As college professors, they fell into fitting roles. For Seiko, the position continued her family's tradition of teaching, and for Bogdan, he could impart his knowledge of international economics to students while delving into the research and writing he enjoyed.

Their backgrounds endowed Bogdan and Seiko with an opportunity for scholarship, and both published about their respective countries. In 1974, Seiko published her revised master's thesis in the *Journal of the Illinois State Historical Society* as "Horace Capron and the Development of Hokkaido: A Reappraisal," examining the U.S. commissioner of agriculture during the 1870s and his recommendations for improving farming on Hokkaido. She used her classroom as a laboratory to experiment with innovative pedagogical techniques. She realized that a gap existed in the Japanese language textbook literature; no books were available for English-speaking students who wished to pursue their study of Japanese beyond the introductory level. Thus, in 2016, she published *A Tie Between People: Advanced Japanese Reader*, a textbook designed to allow students to continue studying Japanese once they acquired some facility with the language.

In 1975, Bogdan published *Personal and Social Consumption in Eastern Europe*, which examined consumption—the ultimate goal of producers, after all, is to get their goods consumed in one form or another—in Poland, Hungary, Czechoslovakia, and East Germany. While Bogdan found that consumption patterns, including diets, had improved in Eastern Europe after the war, he concluded that countries behind the Iron Curtain lagged behind their Western European counterparts. His follow-up book, *Transportation in Eastern Europe* (1978), reported similar findings, noting that transportation—both for people and freight— improved in Eastern Europe in the postwar years but overall, transport systems in Communist-controlled countries were inadequate. Clear evidence drove his conclusions: centrally planned economies imposed great costs and inefficiencies on the region and retarded its overall development.

The collapse of the Iron Curtain in 1989 and independence for Eastern Europe allowed Poland to breathe freely again. Bogdan took advantage of the country's newfound freedom to make an extended visit in 1994, marking the first time he set foot on Polish soil in more than three decades. He made a number of return trips after that and was glad to see the country's economy modernize after decades of stunted growth.

Seiko made regular visits to her relatives in Japan. In 1958, Hiroshi

Seiko and Yanek Mieczkowski with former Japanese Prime Minister Yasuhiro Nakasone during a 2016 visit to Tokyo. On the table before Prime Minister Nakasone is Seiko's newly published textbook, *A Tie Between People*.

and Echi retired and moved to Tokyo, as did Suguru, Shizuko, and Kazutoshi, who were all married with children. In 1982, lung cancer claimed Hiroshi's life. He had always been a heavy smoker, but he lived to the age of 84, and Seiko theorized that he lived as long as he did because of another habit—his consumption of green tea, which contained powerful antioxidant catechins and anticancer properties that might have inoculated him against cancer for a long period. Following his death, Echi lived with Shizuko's family until her passing in 1989.

Bogdan continued teaching until the age of 75, showing the physical stamina and drive that were his trademarks, retiring in 2000. At that time, he and Seiko left the snowy winters of Central New York and relocated to Florida. Bogdan had a chronic cough that cold weather exacerbated, and they found the year-round warmth a tonic. Both of them pursued writing into retirement, with Bogdan completing his final book in 2003 and Seiko publishing her textbook in 2016.

IV. *The War's Lasting Impact*

World War II was the twentieth century's seminal event. It pulverized Japan, but in an unexpected turn of events, that battering allowed the country to rebuild and ascend as an international economic giant. It pummeled Europe, already scarred from World War I, sentencing its countries to a long period of reconstruction and reconciliation. Into the world power vacuum stepped the U.S., which emerged the unquestioned international leader.

On a personal level, World War II became a defining moment for those people who lived through it. For Bogdan and Seiko, the war stayed with them. For the rest of their lives, they could not forget that conflict, and it continued to shape their behavior. For example, having lived through the scarcities of World War II, they both retained frugal habits, shopping for bargains and avoiding debt. "The personal penury of war and postwar experiences," Bogdan recalled, "persisted for a long time." Waste always shocked them, and the throw-away habits of the younger, post–World War II generation often surpassed their understanding. For survivors of that conflict, every morsel of food was precious, every raiment of clothing valuable.

The unsettling cat-and-mouse existence in wartime Warsaw made Bogdan avoid behavior that attracted attention—including conspicuous consumption. He bought small, run-of-the-mill cars and shunned trendy clothes and jewelry of any kind. Rather than frequent restaurants, he preferred to eat at home. Many of these habits dovetailed with the thriftiness that the war inculcated, but they also stemmed from Bogdan's desire to blend in with his environment and go unnoticed.

Bogdan's wartime experiences affected him in unexpected ways. Into middle age and beyond, he impressed his family and friends with his physical stamina and energy. In his mid-fifties, he achieved the dream of many homeowners by having a new, five-bedroom house built, and he and his sons went to the construction site to work on it and perform landscaping, including lifting heavy flagstones to form ornamental walkways. The new Mieczkowski home was less than a mile from the Ithaca College campus, and for the next twenty years, Bogdan walked to work through the woods that separated their house from the school, tallying thousands of commuter miles, all by foot. Luckily, Bogdan's feet functioned well, and he suffered no debilitating effects from the frostbite he had suffered as a POW.

Both he and Seiko also took up lap swimming, with Bogdan easily racking up a mile daily during the summer. He even made double-crossings of Cayuga Lake, which were three-mile swims. During summers in Ithaca, along with his sons, he used a chainsaw to cut firewood, felling large trees, slicing up the trunks into manageable pieces, loading them onto off-road vehicles, and driving them to his house. There, he cut and stacked them into pieces to feed into a wood stove during winter. These physical exploits would have taxed the energies of men half his age. When asked where he got his stamina, Bogdan replied, "I survived prisoners-of-war camps." He felt that the months as a POW had annealed his entire physical system, ratcheting up his body's endurance levels for the rest of his life and giving him a psychological edge as well.

The war experience shaped Bogdan's scholarship as well. During the last two decades of his academic career, he developed an interest in what he termed "dysfunctional bureaucracy in academia." Throughout much of his time in academe, he battled college administrators, who struck him as overcompensated rulers that encrusted a school like barnacles on a ship, securing their places with what he dubbed a "protective strata" of like-minded bureaucrats, all the while impeding an institution's proper functioning. Bogdan used his economics training to analyze the problem's financial and social costs, and he wrote four books on the topic, including *Dysfunctional Bureaucracy: A Comparative and Historical Perspective* (1991), *The Rot at the Top: Dysfunctional Bureaucracy in Academia* (1995), and *The Bureaucratic Campus: Politicizers, Corrupted Standards, and Bias* (2003).

He had seen too much bad government before and during World War II. He explained that the war inculcated a heightened sense of duty to resist the unethical behavior he witnessed on campus. "I survived the war," he wrote, "and among the lessons I learned from my experiences was an important one: Submission to tyranny is craven, and the life of a slave is not worth living, people have a moral obligation to fight against evil for the sake of future generations and for the sake of one's own future, too." Anyone who fails to resist, Bogdan warned, ultimately will surrender freedom and forsake the opportunity to improve conditions for their children and grandchildren.

In 2015, Bogdan attended a ceremony at the Polish Embassy in Washington that recognized his fighting in the Warsaw Uprising, and he received a special commemorative medal. But he remained modest about his contributions to the effort. In 2019, his son Yanek visited Warsaw and observed ceremonies that marked the 75th anniversary of the Uprising, which included enormous street celebrations and media interviews with surviving veterans. Bogdan was too frail to travel, but when Yanek returned to the U.S., he commented to his father that he was a hero. Bogdan demurred. "The real heroes," he replied, "are the ones who sacrificed their lives for the cause."

In July 2020, Bogdan fell ill with a thrush infection and went into complete renal failure; he was hospitalized in an intensive care unit. He appeared to rally, and his tough survival instincts, tested so severely during World War II, kicked in. Over the next month Bogdan fought valiantly for his life. But on August 26, 2020, he died at the age of 95. He was one of the last surviving veterans of the Warsaw Uprising.

Bogdan and Seiko Mieczkowski in 2012.

Conclusion

Seiko orchestrated a lasting tribute to her husband. Growing up in Otaru, she always regretted that the city's public library was small, hardly enough to slake her thirst for knowledge. She arranged to have a new addition built to the Otaru Public Library in her husband's name, commemorating Bogdan's scholarship, his love of books, and her fellow immigrant to the U.S. who became her partner for more than sixty years. Upon entering the library's new children's room, visitors see a plaque with Bogdan's face and name. In the city where his wife experienced World War II, children glimpse a veteran who fought in that conflict on the other side of the globe. It brings to mind the motto of the Armia Krajowa, "We remember." This book constitutes part of that remembrance.

Recalling conflict is tough, and World War II was especially cruel. In Poland and Japan, it hit hard, and Bogdan and Seiko witnessed how it killed citizens, destroyed property and livelihoods, and snatched away happiness, innocent childhoods, and opportunities to lead normal lives. Dwight D. Eisenhower once commented, "War is the ultimate failure of everything you try to do as a country. It's the ultimate failure of diplomacy. It's the ultimate failure of civil behavior." He was right.

The war devasted Bogdan and Seiko and defeated their countries,

The Mieczkowski family at their home in Ithaca, New York. Left to right: Van, Yanek, Dean, Seiko, Bogdan

but it also taught them vital lessons, which they in turn could impart to future generations. What helped Bogdan and Seiko to survive the war also gave them purpose in their lives—a purpose that seemed even larger than themselves. Here, two factors were essential. One was family. For both, their family bonds endowed them with the emotional strength to endure war's shattering hardships, especially the deaths of Bogdan's mother and Seiko's sister, at a time when cherished support struts—for Bogdan, his Catholic faith; for Seiko, her belief in the emperor—lay broken beyond repair. As bleak as the early 1940s were, Bogdan and Seiko had the love and support of their family, as well as a home to repair to at day's end. When they were shorn of an immediate family presence, as Bogdan was in his POW camps and Seiko at Berea College, they thought of their parents and siblings daily, and they resolved to live up to their families' expectations and standards of conduct and success.

A second factor was education. Bogdan and Seiko's learning was a critical pillar of support, during the war and after. No matter how war devastated their classroom study, Bogdan and Seiko never abandoned learning. In fact, they used reading and studying as a way to cushion themselves from war's harsh hand, diverting their attention to more positive channels. They found ways to edify themselves, whether it was through Bogdan's participation in the Warsaw *komplety* system or Seiko's imbibing music and chemistry lessons at the Asari factory. They continually set new reading and learning goals, which kept them focused on personal growth that could transcend the conflict engulfing everything around them.

World War II was tragic. But Bogdan and Seiko were optimists, and for them, the war was also serendipitous. If not for that conflict, they might have remained in their countries, perhaps staying in their hometowns, living comfortable lives without risking other ventures. Just as the war forced their countries to rebuild, it compelled them to restructure their futures. In the U.S., they created new lives for themselves and their family. The war that was so devastating opened opportunities to emerge from its dark shadow and step into sunshine. For that, Bogdan and Seiko were grateful.

Sources for Further Reading

Anders, Wladyslaw. *An Army in Exile: The Story of the Second Polish Corps.* Nashville: The Battery Press, 2004.
Baluk, Stefan. *Silent and Unseen: I Was a Polish WW II Special Ops Command.* Warsaw: Askon, 2009.
Bartoszewski, Wladyslaw. *Abandoned Heroes of the Warsaw Uprising.* Krakow: Bialy Kruk, 2008.
Borgsen, Werner, and Klaus Volland. *Stalag X B Sandbostel. Zur Geschichte eines Kriegsgefangenen-und KZ-Auffanglagers in Norddeutschland 1939–1945.* Bremen: Edition. Temmen, 1991.
Czajkowskik, Zbigniew. *Warsaw 1944: An Insurgent's Journal of the Uprising.* Barnsley: Pen & Sword Military, 2012.
Davies, Norman. *Rising '44: The Battle for Warsaw.* New York: Macmillan, 2003.
Ferrell, Robert. *The Dying President: Franklin D. Roosevelt, 1944–1945.* Columbia: University of Missouri Press, 1998.
Fleming, Thomas. *The New Dealers War: F.D.R. and the War Within World War II.* New York: Basic Books, 2001.
Hanson, Joanna. *The Civilian Population and the Warsaw Uprising of 1944.* New York: Cambridge University Press, 1982.
Jowett, Philip. *The Japanese Home Front 1937–45.* New York: Bloomsbury, 2021.
Korbonski, Stefan. *Fighting Warsaw: The Story of the Polish Underground State, 1939–1945.* New York: Hippocrene Books, 2004.
Koskodan, Kenneth. *No Greater Ally: The Untold Story of Poland's Forces in World War II.* Oxford: Osprey Publishing, 2011.
Lukas, Richard. *The Forgotten Holocaust: The Poles Under German Occupation, 1939–1944.* Lexington: University Press of Kentucky, 1986.
Marian Mazgaj. *In the Polish Secret War: Memoir of a World War II Freedom Fighter.* Jefferson NC: McFarland 2009.
Miron Bialoszewski. *A Memoir of the Warsaw Uprising.* New York: Penguin Random House, 2015.
Moorhouse, Roger. *Poland 1939: The Outbreak of World War II.* New York: Basic Books, 2020.
Ogura, Toyofumi. *Letters from the End of the World: A Firsthand Account of the Bombings of Hiroshima.* Tokyo: Kodansha, 2001.
Richie, Alexandra. *Warsaw 1944: Hitler, Himmler, and the Warsaw Uprising.* New York: Farrar, Straus and Giroux, 2013.
Sakamoto, Pamela Rotner. *Midnight in Broad Daylight: A Japanese American Family Caught Between Two Worlds.* New York: HarperCollins, 2016.
Snyder, Timothy. *Bloodlands: Europe Between Hitler and Stalin.* London: Random House, 2010.
Walker, Jonathan. *Poland Alone: Britain, SOE, and the Collapse of the Polish Resistance, 1944.* Stroud: History Press, 2008.

INDEX

Numbers in **_bold italics_** indicate pages with illustrations

ABCD Powers 27
academic bureaucracy 201–2
acetylene gas 53
Aerated Bread Company 168
Ainu people 29, 30
air defenses of Japan 120
air defenses of Poland 86
Aleutian Islands 112, 180
Allied Powers 19, 63, 73, 90, 117, 118, 119, 120, 121, 138, 140, 142, 144, 145, 146
Alton, Thad 173, 177
Amaterasu (Sun Goddess) 74
Anders, Wladyslaw 142
Anglo-Polish Alliance 18
Anna Smith Residence Hall (Berea College) 181, 182, 189
Arc de Triomphe 140
Argentina 164
Anschluss 17, 59
Armia Krajowa: 59, 78, 79, 203; homemade weapons 84, 85; shortages and lack of armaments 78, 81, 84, 86; surrender 105, 107
Armour Institute 10
Article 9 of the postwar Japanese constitution 153
Aryan superiority 47
Asari, Hokkaido 113, 119–20, 148, 180
Ash, William 134
Atlantic Charter 144
Atlee, Clement 146
atomic bombs 121–22, 148–49, 150
Attu (Aleutian Islands) 69
Auschwitz concentration camp 55, 129
Austin, Steve 76–77
Australia 68, 164, 168
Austria 8, 16–17, 52, 173
Austria-Hungary 8
Axis Powers 69, 152, 160

B-17 Flying Fortresses 90
B-24 Liberator 145
B-29 bombers 112
"bakudan" (bomb) 196
Baltic Sea 15, 69, 175
barricade building during Warsaw Uprising 79, **_80_**
basketball 184
bathing during war 35, 55–56, 77, 89, 128
bathroom practices 35–36, 128
Battle of Britain 45, 146
Battle of Coral Sea 68
Battle of Guadalcanal 69
Battle of Leyte Gulf 118
Battle of Midway 69
bedbugs in Warsaw 53
Beethoven, Ludwig von 52, 67
Beijing, China 27
Belarus 20, 21
Berea, Kentucky 161, 181
Berea College 161, 183–84, 192; desegregation 188–89; work-study program 161, 186
Bergen-Belsen POW camp 129, 132
bigos 51
Binghamton University 198
Biuletyn Informacyjny 57
Black Sea 143
blitzkrieg 18, 45
Bolshevik Revolution 8
Bonaparte, Napoleon 45
Boone Tavern 186
Boston College 196
The Bourne Identity 181
Brda River 12
Bremen, Germany 132
Brenner Pass 52
Brest, Poland 21, 22
Brest-Litovsk Treaty 21

British Malaya 27
British soldiers as liberators 138–40
Brooklyn, New York 194
Brown v. Board of Education 188
Bug River 22
The Bureaucratic Campus 201
burials in Warsaw 88, *104*
Burlington, Vermont 173
Bydgoszcz, Poland 3, 7, 54, 61, 64, 109, 130, 137, 140, 164; downtown 12; Germans in 15, 19–20; Mieczkowski home in *13*, *14*

Canada 134, 164, 175
Cape Erimo, Japan 114
Capron, Horace 198
carbide lights 53
Carpathian Mountains 15
Cascadilla Creek (Ithaca, New York) 197
cats, Japanese fondness for 72
Cayuga Lake, New York 197, 201
Chamberlain, Neville 17, 45, 144
Chicago 10, 169–70, 171, 180, 181
China 26, 27
chiropractor 83
chocolate 74, 155–56
"choose freedom" 175
Chopin, Frédéric 43
Christmas 10, 184
Chrysanthemum Throne 75
church services *see* religion
Churchill, Winston 45, 122, 143, 144
cigarette smoking 49–50, 140, 167
Cincinnati, Ohio 181
civil rights movement 188–89
Clay, Henry 185
clothes washing 36, 187
clothing during wartime 51, 74, 81, 111, 114, 117, 135
coffee 51
Cold War 146, 152, 153, 175
colonialism 27, 117–18
Columbia University 173, 177, 190, 191
Columbus, Christopher 29
Communism 192, 199; control of Poland 172–73, 174–77
Compiègne Forest (France) 45
Congress, U.S. 26
Copernicus, Nicolaus 43
Covid-19 virus 3
Crown Can Company 171
Curie, Marie 43
Czapska, Marysia 20–21
Czechoslovakia 17, 144, 199

D-Day 62, 106, 108, 138
Damon, Matt 181

DDT 139
disillusionment with Japanese government after WWII 3, 150, 151–52
"displaced persons, Polish 147
doctors *see* physicians
Dodge, Joseph 160
donut factory, Bogdan's work in 171
Dresden, Germany 128
Dutch East Indies 128
"dying president" (Franklin Roosevelt) 145
Dysfunctional Bureaucracy 201

East Germany 177, 199
Easter 10
Eastern Europe 145, 168, 175, 176, 198–99
economics, Bogdan's study of 167
Eisenhower, Dwight D. 140, 198, 203
Eisenhower College 198
electricity rationing during war 36, 53, 103
England *see* Great Britain
English Channel 62
enigma encryption machine 144
Eramizawa, Japan 29
Esashi, Japan 30
espionage in wartime Warsaw 54
Estonia 163
ethnic cleansing by Germans 46
Etorofu, Japan 152
European Recovery Program 175, 176
executions in Warsaw 55, 57, 58, 64

Fallingbostel, Germany 129, 132
Ferrell, Robert 145
filipinki (Molotov cocktail) **80**, 83, 84, 106
Final Solution 55
Finland 171
fires in Warsaw 84, 85, **87**
Fleming, Thomas 145
Florida 200
food, Bogdan's 51–52, 89–90, 109, 129, 134–35, 140, 143, 168, 169, 173, 193
food, Seiko's 71, 73, 74, 114, 155–56, 181, 183–84, 193
football 184
Four Power Treaty 26
France 26, 45, 56, 61, `46
RMS *Franconia* 169, 170
frostbite, Bogdan's struggles with 131–32, 162, 201
Fujinotomo (*Friends of Females* magazine) 161

gangrene 91
Gdansk, Poland 137, 175

Index

Geneva Convention 107, 110–11
Georgia 149
German Americans 119
Germany 17, 26, 82, 84, 113, 120, 138, 171; bombing campaign against Warsaw 44, 86–89, 98, 102–3; ethnic cleansing practices 54–55; manpower shortages during WWII 62, 136; Poland, invasion 18–20, 46, 133, 174; Soviet Union, invasion 17, 50, 60, 52, 69, 82, 146; tanks 80, 81, 83, 106
GI Bill of 1944 150, 192
Gibraltar 145
Glasgow, Scotland 143, 164
Goebbels, Joseph 61
Goliath (robotic tank) 85
Gomulka, Wladyslaw 192
Great Britain 34, 138–39, 143, 146, 164, 168
Great Depression 71
Great Synagogue 63
Greater East Asia Co-Prosperity Sphere 27
grenades 64, 84, 85, 99, 101, 102
Greyhound bus 181, 188
Grossborn, Germany 129, 132
guerrilla warfare during Warsaw Uprising 84, 106
Gulag 21
Gypsies 54–55

Habomai, Japan 152
hakama (Japanese skirt) 30
Hakodate, Japan 121, 178
Halifax, Canada 169
Halloween 197
Hamburg, Germany 129, 132
Harnas, Gustav 64
Harrod's Department Store 168
Hercules bicycle 167
Herring 32
Hershey *see* chocolate
Hikama-maru 178, 179, 180
Himmler, Heinrich 108
hina dolls 96–97
Hirohito, Emperor 3, 74–75, 204; dedication of the Japanese people to 3, 152; divinity 154; postwar status 153–55; radio address to Japan 122–23
Hiroshima, Japan 121, 141, 149
history, "top down" versus "bottom up" 2
Hitler, Adolf 16, 17, 18, 44, 52, 55, 60, 86, 107–8, 144, 162
hoanden 75
Hokkaido 28–29, 31, 32, 120, 121, 149, 152; possible invasion by the Soviet Union 121–22, 151

Hokkaido Prefectural Office 29
Hokkaido Shinbun 157
Honshu 34, 120, 121, 149, 178
Hudson River 191, 193
humor during wartime 52, 74
Hungary 19, 187, 199

idioms, Japanese, during wartime 67–68
Imperial Hokkaido University 29
Imperial Rescript 154
imperial system (weights and measures) 183
Impregnacja 11–12, 14, 15, 20, 46, 54
independence day in Poland 8, 18
Indochina 28
inflation during WWII 49
Iron Curtain 176, 177, 199
"island hopping" campaign of WWII 119
Italy 52, 141–42
Ithaca, New York 1, 150, 188, 197, 201
Ithaca College 196–97, 201
Ivey, Doris 1
Ivey, John 1
Iwo Jima 119

Japan 26–27, 34, 68, 70, 71, 112–13, 120, 121, 143
Japanese-American relocation camps 180
Japanese economy during wartime 117–18
Japanese government wartime controls 66–67, 68, 69, 71, 73, 121
Japanese Ministry of Education 70
jaundice, Bogdan's bout with 143
Jewish Uprising in Warsaw (1943) 63
Jews during WWII 52, 53
Jodl, Alfred 140
Jones Beach, New York 194

kamikaze warrior 118
kan (Japanese unit of weight) 114
Kapelska, Jozef 12
kapos 136
Katyn Forest Massacre 61, 131, 176–77
Kawakami, Echi 29–30, 32, 37, 70, 72, 73, 74, 92, 94, 96, 97, 113, 123, 150, 156, 200
Kawakami, Hiroshi 29–30, 32, 37, 70, 72, 73, 74, 92, 94, 96, 97, 113, 123, 150, 156, 199–200
Kawakami, Seiko: closeness to Yasuko 93, 96; college teaching 198; correspondence with parents 184; departure from Otaru 178; elementary school education 25–26, 37–38; English language learning 66, 160, 161, 181–83, 190; factory work 113–16, 186; graduate studies 189, 192, 196; jobs at Berea

College 186; ocean voyage to the U.S. 180; teaching career, start of 158–59
Kawakami, Shizuko 30, 32, 35, 36, 156, 178, 179, 200
Kawakami, Suguru 25, 30, 35, 36, 156, 193; kamikaze training 70, 94, 123, 148, 200
Kawakami, Yasuko 35, 36, 96, 109, 156, 178; death 94, 193, 204; diagnosed with tuberculosis 91; graduation from high school 92; qualities as a sister 92–93; sanitarium 93–94
Kawakami family 30, 32, 35–37, 155–57; cats 72–73; vegetable garden 95
Kentucky 189
The Kentucky Story 185
Khrushchev, Nikita 192
Kierbedz bridge 79
Kobryn, Poland 20
Koiso, Kuniaki 112
Komorowski, Tadeusz 78
komplety education 47–48, 49, 60, 63, 102, 135, 142, 163, 164, 204
konbu 114
Korean War 170, 176
Krakow, Poland 109
Kruszewski, Wacek 163–64
Kunashiri, Japan 152
Kunikida, Doppo 38
Kyushu 118, 120
kyusu 30

labor shortages in Japan 70, 112–13
Lagerlof, Selma 38
Lake District, Great Britain 143, 164
Latin language 47
Latvia 163
laundry *see* clothes washing
League of Nations 26–27
lebensraum 18, 26, 108
Leipzig, Germany 128
Lenin, Vladimir 16
Leningrad, siege of 69, 171
Lexington, Kentucky 189
Liaodong Peninsula (China) 26
Lincoln, Abraham 189
Lithuania 163
Liverpool, England 143, 169
Lohman, Philipp 173
London 44, 45, 60, 61, 62, 78, 147, 164, 167, 169
London University 164, 165
Lublin 61, 145
Lucancia, Italy 142
Ludlum, Charlotte 181–82
Ludlum, Robert 181
Luftwaffe 45, 86

Lutomek farm 15–16
Luzon, Philippines 68

MacArthur, Douglas 68, 124, 153–54, 192
Madja, Przemek 64
Majdanek, Poland 129
Manchester, England 143
Manchuria 26, 112
Manhattan, New York 190, 191, 195
Manila, Philippines 68
manniki nekko 72
Marco Polo Bridge Incident 27
Marconi, Leandro 63
Margrabianka hotel 15
Marianas Islands 112
Marison, Boyden 176–77
marriage of Bogdan and Seiko 195–96
marriages, arranged 30
Marshall, George 175
Marshall Plan *see* European Recovery Program
Marszalkowska Street 24, 44, 78, **110**
Maryanski, Antek 102
Matera, Italy 142
mentorship from professors 167, 185–86
Meppen, Germany 141
metric system 183
MG-42 machine gun 86
Michigan 160
Mieczkowski, Aniela 12, 20, 51, 53, **59**, 85, 101, 109, 147, 164; Catholic faith 10, 52; death 103–4, 141, 193, 204
Mieczkowski, Bogdan: agnosticism 162, 196; arrival in the U.S. 170; avoidance of Warsaw streetcar fee 56; books written by 198–99; debates returning to Poland 162, 163, 164, 166; diet during war 51–52; doctoral dissertation 172–73, 192; education during WWII 46, 47–48; English language 135, 140, 166, 171; German language knowledge 16, 58–59, 171; image as a hungry teenager 49, 50, 52; injured during Uprising 99–100; jobs in Nazi-occupied Warsaw 49–51; medical care for wounds 100–2; "museum education" 166, 193; officers school 141; patriotism 3, 140–41, 162; thumb wound 129, 139, 141, 162; underground courier 57
Mieczkowski, Dean 197
Mieczkowski, Hala 15–16, 53–54, 55, 64
Mieczkowski, Janusz 9, 57, **59**, 85, 87–88, 101, 103, 104, 109, 164, 174
Mieczkowski, Ludwig 15
Mieczkowski, Sozosia 174
Mieczkowski, Tadeusz 10, 19, 20, 21, 85,

104, 109, 137, 147, 170, 174, 197; daily routine in Bydgoszcz 12; education 10–11; hobbies 13; hotel 15; support of boys' education 16; work during WWII 49
Mieczkowski, Van 196, 197
Mieczkowski, Wlodzimierz ("Walter") 169, 170
Mieczkowski, Yanek *133*, 197
Mieczkowski, Zbigniew 9, 55, 57, 64, 104, 109, 130, 174–75
Mieczkowski apartment in Warsaw 24, 53–54, 59
Mieczkowski family crest 12
Mikolawjczk, Stanislaw 107
minshushugi (democracy) 151
Miracle on the Vistula 16
miso soup 73
USS *Missouri* 124
Mitchell, Lee 184, 188, 190
Mitsui Bank 190, 191, 192
Molotov, Vyacheslav 17, 80
Molotov-Ribbentrop Line 22
Mongols 118
Monte Cassino, Italy 142
Montgomery, Bernard 138
Mount Killington 173
Mount Moiwa 29
Mount Suribachi 119
Mount Teguyama 32, 33
Muehlberg, Germany 129, 132
Mukden, China 26
Munich Conference 17, 144
Murnau am Staffelsee, Germany 141
music 52, 67
Mussolini, Benito 45, 52

Nagasaki, Japan 150
Nagoya, Japan 119
Nakamichi, Hiroko 92
Naklo, Poland 11
Name Day, Polish 195
Nanking, China 27
napalm 119
Naples, Italy 143
national anthem, Japan 75
national anthem, Poland 8
National Cosmopolitan Bank 170
National Origins Act (1924) 26
navy, Japanese 26, 28, 34, 68–69, 70, 123
navy, United States 68, 69
Nazi destruction of Polish leadership 7, 19, 46–47
Netherlands 27, 129
The New Dealers' War 145
New Jersey 193
New Year's Day in Japan 154

New York City 170, 173, 177, 192–96
The New York Times 154
New Zealand 168
Nimitz, Chester 118–19
no-tipping policy 186
Nobel Prize 43
North Carolina 188
Northern Territories of Japan 152, 193
nurses during WWII 83, 100

Oata, Minoru 91
obedience of Japanese people 28, 36, 71, 149, 151
Obon 156
Oda, Mikio 26
Okinawa, Japan 120
Old Town section of Warsaw 44, 86, 98, 99, 106
Olympics: 1927 Summer, Amsterdam 26; 1932 Winter, Lake Placid 173; 1972 Winter, Sapporo 151; 1980 Winter, Lake Placid 173
onions, Bogdan's request for 134
Onoda, Hiroo 77
onsen (hot springs) 29
Operation Barbarossa *see* Soviet Union, invaded by Germany
Operation Sealion 45
Operation Starvation 118–19
Order for Warsaw 108
Osaka, Japan 119
Otaru, Japan 34, 36, 37, 66, 113; location 32; reaction to atomic bombs 149; street vendors 70–71; veterans 149–50; wartime economy 34–35, 70
Otaru Bay 75–76
Otaru Prefectural Girls High School 37
Otaru School of Economics and Commerce 157, 158

Pabst, Frederick 44
Panay, sinking of 27–28
Paris 60, 62, 108
"Paris of the East," Warsaw as 44, **89**
partitioning of Poland 8
Pas de Calais, France 62
patriarchal nature of Japanese society 30, 158
Patton, George 138–39
Pearl Harbor 25, 28, 34, 37, 68
Perry, Matthew 154, 181
Personal and Social Consumption in Eastern Europe 198–99
Philippines 27, 68, 77
physicians during WWII 91, 101, 102, 139
Pilsudski, Jozef 16

Poland: borders 8, *9*, 163; casualty rate during WWII 34; consumer economy after WWII 175–77; contributions to Allied war effort 108–9, 144; government-in-exile 59–60, 61, 62, 78, 107, 145; invaded by Germany and the Soviet Union 18–20, 147, 163, 193; leadership classes destroyed 47; rebellions against Russian rule 8, 10; rebirth as a nation 8, 18; refugees from 19, 23; wartime economy 49, 51
Polish Armed Division 141
Polish Home Army *see* Armia Krajowa
Polish-Lithuanian Commonwealth 8
Polish National Income and Production 177
Polish Resettlement Corps 169
Polish University College (PUC) 164, 165, 166
Pollack, Jackson 179
polonium 43
Polska Walczy ("Poland Fights") 59
Pomerania 8
Poniatowski bridge 79
post-traumatic stress disorder (PTSD) 149, 163
potatoes 50, 51, 73, 75, 95, 116, 132
POWs (prisoners-of-war) 62, 127–28, 131, 134, 137; food 129, 132, 134–35
Poziomak (original Mieczkowski family name) 57
prejudice in the American South 187–89
Prudential Building in Warsaw 100
Prussia 8
Pullman Palace cars 127
pumpkins 73, 95

racism *see* prejudice in the American South
radio 25, 37, 52, 67, 68, 122–23, 148, 160
railroads 45, 113, 127–28, 129, 132, 140, 164, 178, 180–81, 198–99
reading 16, 38–39, 47–48, 52, 137, 142, 157–58, 161, 166, 183, 190, 204
Red Cross 61, 86, 134, 140, 169
Reims, France 140
Rejewski, Marian 144
religion in Japan 66, 76
religion in Poland 10, 52–53, 89
restaurants, Seiko's work in 186, 190
Ribbentrop, Joachim von 17
Ribbentrop-Molotov Pact *see* Soviet-German Non-Aggression Pact
rice 73, 183–84
River Mersey 169
Riverside Park (New York City) 177

Rolls-Royce 26, 155
Roma *see* Gypsies
Romania 19, 49, 60, 177
Rome 108
Roosevelt, Franklin 61, 68, 122, 143–45
The Rot at the Top 201
Rotterdam, Netherlands 174
Rousseau, Jean-Jacques 8
Rudzki, Adam 166, 169
Rudzki, Alec 169
Rudzki, Marek 165–66, 170, 195
Rudzki, Walunia 166
Russia 8, 26; *see also* Soviet Union
Russo-Polish War 16
ryakyu (baseball) 66

Saipan 112
Sakhalin 34, 112
Sandbostel POW camp 132–39
sappers (combat engineers) 99
Sapporo, Japan 29, 151, 157
Scottish bagpipers 138
Sea of Japan 32, 178
seaweed 114–15, 116–17
Second Polish Corps 142
seerafuku (Japanese school uniform) 114, 156
Seikan train 120
seisen (holy war) 67
Seneca Falls, New York 198
sennin bari (one thousand people's needlepoint) 76–77
"sensei" 159
Serbs 132
Shanghai, China 27
Sherman tanks 142
Shigemitsu, Mamoru 124
Shikoku, Japan 34, 149
shinkansen 178
Shinto religion 66
Shitokan, Japan 152
Siberia 21, 22, 32, 163
Siemienski, Zbigniew 167
Sikorski, Wladyslaw 60, 145–46
Sino-Japanese War 26, 34
Sinti *see* Gypsies
sitzkrieg 45
The Six Million Dollar Man 57
"slavery," origins of the term 57
Sloan Square, London 165
Smolensk, Russia 61
snipers, German 85
Sobocinski, Dr. (Bogdan's dentist) 7, 19, 47
social stratification in Great Britain 168
Solomon Islands 69

Soseki, Natsume 38
Southeast Asia 68
Soviet-German Non-Aggression Pact 17, 60, 146
Soviet Union: control of Poland after WWII 1, 131, 141–42, 163–64, 176, 193; declaration of war on Japan 121–22, 193; destruction of Polish leadership 21, 61; failure to help during Warsaw Uprising 90, 106–7, 146; global standing 70; invaded by Germany 50, 60, 69; invasion of Poland 18–19, 21, 163, 193; non-aggression pact with Japan 152
Spain 166
Spitfire planes 134
Stalag XB see Sandbostel POW camp
Stalin, Joseph 16, 17–18, 22, 61, 106–7, 122–23, 143, 162
Statue of Liberty 170
Sten submachine gun 64
Stettin, Germany 132
Stettinius, Edward 145
streetcar segregation in Nazi-occupied Warsaw 56
Studebaker car 173
Stuka dive bombers 86, 98
Stutthoff concentration camp 137
Suehiro restaurant 190
Sueoka, Akio 156
sugar 51, 74
suicides among Japanese soldiers 149
Supreme Court (United States) 188
surrender of Germany 120, 142
surrender of Japan 3, 123, 124, 143
survival instincts 95, 109, 122, 137, 167
swimming 15, 75–76, 139, 197, 201
Syrena 43, 44
Szczecin, Poland 132

Takakura, Kunimatsu 38
tatami mats 36
Tatra car 14
Tatra Mountains 14
teaching, first experiences in 158, 172, 173
Teheran Conference (1943) 145
Thanksgiving 173
Thirteenth Amendment 189
Thor (German howitzer) 86
Tito, Josef 106
tobacco 49–50
Tojo, Hideki 25, 27, 112, 152
Tokyo 178; firebombing 36, 119, 120, 149
tonarigumi 71
torture 21–22, 58
"total war" 149
Toyohama, Japan 31–32

Toyohira River 29
trade schools in Warsaw see vocational training
Trafalgar Square 140
Transportation in Eastern Europe 199
Treaty of Riga 16
Treblinka, Poland 63, 129
Tripartite Pact 45
Truman, Harry 124
Truman Doctrine 176
Tsugaru Strait 120
tuberculosis 91–92
"two Warsaws" 86–87
Tymowski, Zbigniew 11, 46, 64
typewriter, Bogdan's purchase of 167

underground newspaper in Warsaw see *Biuletyn Informacyjny*
United Nations 144
United States: attraction to Bogdan after WWII 168–69; automobiles 170; Civil War 149, 189; embargoes against Japan 28; GIs in Japan 151, 155, 156, 158, 180; industrial efficiency 160
United States Occupation of Japan 149, 150, 151, 160, 180, 181; reforms 153, 155, 156, 158, 160
University of Illinois 171–73
University of Kentucky 184, 189
University of Vermont 173
University of Warsaw 44
University of Winnepeg 175
Urbana-Champaign, Illinois 171, 173

vacuum cleaners 171
Van Hook, Joseph 185
V-E Day 140
Verden, Germany 139
Versailles Treaty 8, 26
veterans, Japanese 148–50
Vienna 174, 175
Viking Apartment building 190, 191
Vistula River 16, 43, 79, 89, 90, 107
vocational training in Warsaw 47
Voice of America 176–77
von Stauffenberg, Claus 108

"W" hour 78
Wall Street 172, 190, 191
Warsaw 22, 24, 43, 81–82, 108, 169–70; citizens resist German occupation 56, 59–60; courier system 82, 83–84; German invasion and occupation 44, 55
Warsaw Uprising (1944): Allied aid 90, 102; citizen participation 79, 88; death toll 105–6; decentralized nature 64, 78,

81–82, 106; end 105, 109, 133; females during 90; lack of water 88; reasons for defeat 106–7; turning point of WWII 108–9
Washington Naval Conference of 1921 26
Warsaw Uprising of 1943 89
Wehrmacht 44, 45, 62
West Germany 175
West Virginia 187
Western Europe 57, 175, 199
White House 145
Willys-Overland car 14, 20, 21, 22
winter in Otaru 32, 36, 37, 184
winter migration of Americans 184
"winter of the turnip" 134
Wlochy (Warsaw locality) 85
World War I 8, 14, 26, 134, 169, 185, 199
World War II: beginning 7, 18; conclusion 143; impact on Bogdan and Seiko's personalities 194, 200–1; Pacific theater 68, 69, 76; popular culture and 76–77; survival lessons for Bogdan and Seiko 202–4

Yalta Conference 122, 143–45
Yamamoto, Isoroku 28, 68, 152
Yamato class battleships 34
Yellow Sea 26
YMCA 164, 170
Yoichi, Japan 29
Yokohama, Japan 178
Yugoslavia 106
YWCA 181

Zakopane, Poland 127
Zeithan, Germany 128, 132
Zemelka, Stanley 171–72
Zhukov, Georgy 106
zloty (Polish currency) 172–75
Zoom calls 4

www.ingramcontent.com/pod-product-compliance
Lightning Source LLC
Chambersburg PA
CBHW032042300426
44117CB00009B/1156